...to Create

"*Wired to Create* is an empowering manifesto for creative people. Endlessly relatable and chock-full of wisdom, Kaufman and Gregoire's study of the creative personality will have you saying over and over again, 'This is Me!'"

—Susan Cain, Quiet Revolution cofounder and
New York Times bestselling author of *Quiet*

cutting-edge science and timeless wisdom, Carolyn Greg-
d Scott Barry Kaufman shine a light on the habits, practices,
chniques that can help us tap into our deepest creativity."

—Arianna Huffington, *New York Times*
bestselling author of *Thrive*

t Barry Kaufman has just written the go-to book on
ivity and genius. He puts together the newest scientific
gs from the brain, from mental life, and from the messy
of emotion to whiz us to the cutting edge of the highest
n accomplishments."

—Martin Seligman, director of the Positive
Psychology Center, University of Pennsylvania

re are numerous books telling readers what they can do to
ne more creative. For the most part, the suggestions are
up: They have no basis in scientific fact. This book is
al and perhaps unique not only in explaining what creativ-
but also in showing scientifically how people can unlock
evelop their creative talents. If you are interested in
u. shing your own creativity, you will want to read this book!"

—Robert J. Sternberg, professor of human development,
Cornell University, and author of *Successful Intelligence*

"*Wired to Create* is an exquisite tour through the science of that most prized but often frustratingly ineffable quality: creativity. By weaving research through portraits of the lives of great creators, Kaufman and Gregoire bring creativity into our grasp, and provide a rubric for how each of us can have more of it in our lives."

—David Epstein, *New York Times* bestselling author of *The Sports Gene*

"Through science and storytelling, Kaufman and Gregoire reveal the inner workings of the creative mind. It all adds up to a fascinating and instructive read."

—Robert Greene, *New York Times* bestselling author of *Mastery*

"One of my favorite thinkers and one of my favorite writers came together to write a book about one of my favorite topics: creativity. There is so much here, start now."

—Ryan Holiday, author of *The Obstacle Is the Way*

"At last there is a book on creativity that is accessible, engaging, and highly readable that does not sacrifice scientific rigor in the name of communication. Filled with stories and anecdotes, this is a must read." —James C. Kaufman, author of *Creativity 101*

"A lively, intimate glimpse into the creative mind from one of the most creative psychologists I know. Don't miss it."

—Angela Duckworth, professor of pyschology at the University of Pennsylvania, cofounder and scientific director of the Character Lab, and 2013 MacArthur Fellow

"*Wired to Create* is the state of the science on the personalities behind innovative ideas. It cleans up the messy minds of creative people."

—Adam Grant, Wharton professor and *New York Times* bestselling author of *Give and Take*

"*Wired to Create* is both broadly entertaining and deeply informative. Few books on creativity integrate the two so well!
—Dean Keith Simonton, editor of *The Wiley Handbook of Genius*

"Scott Barry Kaufman is the leading researcher who I'm watching for the next paradigm on how the creative mind works. This very well-crafted book, written with Carolyn Gregoire, lays the foundation."
—Peter Sims, cofounder and president of Silicon Guild Inc.
and author of *Little Bets: How Breakthrough Ideas
Emerge from Small Discoveries*

"This book brings a very fresh perspective to a field that has, inexplicably, been struggling to 'create' new ideas for several decades. With scientifically based research on imagination, daydreaming, intuition, and mindfulness, it opens up new avenues of thinking about this critical human capacity. It is a must read for both scientists and anyone else interested in the 'inner world' of creativity."
—Rex E. Jung, PhD, editor of the forthcoming *Cambridge
Handbook of the Neuroscience of Creativity*

"Groundbreaking creativity scholar Scott Barry Kaufman and talented science journalist Carolyn Gregoire shed light on one of the most mysterious phenomena of the human psyche: creativity. *Wired to Create* is a page-turner that masterfully blends cutting-edge research with historic and contemporary real-world examples of artists and geniuses, inspiring the reader to get in touch with her own inventive spirit."
—Emma Seppälä, PhD, author of *The Happiness Track: How to
Apply the Science of Happiness to Accelerate Your Success*
and science director of the Stanford Center for Compassion
and Altruism Research and Education

WIRED to CREATE

Discover the 10 things great artists,
writers and innovators do differently

Scott Barry Kaufman
and Carolyn Gregoire

Vermilion
LONDON

1 3 5 7 9 10 8 6 4 2

Vermilion, an imprint of Ebury Publishing,
20 Vauxhall Bridge Road,
London SW1V 2SA

Vermilion is part of the Penguin Random House group of
companies whose addresses can be found at global.penguin-
randomhouse.com

Copyright © Dr Scott Barry Kaufman and Carolyn
Gregoire 2015

Dr Scott Barry Kaufman and Carolyn Gregoire have asserted
their right to be identified as the authors of this Work in
accordance with the Copyright, Designs and Patents Act 1988

First published in the United Kingdom by Vermilion in 2016
First published in the United States by TarcherPerigee in 2015

www.eburypublishing.co.uk

A CIP catalogue record for this book is available from the
British Library

ISBN 9781785040641

Printed and bound in Great Britain by Clays Ltd, St Ives PLC

Penguin Random House is committed to a sustainable future
for our business, our readers and our planet. This book is
made from Forest Stewardship Council® certified paper.

To Jerome L. Singer, the father of daydreaming.

—SBK

To Nick, Keep on playing.

—CG

Contents

Preface

When the artist is alive in any person, whatever his kind of work may be, he becomes an inventive, searching, daring, self-expressive creature. He becomes interesting to other people. He disturbs, upsets, enlightens, and opens ways for better understanding. Where those who are not artists are trying to close the book, he opens it and shows there are still more pages possible.

—ROBERT HENRI, AMERICAN PAINTER

The creative genius may be at once naive and knowledgeable, being at home equally to primitive symbolism and to rigorous logic. He is both more primitive and more cultured, more destructive and more constructive, occasionally crazier and yet adamantly saner, than the average person.

—FRANK X. BARRON, PSYCHOLOGIST AND
CREATIVITY RESEARCHER

Several years ago, Scott gave a popular science rapper an extensive battery of personality tests. At the time, this Canadian entertainer, known as Baba Brinkman,[1] was starring in an Off-Broadway show called *The Rap Guide to Evolution*, a hip-hop tribute to Charles Darwin and the theory of natural selection. In the show, an animated Brinkman jumps energetically onstage, drops rhymes such as "The weak and the strong, who got it goin' on? We lived in the dark for so long," and "Getting pregnant before marriage; it's such a tragedy. Apparently it's also a reproductive strategy." He was one of the most bold and magnetic performers Scott had ever witnessed on the stage.

Brinkman's test results were perplexing, revealing a personality riddled with contradictions. On the one hand, Scott noticed that Brinkman scored high in "blirtatiousness"—a personality trait characterized by the tendency to say whatever is on one's mind. But at the same time, Brinkman didn't seem extraverted offstage.

He then found that while Brinkman scored high in assertiveness—one hallmark of extraverted personalities—he was only slightly above average in enthusiasm, another big marker of extraversion.[2] How could this charismatic performer, who seemed so full of energy, be only slightly above average in expressiveness behind the curtain? Scott dug deeper into the data to try to make sense of Brinkman's puzzling personality.

"I get that remark all the time with people who hang out with me after the show," Brinkman told Scott. "They say, 'You're so quiet, what happened to the guy onstage?' I get in front of a crowd, I get charged up, and it's like 'I'm gonna get everybody into this.' There has become this huge split, where I'm quite a temperate personality most of the time until I get on a stage and have a job to do, and then it's like *bam*."

As Scott delved deeper into Brinkman's psyche, further paradoxes emerged. For one, he noticed that Brinkman was low in narcissism—a trait that can be rampant among performers (and often rappers in particular). However, Brinkman *did* possess some of the individual qualities that together make up narcissism. Brinkman scored high in exhibitionism and superiority—two aspects of narcissism that had likely proved helpful to his career as an entertainer—while scoring low in the exploitativeness and entitlement aspects of narcissism. Brinkman also scored high in several positive characteristics that were undoubtedly beneficial to his career in music: emotional intelligence, social awareness, and the ability to manage stress. Scott noticed too that Brinkman was simultaneously oriented toward short-term romantic affairs while demonstrating a strong ability to sustain relationships.

Brinkman's personality was a case study in one of the most well-known findings in the history of creativity research: *Creative people have messy minds.*

Creative people also tend to have messy processes.

* * *

Picasso went through a rather chaotic process in creating his most famous painting, *Guernica.*

After being asked to create a mural for the Spanish Pavilion at the 1937 World's Fair, the painter found himself spinning his wheels for three months while he searched for creative inspiration. Then, inspiration struck alongside tragedy. In the wake of the Nazis' bombing of a small Basque town at the behest of the Spanish Nationalist forces, Picasso set out to illustrate the atrocities of Spain's bloody civil war.

Just fifteen days after the bombing, Picasso went to work on a series of forty-five numbered sketches. He painstakingly drew numerous versions of each of the figures that would appear in the painting—the bull, the horse, the warrior, the woman crying, the mother with her dead child—before touching a single drop of oil to the eleven- by twenty-five-foot canvas on which he would paint the mural.

For each figure, Picasso sketched a diverse set of variations. These sketches often did not exhibit a clear upward progression. In several cases, the figure he selected to appear in the finished painting ended up being one of the earliest he had sketched. The figure of the mother with her dead child featured in the final work, which depicted the mother holding the child in her arms and weeping, was very similar to the first two versions he sketched. But then, he went on to create two images that were wildly different—instead of the mother holding the child in her arms (as she appears in the painting) the discarded sketches show the mother carrying her child up a ladder. Picasso continued his experimentation with new figures even after moving on to the canvas, which often required him to paint over what was already there. He also explored a number of creative possibilities, such as a bull with a human head, that he ultimately didn't pursue.

Although Picasso was a seasoned painter who had been creating masterpieces for decades by the time he took on the project, his process in painting *Guernica* appeared to be more chaotic than controlled, more spontaneous than linear. The surplus of ideas and sketches that Picasso produced did not show a clear progression toward the final painting. The process was characterized by a number of false starts, and as some art historians have noted, many of the sketches he drew appear to be superfluous to the final product.[3]

Exploration and seemingly blind experimentation were key to Picasso's creative process. Rather than creating a painting to reflect his own preexisting worldview, he seemed to actively build and reshape that worldview through the creative process. While he may have had a rough intuition, it's likely that Picasso did not quite know where he was going, creatively, until he arrived there.[4]

Picasso said of his own creative process, "A painting is not thought out and settled in advance. While it is being done, it changes as one's thoughts change. And when it's finished, it goes on changing, according to the state of mind of whoever is looking at it."

The progression of Picasso's *Guernica* sketches offers a fascinating glimpse into his imagination, but it raises as many questions as it offers answers. To what extent did the painter have even the slightest idea what he was doing? And if he didn't know what he was doing, then how are we to make sense of his creative process—or of the creative process more generally?

Attempting to analyze Picasso's personality offers little in terms of answers. The painter was a protean shapeshifter as both artist and man; he has been described as a difficult personality,[5] who was intensely passionate and deeply cynical; "a towering creative genius one moment . . . a sadistic manipulator the next."[6] Picasso himself hinted at these paradoxes in his life and work when he said, "I am always doing that which I cannot do," and described the act of creation as one of destruction.[7]

So how are we to make sense of the complex creative process and personality? It starts with embracing a very messy set of contradictions.

Introduction: Messy Minds

Do I contradict myself? Very well, then I contradict myself, I am large, I contain multitudes.

—Walt Whitman

The debate over the creation of *Guernica* reflects a much larger schism in our understanding of the creative mind.

The history of scientific thinking about creativity has been defined by polarization, starting with a popular 1926 theory of the creative process that set the stage for decades' worth of debate among psychologists.

In his book *The Art of Thought,* British social psychologist Graham Wallas outlined the popular "four-stage model" of creativity. After observing and studying accounts of eminent inventors and creators, Wallas proposed that the creative process involves the following stages: *preparation*, during which the creator acquires as much information as possible about a problem; *incubation*, during which the creator lets the knowledge stew as the unconscious mind takes over and engages in what Einstein referred to as "combinatory play";[1] *illumination*, during which an insight arises in consciousness—the natural culmination of a "successful train of association"; and a *verification stage*, during which the creator fleshes out the insights, and communicates their value to others.[2]

If only the creative process was so tidy. While psychologists continue to vigorously debate its workings, most agree that the traditional four-stage model is far too simplistic.[3] In his presidential address to the American Psychological Association in 1950, J. P. Guilford made a bold call for psychologists to take a closer look at creativity. He rejected the four-stage model, calling it "very superficial from a psychological point of view,"[4] because it tells us so little about the mental processes occurring during the act of creation.

As psychologists continued to put artists under the microscope to examine the creative process in action, they continued to find it to be far from a clear-cut, step-by-step process.[5] Further research showed creative people to engage in rapid switching of thought processes and to exhibit nearly simultaneous coexistence between a number of these processes, from generating new ideas to expanding and working out the ideas, to critical reflection, to taking a distance from one's work and considering the perspective of the audience.

These processes, of course, differ from one type of artist to another. When creating fiction, writers tend to exhibit a complex process of their own. Research conducted on a group of novelists painted a picture of the fiction-writing process as a "voyage of discovery" that begins with a *seed incident*—an event or observation that inspires fascination and exploration and becomes the fertile ground on which creative growth occurs. Seed incidents tend to break the mind out of ordinary understanding and create new meanings for the writer, as evidenced by the writers' descriptions of these events as "touching," "intriguing," "puzzling," "mysterious," "haunting," and "overwhelming." Commenting on a family incident that became the seed for a story, one writer said that the event seemed "full of meanings I couldn't even begin to grasp."[6]

The seed incident is followed by a period of navigation between different creative worlds. At this stage, the writers oscillated between the "writingrealm"—a place of retreat from the world where the writer can plan and reflect on what has been written—and the "fictionworld" of their own making: an imaginative place in which the author engages with fiction characters and events as they unfold. For instance, after one writer began her story with the line "I am a poodle," she imaginatively transformed herself into a dog, "allowing the sounds and sights and smells of a dog's world to come to her." She then switches mental gears, returning to the writingrealm to reflectively evaluate and improve upon what she had written. This fictionworld, which consists of imagination and fantasy, is a distinctly different realm of experience from the writingrealm, where reflective thinking and rational deliberation occur. This constant toggling between imaginative and rational ways of thinking suggests a more complex, less linear account of fiction writing than the four-stage model can accommodate.

Further analyses of creative writers continued to reject a step-by-step account of the creative process, suggesting that writing is likely to be considerably less controlled. Focusing on the contemporary novelist's search for meaning and struggle to express a specific experience,[7] another study emphasized that the writing process often moves forward even without the novelist's full understanding of where the work is going. As the writer slowly gains a sense of the direction in which he is moving, he can begin to move forward deliberately and with greater clarity. The process reflects what *Calvin and Hobbes* creator Bill Watterson said of creativity and life, "The truth is, most of us discover where we are headed when we arrive."[8]

Psychologist Dean Keith Simonton, who has extensively studied the career trajectories of creative geniuses across the arts, sciences, humanities, and leadership, came to a strikingly similar conclusion. Based on a detailed case study of Thomas Edison's creative career, Simonton suggested that even at the level of genius, creativity is a "messy business."[9]

Even at the level of genius, creativity is a "messy business."

Given the complex and ever-changing nature of the creative process, it should come as little surprise that creative people tend to have messy minds. Highly creative work blends together different elements and influences in the most novel, or unusual, way, and these wide-ranging states, traits, and behaviors frequently conflict with each other within the mind of the creative person, resulting in a great deal of internal and external tension throughout the creative process.[10]

One of the most fascinating things about creative work is that it brings together and harmonizes these conflicting elements, which exist to some extent in everyone. Creative people are hubs of diverse interests, influences, behaviors, qualities, and ideas— and through their work, they find a way to bring these many disparate elements together. This is one of the reasons why creativity feels so ineffable—it is so many different things at the same time! After interviewing creative people across various fields for over thirty years, the eminent psychologist of creativity Mihaly Csikszentmihalyi observed: "If I had to express in one word what makes their personalities different from others, it's *complexity*. They show tendencies of thought and action that in most people are segregated. They contain contradictory extremes; instead of being an 'individual,' each of them is a 'multitude.'"[11]

Case in point: The brilliant journalist David Carr—a creature of many contradictions and a protean shapeshifter if there ever was one—said that he often reflected upon the many "selves" that he had possessed over his lifetime, from drug addict to media celebrity. "I spent time looking into my past to decide which of my selves I made up—the thug or the nice family man—and the answer turned out to be neither," he reflected. "Whitman was right. We contain multitudes."

Another prototype of the messy creative mind is the iconic Jazz Age entertainer Josephine Baker. The famous American in Paris—who will forever be remembered for dancing in a banana skirt in *La Revue Nègre*—was not only a singer, dancer, and actress but also a French spy during World War II, a civil rights activist, a mother of twelve adopted children from around the world (her "rainbow tribe"), a rumored lover of men and women numbering in the thousands, and an eccentric character described as both deeply loving and volatile by those who knew her well. Baker's "adopted" son Jean-Claude Baker wrote in his biography of the star, "I loved her, I hated her, I wanted desperately to understand her."

Efforts to peel back Baker's many masks seem to have only brought further questions to light. Feminist studies scholar Alicja Sowinska shines a light on Baker's complexities:

> If she embodied a savage on stage, she would behave like a lady on the street; if men were dying for her as seductress, she would put on a man's suit and bend gender boundaries; if she was called a "black Venus," she would treat her head with a blonde wig. When the perception of her became too refined, she walked her pet leopard down the Champs-Elysées.[12]

David Foster Wallace proved to be similarly perplexing to those who attempted to understand him. Commentators have described the virtuoso author of *Infinite Jest* as both deeply fragile and intensely strong willed, at different times politically conservative and fiercely liberal, a writer of prose that is as precise as it is unwieldy, a master of writing about both highbrow and lowbrow topics. Wallace's biographer, D. T. Max, said that he found himself surprised by the "intensity of violence" in the writer's personality. However, he said, "On the other end of the spectrum, he was also this open, emotional guy, who was able to cry, who intensely loved his dogs. He was all those things."[13]

This delicate, and sometimes extreme, dance of contradictions may be precisely what gives rise to the intense inner drive to create. In the 1960s, the research of Frank X. Barron examined this fundamental motivation.[14] In a history-making study, Barron invited a group of high-profile creators to live on the University of California, Berkeley campus for a few days. The group—which included Truman Capote, William Carlos Williams, and Frank O'Connor, along with leading architects, scientists, entrepreneurs, and mathematicians—arrived, suitcases in hand, to bunk at a former fraternity house for several days.[15] They spent time talking to one another, being observed, and completing various evaluations of their lives, work, and personalities, including tests of mental illness and creative thinking, which required them to answer some very personal questions.[16]

What did Barron find that these highly creative people did differently? One thing that became quite clear is that while IQ and academic aptitude were relevant (to a moderate degree), they did not explain the particular spark of the creative mind.[17]

This led Barron to claim that creativity might be distinct from IQ—a fairly revolutionary idea at the time, as it ran counter to the longtime assumption that intelligence, as measured by

IQ tests, was the special sauce of creative genius. IQ testing was seen as the best route to understanding creativity by many academics in the first half of the twentieth century, but even their own data sets suggested that additional personality traits were important,[18] and Barron's findings added more cause for skepticism.

The Berkeley study also showed that the ingredients of creativity were too complex and multifaceted to be reduced to a single factor. The findings demonstrated that creativity is not merely expertise or knowledge but is instead informed by a whole suite of intellectual, emotional, motivational, and ethical characteristics.[19] The common strands that seemed to transcend all creative fields was an openness to one's inner life, a preference for complexity and ambiguity, an unusually high tolerance for disorder and disarray, the ability to extract order from chaos, independence, unconventionality, and a willingness to take risks.

This new way of thinking about creative genius gave rise to some fascinating—and perplexing—contradictions. In a study of writers, Barron and Donald MacKinnon found that the average creative writer was in the top 15 percent of the general population on all measures of psychopathology covered by the test.[20] But here's the kicker: They also found that *creative writers scored extremely high on all the measures of psychological health*!

The writers scored high on some measures of mental illness, but they also tended to score very high on "ego-strength," a trait that's characterized by "physiological stability and good health, a strong sense of reality, feelings of personal adequacy and vitality, permissive morality, lack of ethnic prejudice, emotional outgoingness and spontaneity, and intelligence."[21] Barron's creators were just as strong in adaptability and resourcefulness as they seemed to be pathological by other measures. They

appeared to be little more than a loosely assembled bundle of paradoxes and perplexities. In order to determine how these writers
could be simultaneously mentally healthier and more mentally ill
than the average person, Barron began to question the value of the
tests themselves and the labels we put on individual personalities.

As Barron began to make sense of what he observed, he
came to identify a key consistency among creative people.
Namely, these people seemed to become *more intimate with
themselves*—they dared to look deep inside, even at the dark and
confusing parts of themselves.[22] Being open to and curious about
the full spectrum of life—both the good and the bad, the dark
and the light—may be what leads writers to score high on some
characteristics that our society tends to associate with mental illness, while it can also lead them to become more grounded and
self-aware. In truly facing themselves and the world, creative-
minded people seemed to find an unusual synthesis between
healthy and "pathological" behaviors.

Armed with mounting evidence of these deep paradoxes,
scientists now generally agree that creativity is not a single characteristic but a *system* of characteristics, and many theories now
emphasize the multifaceted nature of creativity.[23] The characteristics highlighted by these theories include general intellectual
functioning, knowledge, and skills relevant to the activity; creative skills and thinking styles; psychological resources such as
confidence, perseverance, and a willingness to take risks; inner
motivation and a love of one's work; a complex suite of positive
and negative emotions; and environmental factors such as access
to gatekeepers in the field and key resources.

To be creative, you don't need to score off the charts on every
single one of these characteristics. Creativity is not so much a sum
as it is a *multiplication* of factors.[24] What does that mean? Well, it
may be possible to compensate for lower values on one dimension

(like IQ) by capitalizing on another set of strengths (like motivation and perseverance). Indeed, these factors often interact and feed off each other over time, which can amplify levels of creative output.[25]

Creative people not only cultivate a wide array of attributes but are also able to adapt—even *flourish*—by making the best of the wide range of traits and skills that they already possess. This ability to adapt to changing circumstances with fluidity and flexibility is reflected in three main "super-factors" of personality that are highly correlated with creativity: plasticity, divergence, and convergence.[26] *Plasticity* is characterized by the tendency to explore and engage with novel ideas, objects, and scenarios.[27] Characteristics like openness to experience, high energy, and inspiration are all related to each other, forming the core of this drive for exploration. *Divergence* reflects a nonconformist mindset and independent thinking and is related to impulsivity and lower levels of agreeableness and conscientiousness. Finally, *convergence* refers to the ability to conform, put in the hard effort necessary to exercise practicality, and make ideas tenable. Convergence consists of high conscientiousness, precision, persistence, critical sense, and sensitivity to the audience. Individually and together, these diverse qualities encourage the development and expression of creativity.

These characteristics come into play during the two broad stages of the creative process: *generation*—in which ideas are produced and originality is sought out—and *selection,* which involves working out ideas and making them valuable to society. While characteristics associated with plasticity and divergence are most relevant when generating ideas, convergence is most important during the stage when ideas are being ironed out and made tenable. Considering that creativity involves both novelty and usefulness, this makes a lot of sense. While exploration and independent thinking can foster the generation of novel ideas, the more practical quality of convergence can help make them useful.

Divergence and convergence are just two of many seeming polarities associated with creativity. This is precisely the point. Creative people, *being human*, have at least some level of these varying characteristics within themselves, and they can choose to flexibly switch back and forth depending on what's most helpful in the moment. Creative people seem to be particularly good at operating within a broad spectrum of personality traits and behaviors. They are both introverted and extraverted, depending on the situation and environment, and learn to harness both mindfulness and mind wandering in their creative process. As Csikszentmihalyi put it, "What dictates their behavior is not a rigid inner structure, but the demands of the interaction between them and the domain in which they are working."[28]

The Many Networks of Creativity

Today, we're seeing evidence of this complexity at the neural level. It turns out that creativity does not involve only a single brain region or even a single side of the brain, as the "right brain" myth of creativity would have us believe. The creative process draws on the *whole* brain.

The creative process draws on the *whole* brain.

This complex process consists of many interacting cognitive systems (both conscious and unconscious) and emotions, with different brain regions recruited to handle each task and to work together as a team to get the job done.[29]

One of the most important networks at play here is the "default network" of the brain—or as we'll call it, the "imagination network."[30] Considered an exciting discovery by many cognitive neuroscientists, the identification of the default mode network has been described as a fortunate accident.[31] For years, cognitive neuroscientists treated the subjective realm of inner experience as mere "noise," useful only as a comparison to the more "productive" mental activity involved in sensory perception and engagement with the outside world. But when a few rogue cognitive neuroscientists began wondering what the brain actually *does* when it's not engaged in an externally directed task, the importance of this network became abundantly clear.[32]

Even that may be a huge understatement. Some scientists believe that the discovery of this brain network represents nothing less than a *paradigm shift* in cognitive neuroscience, from a focus on external, goal-directed task performance to the more nebulous yet omnipresent phenomenon of *inner experience*. As cognitive neuroscientist Kalina Christoff puts it, "Such a paradigm shift may help us accept our drifting mind as a normal, even necessary, part of our mental existence—and may even enable us to try to take advantage of it in some creative, enjoyable way."[33]

What does the imagination network do? Well, let's start with what it does *not* do. For starters, this brain network is not highly active when we take on leadership roles that focus on getting tasks completed (as opposed to leadership roles that focus on developing relationships), when we reason about physical objects ("I wonder what would happen if the wheels of this skateboard could rotate 360 degrees"), or when we imagine what another person knows about something (as opposed to their mental and emotional state).[34] See the similarities? All of these activities have to do, in some way, with our engagement with the immediate, concrete world outside our minds, which makes up much of our lives.

Nevertheless, external focus is only one part of the creativity puzzle. Another critical aspect of creative cognition comes from the imagination network, which is involved in as much as *half of our mental lives.* The processes associated with this brain network make us each unique and help breathe meaning into our lives. In fact, the functions of the imagination network form the very core of human experience. Its three main components—personal meaning making, mental simulation, and perspective taking—often work together when we're engaged in what researchers call "self-generated cognition."[35] Engaging many regions on the medial (inside) surface of the brain in the frontal, parietal, and temporal lobes, the imagination network enables us to construct personal meaning from our experiences, remember the past, think about the future, imagine other perspectives and scenarios, comprehend stories, and reflect on mental and emotional states—both our own and those of others.[36]

In recent years, the imaginative and social processes associated with this brain network have also been found to be critical for the healthy development of compassion and empathy as well as the abilities to understand ourselves, create meaning from our experiences, and construct a linear sense of self.[37] It should come as no surprise that the activity of the imagination brain network can also help inform not only our most deeply personal but our most creative ideas.[38]

Creative thought doesn't emerge solely from the imagination network.[39] A different brain network—the "executive attention" network, which helps us direct our attention—is also crucial here. Executive control processes support creative thinking by helping us deliberately plan future actions, remember to use various creative tactics, keep track of which strategies we've already tried, and reject the most obvious ideas.[40] They also help us *focus* our imagination, blocking out external distractions and allowing us to tune in to our inner experience. The imagination network and the executive attention network cooperate with each other whenever we have to evaluate personal information, from future planning to keeping track of social information, to evaluating a creative idea, to planning and carrying out a project.[41]

When we generate new ideas, these networks—along with the salience network, which is responsible for motivation—engage in an intricate dance. Researchers have observed this cognitive tango in action through the brain scans of people engaged in their personal creative process—from study volunteers thinking up creative uses for everyday objects like a brick, to published poets generating new verses, to jazz musicians and rappers deep in improvisation.[42] Initially, their brain states resemble a state of *flow*, or complete absorption in the task. The imagination and salience networks are highly active, while the more focused executive attention network is relatively quiet. As they further hone and refine their work or engage in collaboration with others, however, the executive attention network becomes increasingly more active.

Creative people are particularly good at exercising flexibility in activating and deactivating these brain networks that in most people tend to be at odds with each other. In doing so, they're able to juggle seemingly contradictory modes of thought—cognitive and emotional, deliberate, and spontaneous.[43] Even on a *neurological* level, creativity is messy.

Living More Creatively

In this book, we'll discuss creativity as a habit, as a way of life, and as a style of engaging with the world.[44] Following in the footsteps of psychologists J. P. Guilford, Frank Barron, E. Paul

Torrance, Robert J. Sternberg, and Abraham Maslow, we'll argue that we are all, in some way, *wired to create* and that everyday life presents myriad opportunities to exercise and express that creativity. This can take the form of approaching a problem in a new way, seeking out beauty, developing and sticking to our own opinions (even if they're unpopular), challenging social norms, taking risks, or expressing ourselves through personal style.

We are all, in some way, *wired to create.*

We can display creativity in many different ways, from the deeply personal experience of uncovering a new idea or experience to expressing ourselves through words, photos, fashion, and other everyday creations, to the work of renowned artists that transcends the ages.[45] All these types of creativity are rooted in the same fundamental thought processes, creative problem-solving skills, and ways of being. In this book, we'll explore the ten habits of mind that foster them.[46]

Creative self-expression, in its many forms, can be a particularly powerful means of coping with life's inevitable challenges. There's a great myth that creativity requires mental illness or suffering, but as we'll see throughout this book, while there are interesting connections between creativity and suffering, they do not suggest that suffering is a necessary or sufficient condition for creativity. Of course, trauma is a part of the human condition— every life has its "ten thousand joys and ten thousand sorrows," as Buddhists have long noted. While creativity—expressions of originality and meaningfulness in daily life—does not require suffering, creative work can be highly therapeutic for those who are experiencing hardship. People who engage in a creative lifestyle—perhaps by drifting off in daydreams, taking photographs just for fun, talking passionately about personal goals, writing thoughtful cards or letters to friends and family, keeping a journal, or starting their own business—tend to be more open minded, imaginative, intellectually curious, energetic, outgoing, persistent, and intrinsically motivated by their activity. They also report a greater sense of well-being and personal growth compared to those who are less engaged in these everyday creative behaviors.[47]

People who set aside a special time and place in their lives for creative thinking and work—for instance, waking up with the sunrise each morning to write in the quiet of the early hours or meditating before a painting session—also tend to score higher on measures of creative potential.[48] In contrast, those who are more *motivated to develop a final product* (agreeing with statements like, "I work most creatively when I have deadlines," "If I don't have something to show for myself, then I feel I've failed") tend to score *lower* in creative potential and intrinsic motivation and *higher* in stress and extrinsic (reward-oriented) motivation. Those who derive enjoyment from the act of creating and feel in control of their creative process tend to show greater creativity than those who are focused exclusively on the outcome of their work.

As with happiness, it seems that the more you strive for creativity, the less likely you are to achieve it. Creativity can't be bottled and sold, or tapped into at will—it works in seemingly mysterious and paradoxical ways, and rarely at our own convenience. But learning to embrace and enjoy the creative process itself—with all its peaks and valleys—can yield immense personal and publicly recognized rewards. This has important implications for the sorts of attributes and processes we value and reward in society. If we want to develop creativity and imagination on a large scale, it's important to begin to foster these skills during childhood and to continue to do so throughout our lives. Repeated engagement of the many networks of creativity are essential for their optimal development.[49]

To build these skills, we must encourage risk tasking and originality, and give people the autonomy to decide how they learn and create. We must offer them the time they need for personal reflection, daydreaming, and inner exploration. We must make tasks more meaningful and relevant to their personal goals and help people find and develop their unique purpose and identity. To foster creativity, it is important to build people's confidence and competence to learn new information and deal with adversity; make tasks conducive to flow by engaging them in the appropriate level of challenges; and help them develop supportive, positive social relationships.[50]

Unfortunately, our society increasingly allows children's creativity and imagination to fall by the wayside in favor of the passive consumption of social media and television as well as superficial learning evaluated by standardized tests—which only serve to increase extrinsic motivation, often at the expense of intrinsic passion. And it's to our own detriment. Learning to solve the increasingly complex world problems of the twenty-first century—and to identify the problems themselves—will require creative qualities like originality, curiosity, risk taking, and a tolerance for the ambiguity inherent in the idea that there is not always a single correct solution.[51] Of course, knowledge, skills, and intelligence in the traditional IQ sense are important, but they're not enough for true innovation. Being creative requires the cultivation of a balance of skills—including the ability to learn and memorize—as well as the ability to *free oneself* from that knowledge and from habitual ways of thinking in order to imagine possibilities that have never been dreamed of before.

The Evolution of the Science of Creativity

Since the 1950s, there has been a dramatic rise in research on creativity. Between the late 1960s and early 1990s, more than nine thousand scientific papers were published on the subject.[52] Between 1999 and 2009, another ten thousand papers were written about creativity from a variety of psychological perspectives, including biological, developmental, social, cognitive, and organizational domains, as well as in other fields including economics, education, and the arts.[53] Today, creativity research is in full bloom, with its own scholarly journals and a division of the American Psychological Association.[54] There are now twenty-one thousand books on or related to creativity on Amazon and an endless array of blogs devoted to sharing tips for living more creatively.

The growth of the field of positive psychology—spearheaded by Martin Seligman and Mihaly Csikszentmihalyi in the late 1990s, and carried on by the numerous positive psychologists featured in this book—has also contributed substantially to our understanding of creativity and has shed light on the many ways that creativity contributes to psychological health and well-being. Indeed, the scientifically rigorous field of positive psychology, which focuses on "nurturing what is best within ourselves,"[55] grew out of the humanistic psychology of the mid-twentieth century, a field that emphasized the whole person and the many paths to personal growth.[56]

In preparing this book, we scoured current and past scientific research over the past hundred years (including new research conducted by Scott and his colleagues) and extracted common themes from within the minds and lives of eminent creators throughout the course of human history. Together, science and art offer a glimpse into the many things that highly creative people do differently. While this list is by no means exhaustive, people who live the creative lifestyle do a good number of these things, and there are very few people with originality and meaningfulness who do *none* of them.

In March 2014, Carolyn's *Huffington Post* article "18 Things Highly Creative People Do Differently" went viral, amassing five million views and more than half a million Facebook likes in a matter of days.[57] The article, which featured Scott's research, explored some of the characteristic traits and habits of creative people and was widely shared and discussed within creative communities. That article became the basis for this book, which explores in greater depth the same questions of the creative mind and personality.

As you'll notice, this book presents many paradoxes—mindfulness and mind wandering, openness and sensitivity, solitude and collaboration, play and seriousness, and intuition and reason. These seeming contradictions capture some of the polarities that come together in the creative person and that are reconciled through the creative process as the creator makes meaning out of her inner and outer experiences. Creative people learn to harness these widely varying skills, behaviors, and ways of thinking as the situation demands and to bring them together in new and unusual ways to come up with novel ideas and products.

The aim of this book is to shed light on the fascinating perplexities of the creative mind and to encourage readers to embrace their own paradoxes and complexities, and in doing so, open themselves up to a deeper level of self-understanding and self-expression. As we'll suggest, it is precisely *this* ability to hold the self in all of its dimensional beauty that is the very core of creative achievement and creative fulfillment.

And so it is here, with the deepest respect for the intimate and complex connections between creativity, personal identity, and meaning, we begin our exploration of the things highly creative people do differently.

Ten Things
Highly Creative People
Do Differently

Imaginative Play

You see a child play . . . and it is so close to seeing an artist paint, for in play a child says things without uttering a word. You can see how he solves his problems. You can also see what's wrong. Young children, especially, have enormous creativity, and whatever's in them rises to the surface in free play.

—ERIK ERIKSON

As a young boy growing up in rural Japan in the late 1950s and early 1960s, Shigeru Miyamoto created fantastical worlds in his imagination. He made his own toys using pieces of wood and string. Miyamoto also created puppets and acted out performances with them, drew cartoons, and explored the mountains and river valley surrounding the village where he lived, in the mountains northwest of Kyoto.

As the boy got older, he spent more and more time in nature. One carefree summer when he was around eight years old, Miyamoto stumbled upon a hidden cave. He passed many happy hours in the dark cavern that summer, letting his imagination roam free.[1] Later in his life, these outdoor excursions would provide the inspiration for some of his most influential work—namely, the creation of the iconic *Super Mario Bros.* video game.

The man who spent his childhood inside an imaginary world of his own making would grow up to share that imagination with the world. Miyamoto—often called the Walt Disney of video games—created and designed not only *Super Mario Bros.* but also the blockbuster's *Donkey Kong*, *The Legend of Zelda*, and the Wii console in addition to overseeing the creation of more than four hundred Nintendo games.

After the collapse of Atari in the 1980s, *Super Mario Bros.*—the classic game that follows a mustached, overalls-clad Italian plumber who must venture on a journey through the Mushroom Kingdom, along with his right-hand man, Luigi, to rescue Princess Toadstool—revived the modern video gaming industry. Through *Mario* and other classic games, Miyamoto inspired the admiration of gamers and aspiring video game creators around the world. His video games are now widely held to be some of the greatest (and most profitable) ever created.

What's Miyamoto's secret to dreaming up some of the world's most beloved games? Nintendo's luminary, as he's grown older, has managed to never lose a sense of play. According to *The Sims* creator Will Wright, "He approaches the games playfully, which seems kind of obvious, but most people don't."[2]

For Miyamoto, childhood play paved the way for prolific adult creativity. As journalist Nick Paumgarten wrote in a 2010 *New Yorker* profile, Miyamoto always sought to re-create the sense of wonderment he experienced as a child in his games.[3] This spirit of childlike curiosity and exploration is palpable in each of his highly imaginative creations. "When you play his games, you feel like you're a kid and you're out in the backyard playing in the dirt," Wright observed.

Miyamoto's philosophy is that anything can be turned into fun and games. While he continues to draw creative inspiration from his childhood, he also channels his personal interests and fascinations into his work—the creation of the Wii Fit, for instance, was the result of a personal attempt to "gamify" his weight loss efforts. Turning the mundane into play and fun, Miyamoto found, could help people get more enjoyment out of their activities, whether it be exercise, working up to the next level of *Zelda,* or learning a new lesson in school.

"Anything that is impractical can be play," Miyamoto told *The New Yorker.* "It's doing something other than what is necessary to continue living as an animal."

From Childhood Play to Adult Creativity

Like Miyamoto, many eminent creators in the arts and sciences engaged in imaginative play as children and maintain that youthful sense of play in their work as adults.[4] Studying the lives of promising young entrepreneurs, innovators, and scientists, psychologist Larisa Shavinina found that great business innovators like Richard Branson, Warren Buffett, and Bill Gates exhibited entrepreneurial behaviors in childhood (Branson, for instance, started a Christmas tree farm at age twelve).[5] She also found that family played a crucial role in the development of scientific and innovative talent. Parents of Nobel Prize winners were encouraging and supportive, valued education, were in professional occupations related to science, and had houses full of books and scientific toys that allowed for experimentation at home. What's more, nearly every Nobel Prize winner "had at least one exceptional teacher" in their school days, Shavinina notes.[6]

Studies conducted by the LEGO Foundation support the importance of this type of play for creativity and cognitive development. In their observations of children building and playing with objects, the researchers saw that the children were often deeply engaged in searching for personal meaning as an ongoing process of understanding themselves and their relationship to the environment. For children, play becomes a way of experimenting with the meanings of objects by using their innate curiosity to turn the unfamiliar into something familiar.[7]

It's important that children grow up in a home environment in which adult interactions support their natural desire to play in this way. Research has shown that pretend play is more common among children whose parents talk to them often, read or tell bedtime stories, and explain things about nature or social issues to them. Research has also found that in schools, encouraging pretend games either in the curriculum or at recess can enhance imaginativeness and curiosity.[8]

Adults, too, need this type of support to dream and play. Drawing on a different set of materials—personal memories, fantasy, and emotions can be objects of play as much as physical items—many highly creative people exhibit a great deal of imaginative playfulness. For these creative minds, creating is itself an act of play. English professor Brian Boyd puts it this way in his 2009 book, *On the Origins of Stories*: "A work of art acts like a playground for the mind, a swing or a slide or a merry-go-round of visual or aural or social pattern,"[9] while the poet Stanley Kunitz emphasized the role of exploring emotions in poetry writing, saying, "The poem has to be saturated with impulse, and that means getting down to the very tissue of experience. How can this element be absent from poetry without thinning out the poem?"[10]

Imaginative play in particular is an important part of many artists' childhoods.[11] Novelist Stephen King's earliest childhood memory was imagining himself as the "Ringling Brothers Circus Strongboy,"[12] while the young Mark Twain would act out stories with his friends, which he adapted from books such as *Robin Hood*.[13] Artist and sculptor Claes Oldenburg—who was known for his monumental replicas of everyday objects—even proclaimed, "Everything I do is completely original—I made it up when I was a little kid."

In Oldenburg's case, this may very well be true. At the age of seven, he invented "Neubern," an imaginary island located somewhere between Africa and South America. These early experiences led to more imagination, as he playfully combined materials and objects, mixing and matching sizes and shapes until the common became enlarged and astonishing.[14] As Oldenburg puts it, the result was "a parallel reality according to the rules of (my) fantasy."[15] Philosopher Stanisław Lem, novelist C. S. Lewis, geologist Nathaniel Shaler, psychologists Carl Jung and Jerome L. Singer, and neurologist Oliver Sacks have all said that they made up fantastical realms in their minds as children.

For many artists—particularly writers—this crucial "tissue of experience" comes from youth, and the ability to access a deep well of early memories and emotions can facilitate their creative work. Flannery O'Connor famously said that anyone who has survived childhood has as much material about life as they'll ever need, while John Updike noted, similarly, "Memories, impressions, and emotions from your first 20 years on earth are most writers' main material: Little that comes afterward is quite so rich and resonant."[16]

Research tells us that imaginative play—whether it's exploring objects, ideas, emotions, or fantasies—is essential to creativity in a variety of disciplines, from science and technology to creative writing, to music, to the visual arts.[17] According to clinical child psychologist Sandra Russ, "Pretend play in childhood is where many of the cognitive and affective processes important in creativity occur."[18] Russ argues that pretend play is a creative act unto itself because "the child is making something out of nothing, as is the artist."[19] Likewise, as creativity scholar Michele Root-Bernstein notes, no matter your walk in life, "in the private country of the mind, you create visions of the way things were and the way they might be. You enter into imagined realms and shape an alternative space and time. To one degree or another, we all do."[20]

Taking Play Seriously

> You can discover more about a person in an hour of
> play than in a year of conversation.
>
> —PLATO

Influential twentieth-century psychologists such as Piaget, Freud, and Erikson accorded play a crucial place in child development, and Russian developmental psychologist Lev Vygotsky went so far as to say that child's play is the very birthplace of the creative imagination. Indeed, if there is one fundamental function of play, it is to contribute to the growth of a flexible brain that is primed for creative thinking and problem solving.

Observing children engaged in imaginative play reveals a wellspring of natural-born creativity; they make up and act out stories, taking on the roles of writer, actor, and director with ease and enjoyment. This occurs naturally, without instruction or guidance, starting at roughly the age of two and a half and lasting until around nine or ten years old, and it can occupy up to 20 percent of a child's time at its peak. When engaged in pretense, children take on multiple perspectives and playfully manipulate emotions and ideas. "Children make up stories based on what they know in their environment, but also what they wish for. . . . They try to conquer their fears in play. They rehearse in play," child psychologist Sandra Russ explained.[21]

In imaginative play, everyday objects are used in a symbolic fashion."[22] The banana becomes a telephone, the stuffed animal a real baby, the LEGO a car, and the backyard an enchanted kingdom. This symbolic behavior involves not only thinking but also emotions. When the child is playing, he is experimenting with ideas, images, and feelings.[23]

Unfortunately, as a culture, we don't tend to view play in such a positive light. Children's free time has been steadily declining since 1955.[24] While this may create more time for valuable activities, it also robs children of not only the enjoyment of pure fun but also the opportunity for the healthy development of many key skills necessary for creativity. These important skills include impulse control, planning, organization, problem solving, literacy and language development, symbolism, comprehension of STEM concepts, mathematical ability, curiosity, divergent thinking ("what if" thinking), cognitive integration of diverse content, flexibility, emotional regulation, stress reduction, integration of cognition and emotions, empathy, respect, social negotiation, collaboration, and tolerance for others[25]—a significant set of skills to allow to fall by the wayside.

In recent years, an increasing number of psychologists, concerned parents, educators, and activist groups have spoken out about the "war on play," and many have launched movements to preserve dwindling childhood playtime.[26] Research suggests they may be onto something very real. Some studies have found that direct instruction in the earliest years of life can *backfire*, making children less curious, less likely to discover new information, and less likely to make new, unexpected connections.[27] In fact, psychologists in New Zealand found that children who learned to read later in childhood had *greater* reading comprehension scores, suggesting that it may not always be beneficial to rush children to learn key competencies.[28] The evidence is loud and clear: Time for play and curiosity *supports* learning.

At Swiss Waldkindergartens, or forest kindergartens, children between the ages of four and seven spend the entirety of their school days playing outside. Come rain or shine, the kids run around in the woods, play games together, build structures with found objects, and explore their natural surroundings. The goals and expectations for the children are fairly minimal— learning how to write their names on the ground, for instance—and math and reading are not taught until first grade.[29] First and foremost, the schools are concerned that the children learn important socio-emotional and motor skills and exercise their natural curiosity, imagination, and creativity through free play. Once this important foundation has been established, there will be time to prepare for the specific academic challenges that lie ahead in elementary school.

As adults, cultivating a childlike sense of play can revolutionize the way we *work*. We tend to think of work—even when it is creative in nature—as being serious and difficult. And of course, successful creative people tend to be very serious about their field and put hours of hard work into what they do. But the most eminent creative minds learn to balance seriousness with fun and enjoyment in one's work. *Playing* with work gives us a certain lightness and flexibility when generating new ideas and also helps motivate us to continue to work long hours without becoming too stressed or depleted. When it comes to creative work, there is a time for seriousness and a time for play, and very often, the best work arises as a result of combining the effort and ease. This false dichotomy we've set up between play, on the one hand, and work, on the other, is a not only illusory but also destructive. The science shows that hybrid forms of work and play may actually provide the most optimal context for learning and creativity, both for children and for adults.[30] Video game designer Jane McGonigal argues, too, that many of the things we do "just for fun," like gaming, actually are crucial to our life happiness, resiliency, work performance, and creativity.[31]

As many of us know well, we tend to lose the spirit of play and fun as we grow older, as our lives become dominated by work and seriousness. In the words of George Bernard Shaw: "We don't stop playing because we grow old; we grow old because we stop playing." But that doesn't mean we can't infuse playfulness back into our adult lives. One experiment asked college students to imagine either that their classes had been canceled for the day or to envision being their seven-year-old selves in the same situation. The students who imagined themselves as excited children gave more creative responses on a subsequent test of divergent thinking. It just goes to show that playful curiosity can help us break free from conventional ways of thinking.[32]

Our widespread play deficit is an important reason to carve out spaces in which play is not only tolerated but *celebrated*. Adults who are more playful report feeling less stressed, being better able to cope with stress, and having greater life satisfaction and other positive life outcomes.[33] And truly, maintaining a spirit of play keeps creativity and vitality alive as we get older. As we'll see next, play and intrinsic joy are intimately connected, creating a synergy that naturally leads to greater inspiration, effort, and creative growth. So go ahead—dance, paint, explore a new place, be silly, and have fun. You just might find that it gets your creative juices flowing!

Imaginary Worlds

As children, we create entire worlds of our own making. The creation of imaginary worlds is the most complex form of pretend play and an important way that children exercise their creative power.

Michele Root-Bernstein has studied the creation of these paracosms—or, as she calls it, "worldplay."[34] Sometimes paracosms grow out of early play with animated toys or imaginary companions, they nearly always thrive in the elementary school years after early pretend play subsides, and they tend to dissipate around the time of puberty. But in some cases, paracosms persist throughout adulthood, providing the fodder for mature creative work.

Many eminent adult innovators created complex imaginary worlds in childhood.[35] Perhaps the most well-known example is that of the imaginary "Glass Town Federation" created by the four Brontë siblings—Charlotte, Branwell, Emily, and Anne. This imaginary world consisted of the kingdoms of Angria (invented by Branwell and Charlotte) and Gondal (invented by Emily and Anne), ruled within the capital city of Glass Town. The Brontë children drew maps, invented characters, and wrote stories about these imaginary worlds, naming themselves the gods ("genii") of the kingdoms.[36]

"To invent and elaborate imaginary worlds is to develop a sense of self as a creator by immersing oneself in the creative process," Root-Bernstein writes in *Inventing Imaginary Worlds*. In a fascinating study, she looked at the imaginary play habits of adults selected for their exceptional creative achievement or potential. She found that over half of the study participants— regardless of whether they invented imaginary worlds in childhood—reported engaging in some aspect of worldplay in their adult work or hobbies. This included the creation of make-believe worlds in paintings, plays, films, and novels as well as the invention of hypothetical models and constructs in the sciences, social sciences, and humanities. She also found that worldplay in childhood was twice as common in the highly creative achievers as it was in typical college students.[37]

Based on these findings, Root-Bernstein proposes that the creation of imaginary worlds may be used as an indicator of advanced creative development. It bears repeating: Whether it's a three-year-old building a LEGO truck or a future novelist's construction of an elaborate sci-fi or fantasy world—the child at play is truly a creator.

2
Passion

One of the most powerful wellsprings of creative energy, outstanding accomplishment, and self-fulfillment seems to be falling in love with something—your dream, your image of the future.

—CREATIVITY RESEARCHER E. PAUL TORRANCE

When four-year-old Jacqueline du Pré first heard the sound of the cello on the radio, she immediately told her mother, Iris, "That is the sound I want to make."[1] According to Iris, the first time she played the cello, the young du Pré exclaimed in delight, "I do so love my cello."[2] Du Pré's mother was amazed at the depth of feeling behind those words, and could envision for her daughter a lifetime commitment to the instrument. What was the essence of du Pré's prodigious talent? In the words of biographer Elizabeth Wilson, it was a "deeply felt inner passion which illuminated her attitude to music from the earliest age, whether it was in her lisping of nursery rhymes, or singing of Christmas carols, or in her immediate identification with the sound of the cello."

Also at the age of four, Yo-Yo Ma asked his parents for a bigger instrument after trying his hand at the violin and viola.[3] Once he made contact with the cello, the speed with which he learned how to play—and play brilliantly—took off at a staggering pace. By age five he was performing for audiences, and at the age of seven he took the stage to serenade Presidents Dwight D. Eisenhower and John F. Kennedy. When cellist Leonard Rose first heard Ma, he was awed by the young musician's skill and intense concentration.[4] As Ma remembered years later, Rose once told him to become "one" with the instrument. "The strings are your voice, and the cello your lungs," Ma recalls being told. Ma's love for his instrument is apparent to anyone who sees him perform, as is the way his cello functions as a direct extension of his own inner feelings, reflections, and strivings.

Not only cello prodigies but also future rock musicians can recall a moment early in life when their passion for music was born. Like so many creative people, Thom Yorke didn't fit into a conventional school system. In a conversation with actor Daniel Craig for *Interview* magazine, he notes that the school system "was set up in a way that was very contrary to how I was built. I was constantly getting in trouble in small and annoying ways."[5] One day, he walked into one of the music rooms and saw a young Thomas Dolby—the recording artist who later became famous for his 1980s hit "She Blinded Me with Science"—playing with his synthesizer. At that moment, Yorke recalls thinking to himself, "I want *that* in my life." He began spending his days hiding in the music/art department, passionately cultivating his craft and experimenting with electronic sounds and beats. He had discovered that music was how he wanted to spend his life. Fortunately, Yorke's music teacher Terry James and his art teachers saw his passion and encouraged him to keep playing music.[6] The result is one of the greatest bands of all time: Radiohead.

National chess champion Josh Waitzkin, similarly, looks back on one particular day when he was six years old, strolling through Washington Square Park hand in hand with his mother. He loved to come to the park to swing on the monkey bars. However, he recalls that on this day, "something felt different." Looking over his shoulder, he was mesmerized by two park hustlers playing a game of chess. "I was pulled into the battlefield, enraptured; something felt familiar about this game, it made sense," he writes in his book *The Art of Learning*.[7]

A few days later, when Waitzkin and his mother returned to the playground, he broke away from her and ran up to one of the players who was setting up pieces on a marble board. Amused at the boy's fascination, the man invited Waitzkin to play a game with him. As the game continued, he soon realized that this wasn't any ordinary kid, but a player with a deep connection to the game. "As we moved the pieces," Waitzkin recalls, "I felt like I had done this before. There was a harmony to this game, like a good song." He would go on to become an eight-time National Chess Champion and the subject of his father's book, *Searching for Bobby Fischer: The Father of a Prodigy Observes the World of Chess*, upon which the blockbuster movie of the same name is based.[8]

The beautiful thing about these kinds of experiences is that you never know when they'll happen. Once stirred—whether early or late in life—passion has no expiration date.[9] When these inner desires arise, they can completely alter and enliven an individual's life and work. Steve Jobs went so far as to say that igniting this kind of passion is "the only way to do great work."

Passion has no expiration date.

Falling in Love with Your Dream

Many highly creative people can vividly remember a "moment, an encounter, a book that they read, a performance that they attended, that spoke to them and led them to say, "This is the real me, this is what I would like to do, to devote my life to, going forward," says psychologist Howard Gardner.[10]

That moment of memorable, dramatic contact with an activity of fascination is known as a "crystallizing experience." It can be like love at first sight. The encounter often activates lasting changes in the person's worldview and self-understanding. Ultimately, *the individual and the activity become one and the same.*

Crystallizing experiences can take many forms. An *initial* crystallizing experience signals that first moment of falling head over heels for a creative activity—like Yo-Yo Ma's discovery of the cello. Then, with a *refining* crystallizing experience, the creator goes deeper and discovers a particular instrument, style, or approach within their activity—like Thom Yorke's impassioned discovery of the Beatles' music after he began playing guitar.[11] Both the initial and refining crystallizing experiences are critical to the development of the creative mind. As author Thomas Armstrong puts it, crystallizing experiences—which he believes propel people toward their destinies—are the "sparks that light an intelligence and start its development toward maturity."[12]

Systematic studies support the importance of these sparks to the overall creative process and suggest that the passionate focus that arises from them plays a major role in helping the creator to persist through the roadblocks and challenges that inevitably arise during the creative process. In her study of prodigies who became successful later in life, developmental psychologist Ellen Winner concluded that talented young people "must be able to persist in the face of difficulty and overcome the many obstacles in the way of creative discovery."[13]

Talent is associated with a "rage to master"—an intense and sustained drive for excellence—in the individual's chosen activity or medium, according to Winner.[14] While important, this drive does not take the place of mundane, everyday hard work. The prodigies she studied *worked intensely hard*, and they were highly motivated to consistently work hard precisely by this internal drive. But what she noticed was that, in addition to hard work, talented young artists shared an intense love of their activity. They were driven less by external rewards and praise and more by a passionate joy in doing their work. While working, they focused like a laser beam, entering a psychological state of flow, which is characterized by complete absorption, concentration, joy, and subjective loss of time.[15]

Flow has been documented as an important contributor to performance in areas ranging from sports to music, to physics, to religion, to spirituality, to sex.[16] Who can forget the 1992 NBA Finals, Bulls against Trail Blazers? Imprinted in the brains of many sports fans is the moment when Michael Jordan hit his *sixth* consecutive three-point shot, looked over at Magic Johnson (who was a network announcer by that point), and just shrugged, as if to say, "This is out of my hands!"[17]

It's likely that our ability to enter flow states is a product of the creative rage to master. Martha J. Morelock, who has worked with exceptionally creative children, is convinced that the intense engagement she saw in the children is a reflection of a deep brain-based impulse to learn—"a craving for intellectual stimulation matching their cognitive requirements in the same way that the physical body craves food and oxygen."[18] In other words, the children didn't just seem internally driven to learn about their craft. It appeared as though they *needed* to master it.[19]

The same finding, of course, applies to highly motivated adults. A love of one's work is key to not only productivity but also high-level creativity. In a famous study of the development of excellence, developmental psychologist Benjamin Bloom found that children who became highly creative later in life showed unusual interests in their field.[20] The adult sculptors recalled drawing nonstop as children and finding great joy in building physical objects with their hands. The mathematicians reflected on being highly inquisitive and fascinated with how things work, often taking toys apart and looking at the gears, valves, gauges, and dials.[21] These unusual interests and their quick learning in their activity led to encouragement and support from parents, peers, mentors, and the community, which only motivated the children to work harder. Another seminal study, led by E. Paul Torrance, asked elementary-school children what they were "in love" with. He was amazed to find that many of the young children were already in love with a personal passion, and that the themes of their interests persisted, and sometimes intensified, as they got older.[22]

One child in the study, Mack, was already creating science fiction drawings when he was in second grade, and by third grade was writing science fiction stories and space dramas that his classmates performed. In high school, he organized a science fiction society that published a science fiction magazine and held annual meetings. Mack went on to complete a PhD in utopian political theory and to share his ideas in a variety of creative formats, from acting performances to musical compositions, to business entrepreneurships, to artworks. But he never forgot that the core theme of his love was *creative writing*, and he viewed engagement in other creative activities as a way to offer him the financial security and raw materials for his imagination to create science fiction and other forms of literature.

After a formal analysis comparing the children who were academically successful ("sociometric stars") with those who became adult creators ("the Beyonders"), Torrance found that those who fell in love with something as a child were more likely to score high on a variety of indicators of creativity more than twenty-two years later.[23] In fact, the extent to which children fell in love with their dreams was a *better* predictor of both personally meaningful and publicly recognized creative achievement than things like scholastic performance.

Basing his conclusion on a lifetime of research on these Beyonders, Torrance wrote, "Life's most energizing and exciting moments occur in those split seconds when our struggling and searching are suddenly transformed into the dazzling aura of the profoundly new, an image of the future."[24]

But of course, having a dream isn't enough. Some people have a clear image of their future but aren't *in love* with it—it doesn't quite scream "This is me!" We must see our true selves and our highest potential reflected in the dream.

The highly creative person may also fall in love with the creative process itself—the imagination, the creation of new forms and figures, and the exploration of new ideas and possibilities. *The Color Purple* author Alice Walker professed that she fell in love with her imagination. "And if you fall in love with the imagination, you understand that it is a free spirit," she said. "It will go anywhere."[25]

The search for a true passion is one of the driving forces that move life forward for those with a creative spirit. Indeed, Torrance firmly believed, "This search for identity is one of the most important things that a person ever does."[26] Research supports the importance of finding a passion, but also suggests that the particular *shade* of one's passion might matter even more.

Passion's Two Paths

"Follow your passion" is one of the most common clichés out there—not to mention some of the most hackneyed, and probably unhelpful, career advice. While the latest science supports the importance of passion in achieving any personally meaningful goal, it also suggests that this thinking is far too simplistic. Mastering the skills necessary to create something valuable takes hard work.[27] Indeed, passion and effort feed off each other—but passion can be a double-edged sword.

Psychologist Robert Vallerand and his colleagues make a distinction between *harmonious* and *obsessive* passion, which are most importantly distinguished by *how* a passion has been internalized in the person's identity.[28]

When engaging in their activity—performing in theater, for instance—harmoniously passionate people feel in control of their passions. They are not following their passions; they are *one with their passions*. They feel that rehearsing and performing onstage is in harmony with their authentic self and is compatible with the other activities that breathe rich meaning into their lives. In other words, performing is an extension of their inner selves. It is a part of who they are.

In contrast, *obsessively* passionate people are less motivated by a love of their work, and they tend to feel as though they are not in control of their passions. They frequently experience anxiety when engaging in their work and feel constant pressure to outperform others because they see their achievements as a source of social acceptance or self-esteem. They are motivated to engage in their activity due to the promise of external rewards, not their inner inclinations. Obsessive passion is an indicator that the activity has not been healthily integrated into a person's overall sense of self.

The ego feeds off of high performance, and the person may find herself pushing too hard with little improvement, sometimes leading to mental and physical injury. In a nutshell: Harmoniously passionate people are *impelled* to create, whereas obsessively passionate people are *compelled* to create by more extrinsic factors.

This difference matters. The shade of one's passion colors the entire journey of creative achievement, from start to finish.[29] Vallerand and colleagues have found two distinct paths to high performance in pursuits as diverse as drama and basketball to synchronized swimming and classical music.[30] The first road—the *harmoniously passionate road*—is the most direct path. It's paved with a focus on mastery, learning, and growth rather than on things like looking good, becoming famous, or beating others. This path is fueled by feelings of vitality, positive emotions, and joy. In contrast, the second road—the *obsessively passionate road*—is far more winding. While it is paved with goals that can sometimes be adaptive for performance—like proving themselves to others—it also involves *avoiding* challenges that could lead to further growth. This road tends to be marked by lower levels of vitality, positive emotions, and enjoyment—a result that has been found across a range of fields.

When Inspiration Strikes

> When your Daemon is in charge, do not try to think
> consciously. Drift, wait, and obey.
>
> —RUDYARD KIPLING

Passion and its companion, inspiration, are critical pieces of the creativity puzzle. The locus of these moments of inspiration, however, is still something of a mystery. Until recently, inspiration was overlooked as a serious subject of scientific investigation, most likely due to its history of being treated as something supernatural or divine. In ancient Greece, inspiration was thought to come from the Muses, goddesses who presided over the creation of literature and the arts by speaking directly with the artist. Over the course of human history, many great poets have incorporated this idea of the Muse into their writings. "I in myself am one who, when Love breathes within me, takes note, and to that measure which he dictates within, I go signifying," Dante writes in the *Divine Comedy*.

There are three defining features of inspiration. It starts with *evocation*. People are usually inspired by something, whether it's a role model, teacher, experience, or subject matter—this could be as significant as a full-on crystallizing experience or as everyday as noticing an eye-catching photo on Instagram. Evocation occurs largely without conscious effort. As psychologists Todd Thrash and Andrew Elliot say, "One cannot actively awaken oneself to better possibilities through an act of will any more than one can awaken oneself from sleep."[31] But that doesn't mean there's nothing we can do to increase the likelihood of inspiration happening. As we'll see, the creative mind can be primed to make inspiration more likely when we come into contact with the right materials, insight, or inspiring person.

Next comes *transcendent awakening*—a moment of clarity and an awareness of new possibilities. Thrash and Elliot note, "The heights of human motivation spring from the beauty and goodness that precede us and awaken us to better possibilities." This moment of beauty or insight is frequently vivid and can take the form of a grand vision, insight, or a "seeing" of something one has not seen before (but that might have always been there).[32]

This awakening is typically set off by a creative idea or insight that compels the person to energetically bring the idea to fruition. Which leads to the third hallmark feature of inspiration: a *striving to transmit, express, or actualize a new idea, insight, or vision.* The actualization process is usually a *response* to a creative idea, material, or inspiring person.[33] Inspiration, then, explains not only the origin of creative ideas but also their *actualization*. It's important to note, however, that preparation is still necessary for insights to arise in consciousness (see Chapter 5).

What does an inspired person look like? People who enjoy a high frequency and intensity of inspiration in their daily lives tend to be more open to new experiences and report feeling greater absorption and flow in their activities.[34] Openness to experience typically precedes inspiration, however, suggesting that those who are more *open* to inspiration are simply more likely to experience it. Inspired people also have a stronger drive to master their work, but are less competitive. They tend to be more intrinsically motivated by the love of their activity and less motivated by extrinsic factors like success or social status. Therefore, what makes an object inspiring is its perceived subjective value—not how much it's objectively worth or how attainable it is.

There are many benefits, creative and otherwise, to being an easily inspired person. One study found that inspiration leads to increased optimism, belief in one's capabilities, self-determination, and self-esteem. Being an expert in a field is both a cause and an outcome of inspiration, which suggests that a focus on learning and growth increases the likelihood of being inspired, and in turn, inspiration leads to even higher levels of expertise. Inspiration favors the prepared mind.

Inspiration favors the prepared mind.

Inspired people also tend to enjoy increased well-being in life. In particular, they enjoy greater levels of gratitude, positive emotions, life satisfaction, vitality, and self-actualization.[35] Thrash and Elliot also found that inspiration is associated with having a greater purpose in life—inspired people feel that their idea or vision is deeply meaningful and transcends their more self-serving concerns. Inspiration seemed to prompt feelings of gratitude, because inspired people are deeply appreciative of their source of inspiration.

In its transformative, transcendent nature, inspiration is truly the springboard for creativity. As you'll notice throughout this book, creativity and imagination involve seeing new possibilities in life. People who are inspired to see these new possibilities also tend to view themselves as more creative and show actual increases in self-ratings of creativity over time.[36] And on days when people feel more inspired, they tend to say that they feel more creative.

While we usually associate inspiration with visual art, it's also important in other artistic fields and in the scientific world. Patent-holding inventors report being inspired more frequently than nonpatent holders, and the higher the frequency of inspiration, the higher the number of patents they held. Being in a state of inspiration also predicts the creativity of writing samples across scientific writing, poetry, and fiction.[37] Inspired writers are more efficient and productive, spending less time pausing and deleting sentences and more time writing. These effects hold even after taking the individual's writing ability into account.

These findings suggest that it might be time to rethink Thomas Edison's famous inspiration equation, which suggests that genius is "1 percent inspiration and 99 percent perspiration." As most creative people are well aware, this is a gross oversimplification. For one, we've seen that inspiration and effort feed off of each other in a dynamic interplay; indeed, they *need* each other for creativity to flourish. Writers who are more inspired, for instance, actually do more work. Inspiration during writing is positively related to the productivity and efficiency of the final product. Inspired people are *more* likely, not less likely, to do the hard work necessary to achieve their goals.

What's more, people who are harmoniously passionate about their activity are more likely to set a goal to become a master in their field, which in turn predicts higher levels of deliberate practice. These individuals actually do more work because they are more driven to master their craft. It should come as little surprise that when we feel that our work is both emotionally interesting and personally meaningful, accomplishing a task is significantly less mentally taxing.[38]

It doesn't make much sense to single out perspiration as important and treat inspiration as unimportant. They are *jointly* important! Instead of pitting hard work against inspiration, we'd do well to recognize that it's the *dynamic dance* between the two that leads to creativity.

Turning Dreams into Reality

Falling in love with a dream—and with an image of one's future self who has achieved that dream—deeply inspires us to make that vision a reality. But just as hard work and inspiration are both critical to creative achievement, nurturing passion requires both a dream and a plan.

To nourish and sustain motivation toward a creative goal, we must not only fall in love with a dream of our future self, as Torrance says, but also love the process of *becoming that person*—including all the unglamorous, everyday hard work. Entrepreneur James Clear argues that dreaming about the results we desire is not enough to truly motivate us to stay focused on our goals, especially when we experience boredom or setbacks. He writes, "If you want to become significantly better at anything, you have to fall in love with the process of doing it. You have to fall in love with building the identity of someone who does the work."[39]

Indeed, passion and effort feed off of each other. Sometimes hard work can lead to passion, rather than it always being the other way around.[40] Highly motivated creative people fall in love with an image of themselves as a person who will do whatever it takes to achieve their dreams—and this identification becomes, in a way, a self-fulfilling prophecy. It's not about just achieving the dream but, as Clear suggests, becoming a person who has the *grit*—the passion and perseverance for a long-term goal—to *do whatever it takes* to realize that dream.[41] Torrance's dreamers—who went on to become creatively fulfilled and successful—used these visions of themselves not only as an expression of passion but also as *a way to fuel their passion*. Holding on to the dream is especially important in times of inevitable rejection and failure during the creative process and the times when motivation is most difficult to find.

Having dreams and goals alone is not enough to push us through the difficult times and, when it comes to creative work, long hours of practice and experimentation. What's clear is that while we need a dream and a positive self-image, we must also develop strategies for keeping sight of those dreams while we work through the investable challenges that the creative journey presents. Grit, optimism, passion, and hope are all strategies that we use to help us achieve our goals. Positive psychologist Charles Snyder's 1991 hope theory posited that having hope involves having both the *will* and the *ways* to achieve your goals and is more effective than both optimism and self-efficacy as a vehicle for success.[42] Snyder suggests that hope is a *dynamic cognitive motivational system* in which emotions follow thoughts, rather than the opposite. Guided by either a hopeful personality or state of mind, people approach their goals with an attitude and a set of strategies that are conducive to success.

People who are hopeful tend to create learning goals (like experimenting with a new type of sound), which support personal growth and improvement. Those without hope, on the other hand, tend to adopt mastery goals (like selling a certain number of records), which are less focused on growth and more focused on outperforming others.[43] Several studies have also linked hope to academic achievement, while one study found that those who were in a hopeful state came up with more original ideas and associations.[44] Hopeful thinking may actually promote creative thinking skills, insofar as it involves coming up with various flexible strategies to achieve a goal.

As much as we need the will, we also need the ways. The work of New York University psychologist Gabriele Oettingen, who studies the science of motivation, emphasizes both the importance of dreaming and the fact that dreaming alone is not sufficient to get us where we want to go.[45] Oettingen explains that simply dreaming about what we want can actually make us complacent—we're already mentally enjoying the fruits of our desired outcome, so we may be less willing to take on the sacrifices and drudgery required to make that outcome a reality.

So what *does* help? Oettingen employs a technique called *mental contrasting*, which involves imagining the desired goal, and then visualizing the obstacles (both internal and external) that might realistically get in the way of your ability to achieve that goal. What you're doing here is looking at the contrast between a desired future outcome and the realities that you currently face and may face in the pursuit of this outcome. This method can help you not only to clearly identify a dream but also to identify obstacles and devise strategies for dealing with those obstacles. "We need the dream . . . this is a good starting point. Then what we need to do is identify and imagine the obstacles that actually hinder us from fulfilling these dreams. Then we understand what we need to do to achieve these dreams," says Oettingen.[46] Indeed, she has found this technique to be effective in boosting creative performance.[47]

Falling in love with a dream is frequently the starting point. Then, people who fulfill their creative dreams over the long haul balance optimism about the future with realistic strategies for getting closer to their goals; inspiration with hard work; and *dreaming* with *doing*.

Nevertheless, the importance of dreaming should not be understated. As we'll see next, there is a great continuity between the dreams of our youth and the more mature daydreams of our adult lives.

Daydreaming

Your visions will become clear only when you can look into your own heart. Who looks outside, dreams; who looks inside, awakes.

—CARL JUNG

"Was it only by dreaming or writing that I could find out what I thought?" Joan Didion once asked.[1]

Although we don't usually look at it that way, daydreaming is an invaluable tool for "finding out" what we think and feel. Daydreamers are often labeled space cadets, absent minded, out of it, and lazy. Even today, psychologists use phrases such as "thought intrusions," "zoning out," "task irrelevant thoughts," "undirected thought," and "mind wandering" to describe the thoughts and images that arise when our attention shifts away from the external environment and toward our private mental canvas of images, memories, fantasies, and interior monologues.[2] A group of Harvard psychologists even concluded that "a wandering mind is an unhappy mind."[3]

A study by those Harvard researchers found that mind wandering consumes an average of 47 percent of peoples' waking hours. This begs the question: If mind wandering is so costly to our well-being, then why in the world are we so willing to spend nearly half of our lives in this mental state?

Creative thinkers know, despite what their parents and teachers might have told them, that daydreaming is hardly a waste of time. But unfortunately, many students learn to suppress their natural instincts to dream and imagine—instead, they're taught to fit into a standardized mold and to learn by the book, in a way that may not feel natural and that very well may suppress their innate desire to create. But as two prominent psychologists recently noted, "Not all minds who wander are lost"—in fact, the mind's wandering is vital to imagination and creative thought.[4]

Nearly fifty years ago, psychologist Jerome L. Singer established that daydreaming is a normal and indeed widespread aspect of human experience. He found that many people are "happy daydreamers" who enjoy their inner imagery and fantasy.[5] According to Singer, these daydreamers "simply value and enjoy their private experiences, are willing to risk wasting a certain amount of time on them, but also can apparently use them for effective planning and for self-amusement during periods of monotonous task activity or boredom."

Singer coined the term *positive-constructive daydreaming* to describe this type of mind wandering, which he distinguished from poor attention and anxious, obsessive fantasies.[6] By making these important distinctions, Singer was able to highlight the positive, adaptive role that daydreaming can play in our daily lives, under the right circumstances.[7] From the beginning of his research, he found evidence that daydreaming, imagination, and fantasy are related to creativity, storytelling, and even the ability to delay gratification.[8]

Of course, mind wandering *can* be costly when it comes at the wrong time, especially in regard to things like reading comprehension, sustained attention, memory, and academic performance.[9] The inability to control your attention when the task at hand requires it often leads to frustration, just as the tendency to get wrapped up in distracting negative thoughts can lead to unhappiness. But when we consider the fact that most of our important life goals lie far into the future, it's easier to see how daydreaming might be beneficial. When our inner monologues are directed toward and measured against goals, aspirations, and dreams that are personally meaningful, the benefits of daydreaming become much more clear.[10]

Over the past decade, scientists have employed newer methodologies to investigate these potential benefits. In a review of the latest science of daydreaming, Scott and colleague Rebecca McMillan noted that mind wandering offers very personal rewards, including creative incubation, self-awareness, future-planning, reflection on the meaning of one's experiences, and even compassion.[11]

Take creative incubation, for starters. Many of us know from experience that our best ideas come seemingly out of the blue when our minds are off wandering elsewhere. Idle though it may seem, the act of mind wandering is often anything but mindless. Research suggests that an incubation period of mind wandering leads to improvements in creative thinking.[12] The next time you're working hard on a creative project or work assignment that requires intense focus and creative chops, try taking a five-minute daydreaming break every hour or so, and see how it affects your ideas and thinking. During this break, engage in a simple activity that will allow your mind to wander, like walking, doodling, or cleaning. Consider this your creative incubation period and see if you feel a renewed sense of creative energy when you get back to work.

Mind wandering can be anything but mindless.

The Artist as Dreamer

Daydreaming is a key part of the creative toolkit for a number of reasons, including its ability to facilitate creative incubation, self-understanding, and even social understanding. And in the long term, positive daydreaming may help artists along in their pursuit of personally meaningful creative goals.

Artists like John Lennon, who wrote the classic song "Imagine" as a tribute to those who dreamed of the possibility of a better world, have self-identified as dreamers. Andy Warhol, too, said that "everybody must have a fantasy." Turning our attention away from the external world and tuning in to the world within—dreams, fantasies, stories, personal narratives, and feelings—not only builds a sense of meaning and hope, as Lennon's anthem suggests, but also allows us to tap into our deepest wellsprings of creativity.

Why? Creative work requires a connection to one's inner monologue, and it is from this stream of desires, emotions, and ways of making sense of the world that new ideas and novel perspectives arise. T. S. Eliot was ahead of his time in recognizing the role of mind wandering in creative incubation, which he referred to as "idea incubation" in his 1933 work, *The Use of Poetry and the Use of Criticism*. Eliot argued that creativity required an "incubation period" during which the mind could unconsciously process preexisting ideas—and for this reason, he believed that illnesses forcing the artist to take to bed and avoid the usual distractions of their daily routines could be surprisingly beneficial for creative work.

Eliot said that an idea that's been given time to formulate within the mind gives the impression of having "undergone a long incubation, though we do not know until the shell breaks what kind of egg we have been sitting on." These moments of insight, he explains, are characterized by the "sudden lifting of the burden of anxiety and fear which presses upon our daily life so steadily that we are unaware of it, what happens is something negative: that is to say, not 'inspiration' as we commonly think of it, but the breaking down of strong habitual barriers."

Eliot's musing, as it turns out, was fairly prophetic. Research has supported the idea that the creative incubation that occurs during daydreaming is critical to creative thought and achievement and also to insightful problem solving (see Chapter 5).[13] But daydreaming goes far beyond giving our ideas time to simmer— it can powerfully connect us to our humanity. Jack Kerouac once called all human beings "dream beings," because, as he puts it, "dreaming ties all mankind together." Research by Singer and others does show that the solitary activity of daydreaming may bring us together, if we allow ourselves to indulge in it, by bringing us closer to our core inner selves.

Research has shown that dreaming about the future is something that nearly all of us naturally spend quite a bit of time doing.[14] In this way, it can help bring us closer to achieving our goals. People who are active dreamers tend to feel that they are the creators and protagonists of their own lives—or as Nietzsche said, they "make life a work of art." By regularly tapping into our own inner stream of consciousness, we personally reflect on the world and visualize our future selves. The first step to creating a future self is indeed to dream of it. Most people have what's known as a "prospective bias," meaning that when they allow time for self-reflection, their thoughts naturally drift toward the future.[15] This bias facilitates "autobiographical planning"—a process in which we imagine future scenarios, including our own emotional and physical reactions in response to the mental simulations. Many of these future scenarios are related to long-standing unresolved desires, such as potential relationships, social interactions, or desired jobs.[16] This sort of introspection can help us make meaning out of our lives or at least to stumble upon some interesting thoughts and realizations in the process.[17]

Psychoanalyst Carl Jung, a champion of inner experience, also advocated daydreaming as a way to connect with the unconscious, which he believed could heal the self from its emotional and psychological ailments. In 1913, Jung came up with a creative visualization technique called "active imagination," which looks to daydreams to harness the wisdom of the unconscious mind to help solve the problems of the conscious mind.[18] Jung claimed that the free visualizations and mind wandering involved in the technique helped him heal from the emotional problems he was undergoing at the time by giving him new insights on his situation. He referred to the communication between the unconscious and the conscious mind that occurs during this process as the "transcendent function"—transcendent because it makes it possible for the mind to shift in and out of consciousness.[19]

To Sleep, Perchance to Dream

Jung believed that, like daydreams, the dreams we have while asleep are a gateway to connecting with the unconscious. Modern science has determined, as Jung theorized a generation earlier, that daydreaming serves a similar function to the dreams we have at night. When most of us fall asleep, the brain network that involves attention to the outside world (the executive attention network, which consists primarily of the lateral frontal and parietal cortices) deactivates and our deep storehouse of personal thoughts and memories takes over.

There is a great continuity between night dreaming and daydreaming, as both involve an exploration of various aspects of who we are, including self-representations, strivings, current concerns, and autobiographical memory. They both help us process information and can help us access a deeper level of creative thought. Perhaps Edgar Allan Poe was right when he noted that genius might require "dreaming by day":

> Men have called me mad; but the question is not yet settled, whether madness is or is not the loftiest intelligence—whether much that is glorious—whether all that is profound—does not spring from disease of thought—from moods of mind exalted at the expense of the general intellect. They who dream by day are cognizant of many things which escape those who dream only by night. In their gray visions they obtain glimpses of eternity, and thrill, in waking, to find that they have been upon the verge of the great secret.[20]

Like daydreaming, night dreaming can be a time for creative incubation—and for this reason, dreams have been a source of inspiration for artists throughout history. Salvador Dalí referred to many of his works as "hand-painted dream photographs," and his iconic 1931 dream landscape, *Persistence of Memory,* with its imagery of melting clocks, was meant to depict how arbitrary our concept of time becomes when we're trapped in a dream state.

Lennon even penned a hit song, "#9 dream," based on a vision that came to him in a dream one night. He even used the gibberish phrase that he heard calling to him in the dream, *Ah! Böwakawa, poussé, poussé,* as the song's chorus. But the "intellectual Beatle" wasn't the only one to tap into his dreams for inspiration: Paul McCartney composed the melody for "Yesterday"—the most covered song in music history—based on a dream he had one night in 1964. As McCartney recalls: "I woke up one morning with a tune in my head and I thought, 'Hey, I don't know this tune—or do I?' It was like a jazz melody. I went to the piano and found the chords to it, made sure I remembered it and then hawked it round to all my friends, asking what it was: 'Do you know this? It's a good little tune, but I couldn't have written it because I dreamt it.'"[21]

Perhaps most famously, Edgar Allen Poe's hauntingly imaginative stories and poems were often inspired by his nightmares. The poet believed that dreams had been a source of valuable wisdom since biblical times. "There appears no reason," Poe wrote in an 1839 essay, "why this mode of divine communication should be discontinued in the present day."[22]

Unblocking the Flow of Ideas

There's one rather simple and prosaic way to tap into this mode of "divine communication": hop in the shower.

We know that showering is relaxing, but it also seems to

have larger benefits for the mind, supporting creative thought and leading to unexpected insights. Research conducted by Scott, in collaboration with the world's largest showerhead supplier, Hansgrohe, found that 72 percent of people around the globe report experiencing new ideas in the shower.[23] In fact, people reported that they are more likely to get fresh insights in the shower than at work!

As creative people stuck in offices know well, your best ideas don't usually come to you when you're sitting in front of a computer straining to think up a solution to a problem or make a project come together—especially when you've been at your desk for hours. But when you get up for a bathroom break or a walk around the block to clear your head—precisely when your attention wanders away from the task at hand—the missing link pops into your mind. More often than not, the elusive *Aha!* moment comes when you give the intensely focused mind a little break and let your thoughts wander free, uninhibited by critical thought.

A shower is also, quite literally, a place of incubation—a change of scenery from the rest of our everyday lives that's relatively free of stimulation and distractions. Showering insulates us from the external world so that we can focus all of our attention on our inner desires, daydreams, and memories—thereby increasing the likelihood that our mind will come up with creative connections. No matter how minor they may seem, new and unexpected experiences can lead to constructive shifts in thinking. Getting off the couch and jumping in the shower may be all you need to see things a bit differently—it can jolt you out of your ordinary awareness and create the necessary distance to force you to entertain a different perspective.

According to Harvard psychologist Shelley H. Carson, author of *Your Creative Brain*,[24] the brief distraction that a shower provides can also be a good thing when it comes to creativity. She explains that interruptions and diversions can help that all-important creative incubation period. "In other words, a distraction may provide the break you need to disengage from a fixation on the ineffective solution," Carson told the *Boston Globe*.[25]

Woody Allen has been using this technique for most of his creative life. The writer and director says he regularly takes showers for inspiration, sometimes standing in the water for close to an hour to explore what's going through his mind and to get those creative juices flowing.

"In the shower, with the hot water coming down, you've left the real world behind, and very frequently things open up for you," Allen said in a 2013 interview with *Esquire*.[26] "It's the change of venue, the unblocking the attempt to force the ideas that's crippling you when you're trying to write."

But it doesn't have to be the bathroom where you go for a little creative inspiration—find your own personal shower-head, a space where you let your mind roam free—whether it's a walk near the ocean, a country drive, or in your reading nook at home. Nikola Tesla had many great ideas, but one of his best occurred to him far from the laboratory: The inventor came up with his idea for alternating electric currents while out on a leisurely stroll. Tesla used his walking stick to draw a picture explaining how the currents would work to his partner. For Gertrude Stein, it was being in her car, looking at cows. She made a habit of writing for just thirty minutes a day, driving around a farm and stopping at different cows until she found the one that most inspired her.

Take a Hike

> How vain it is to sit down to write when you have not
> stood up to live! Methinks that the moment my legs
> begin to move, my thoughts begin to flow.
>
> —HENRY DAVID THOREAU

Tesla's story isn't unusual. According to anecdotal accounts, Immanuel Kant's daily routine was punctuated by an hour-long walk around Königsberg, the German town where he lived. The philosopher embarked on these strolls religiously, at the same time each afternoon, and was said to be so strict and regimented about his daily walkabout that the townspeople set their clocks according to the time he passed by their houses. Kant is documented to have missed his walk only once, when he was reading Jean Rousseau's *Emilie* and became so engrossed that he stayed home for several days to finish the book.[27]

Kant preferred to be alone as he walked along the Philosopher's Walk, a street named for him, so that he did not have to engage in conversation. The physically frail philosopher preferred not to open his mouth, instead breathing solely through his nose, which he found more conducive to meditating on topics of philosophical inquiry.[28]

Charles Darwin was also known for his devotion to daily walks. Darwin took strolls with his white fox terrier, Polly, along the trail he dubbed his "thinking path" in Kent, England. These walks were used not just as an opportunity for physical exercise but also for mental reflection and creative incubation. Darwin's walks had a unique intellectual value, aiding the naturalist in "reorganizing concepts and revitalizing perception," a kind of "moving meditation" that stimulated deep contemplation and creative connections, according to Australian philosopher Damon Young.[29]

Kant and Darwin are part of a noteworthy historical lineage of *thinker-walkers*. By one estimate, William Wordsworth—whose poetry is filled with images of the natural world—may have walked upward of 180,000 miles in his lifetime,[30] while Virginia Woolf was known to wander London's parks extensively for inspiration. In an 1862 essay for *The Atlantic*, Henry David Thoreau said that daily walks were not a luxury but a necessity for his physical and mental well-being. "I think that I cannot preserve my health and spirits, unless I spend four hours a day at least—and it is commonly more than that—sauntering through the woods and over the hills and fields, absolutely free from all worldly engagements," he wrote.[31]

Aristotle, Nietzsche, Freud, Hemingway, Jefferson, Dickens, Beethoven, and many other thinkers made regular strolls a part of their creative process, and Nietzsche went so far as to say that "all truly great thoughts are conceived by walking." Greek philosopher Diogenes proved the law of motion using the phrase *Solvitur ambulando*, "It is solved by walking,"[32] while Thoreau noted that if we spend time outside, "there will be so much more air and sunshine in our thoughts."[33]

Now, scientists are singing a similar refrain. Studies have shown that creative problems, in fact, can be solved by walking, particularly in nature, thanks to physiological changes in the brain that lead to lower frustration and stress, boosted engagement and arousal, and higher levels of meditation and enhanced mood—all of which can help us come up with more creative connections.[34]

Mindful Daydreaming

Walking through nature is a great way to enjoy the benefits of not only mind wandering but also mindfulness, the practice of cultivating a focused, nonjudgmental awareness on the present moment. With meditation, the most common way of practicing mindfulness, recently exploding in popularity, we're told increasingly to focus on the here and now, whether we're in the shower, on our commute, or sitting in the lotus pose for our morning meditation. So where does that leave daydreaming?

There seems to be a tension between mindfulness, which emphasizes the stilling of the thoughts to cultivate a quiet, peaceful mind, and daydreaming—or "spontaneous mental time travel,"[35] as some psychologists have referred to it—which encourages us to let any and all of our thoughts roam free, sometimes, yes, at the expense of being fully aware of our present surroundings. How can the benefits of mind wandering, which beckons us to disconnect from our surroundings, be reconciled with the many mental health and cognitive benefits of mindfulness?

While there are a number of distinct creative benefits associated with mindfulness (see Chapter 7), being distracted isn't always a bad thing. As University of California, Santa Barbara researchers noted in a recent report,[36] a balance between external-directed focus and free-flowing inward attention may be our natural state.

"Consciousness is continuously moving with ever-changing content, but also ebbs like a breaking wave, outwardly expanding and then inwardly retreating," the researchers write.

Successful innovators are often adept in harnessing both of these important mental states as their creative process calls for them. A connection to our inner selves and our stream of consciousness is undeniably what makes us creative. We all have the potential to become artists precisely *because* we dream. We should allow ourselves to balance the focused mind with the wandering mind, and skilled daydreamers do this naturally. Research has found that those whose daydreams are most positive and most specific also score high in mindfulness.[37]

We all have the potential to become artists precisely *because* we daydream.

It may be wise, then, to question whether we should always be living in the moment and whether this is the best way to foster creative thinking. Finding this "middle way" between mindfulness and mind wandering can help us enjoy optimal benefits of both ways of thinking. Mindfulness helps us truly see what's around us—a skill of paramount importance in life and art—but it must be balanced with giving the mind space to dream, fantasize, and simply roam free.

Of course, as Singer's work pointed out, not all daydreaming is created equal—rumination, for instance, distracts us from our present environment with little mental payoff. And of course, attending to one's inner experience isn't always going to be blissful, and daydreaming puts us in contact with the darkness within ourselves as much as it connects us to the light. But as Singer explains, "What his increased inner capacity offers him is a fuller sense of being intensely alive from moment to moment, and this may be worth the frequent pain of a deeper self-awareness."[38]

As we'll see in the next chapter, solitude is an important means for artists and thinkers to cultivate that inner focus. After all, it is only in the stillness of our own company that we can begin to truly bring our attention to the inner landscape of thoughts, ideas, and emotions that is a crucial wellspring of creativity.

Solitude

It is easy in the world to live after the world's opinion; it is easy in solitude to live after our own; but the great man is he who in the midst of the crowd keeps with perfect sweetness the independence of solitude.

—RALPH WALDO EMERSON

In the last decades of his life, Swedish filmmaker Ingmar Bergman sought peace and quiet in a cabin on the remote island of Faro, in northern Sweden. He lived a simple life there, spending his days working, taking walks, and sometimes entertaining visitors in the evening.[1] In his diaries, Bergman wrote of both the need for solitude in order to do his work and also the challenges of being alone in his mind. By himself, he found, there was no place to hide from his own thoughts. "Here, in my solitude, I have the feeling that I contain too much humanity," he wrote.[2]

It is arguably by virtue of this intimacy with his own thoughts that Bergman was able to do his best work. He took that feeling of having "too much humanity"—all the ecstatic and chaotic emotions, fear, pain, and joy of being a human being—and spun it into great cinematic art. Sitting alone and observing the whole spectrum of his emotions, Bergman was faced with the great challenge of turning these passing thoughts and feelings into film.

The creative act is a process that often unfolds in solitary reflection, and indeed, the portrait of any artist is often one of solitude. The trope of the reclusive writer and the introverted artist stems from a significant truth of creativity: In order to make art, we must find the space to become intimate with our own minds.

The metaphorical "room of one's own" is a basic need for many creative people. For Georgia O'Keeffe, it was a desert ranch in New Mexico, which she loved most during the quiet, early morning hours, when the air was crisp and the rest of the world was still asleep. Jonathan Franzen found the solitude he needed, for four years while writing *The Corrections,* in his Harlem studio with the curtains drawn and the lights off.[3] Poet Emily Dickinson deeply valued her privacy, writing more than eighteen thousand poems in her bedroom in her parents' home in Amherst, Massachusetts.[4] Dickinson was known to rarely leave the house, often speaking to visitors through the closed front door.

Zadie Smith describes solitude as an absolute necessity for writers. "Avoid cliques, gangs, groups," she wrote in the *Guardian*. "The presence of a crowd won't make your writing any better than it is." Smith added that a writer's work space must be separate from everyone in their lives: "Protect the time and space in which you write," she advised.[5]

Somerset Maugham called the writer's life a "lonely life," and Frederico Fellini said it was so lonely, in fact, that he chose to become a filmmaker instead.[6] Indeed, when we think of a great literary genius, the image likely to come to mind is that of a disheveled writer bent over his desk, alone in a dark room with crumpled pieces of paper strewn across the floor.

Creative writing can be a particularly solitary affair, forcing the writer to dive into the depths of her own imagination and memories and leaving little room for collaboration, at least in the early stages.

Perhaps no writer is more famous for his reclusive habits than Marcel Proust, who took to spending his days behind closed doors while writing his masterpiece *Remembrance of Things Past* in 1910.[7] The writer would sleep all day and work all night in his one-bedroom Paris apartment on the Boulevard Haussmann. British historian Jon Kear argues that Proust's environment not only created the conditions for him to do his best work but also deeply influenced its content. Proust felt that his earlier literary aspirations had been compromised by his active social life in Paris, and so he committed to a more solitary life as a "way of redeeming his own sense of time lost"—time lost being, of course, the subject of meditation of *Things Past*.[8]

Kear describes Proust as "living at the heart of the new Paris, his bedroom facing onto one of Paris's most fashionable boulevards, but [keeping] the blinds firmly drawn . . . at the centre of Parisian society but simultaneously distanced from it . . . [belonging] to all this but only by way of self-consciously fashioned detachment."[9]

As Proust surely knew, a life lived "in and apart" is not always an easy one, but it can have creative and personal rewards. To become intimate with oneself can yield meaning, insight, and even psychological well-being. Solitude is an essential element of self-discovery and emotional maturity, and the reflection undertaken in its company can give rise to our most profound personal and creative insights. Being alone forces us to reflect upon all aspects of ourselves—even those parts that we normally choose to leave unexamined.[10]

Alone but Not Lonely

Science has confirmed that time for solitary reflection truly feeds the creative mind. The capacity for solitude is a quality that unites successful creators, who are able to turn away from the distractions of daily life and social interactions to reconnect with themselves. But solitude isn't just about avoiding distractions; it's about giving the mind the space it needs to reflect, make new connections, and find meaning.

Although many esteemed artists and thinkers lived lives of relative solitude, our culture has come to overemphasize the importance of constant social interaction, devaluing and mis-understanding aloneness as a result. Of course, meaningful collaboration is important for creativity in many settings, and it's essential to bringing different perspectives together.[11] As prolific author and biochemist Isaac Asimov wrote in a semi-nal 1959 essay on the nature of creativity, collaboration can be very helpful for generating ideas ("One person may know A and not B, another person might know B and not A," says Asimov). However, the act of creating requires us to find time to ourselves and slow down enough to hear our own ideas—both the good and the bad ones. Some degree of isolation is *required* in order to do creative work, because the artist is con-stantly working through ideas or projects in his mind—and these ideas need space to be developed. The creative person's mind is "shuffling his information at all times, even when he is not conscious of it," Asimov wrote in the essay, first published in 2014. "The presence of others can only inhibit this process, since creation is embarrassing. For every new good idea you have, there are a hundred, ten thousand foolish ones, which you naturally do not care to display."[12]

There is reason to believe that what goes on in the human mind while we're alone is every bit as important as what happens in our interactions with others. And yet, we tend to view time spent alone as time wasted or as an indication of an antisocial or melancholy personality. But as Susan Cain makes clear in her bestseller *Quiet: The Power of Introverts in a World That Can't Stop Talking*, alone doesn't necessarily mean lonely.[13] Cain's book and now her Quiet Revolution initiative have sparked a social movement to shift our bias against quiet moments and personalities.[14] Quiet Revolution offers an online hub for introverts and advocates the creation of safe spaces in schools and workplaces for solitude and creativity.[15]

The capacity for solitude may be a sign of emotional maturity.

Far from being an indicator of negative personality traits or mental illness, the capacity for solitude may be a sign of emotional maturity and healthy psychological development. D. W. Winnicott calls the capacity to be alone "one of the most important signs of maturity in emotional development."[16] Regardless of where you fall on the extraversion spectrum, the *capacity for solitude* is a muscle that anyone can strengthen and tap into as a way to facilitate the creative process. Psychologist Ester Buchholz describes solitude as "meaningful alone time" that fuels joy and fulfillment in both interpersonal relationships and creative work. "The need for genuine and constructive aloneness has gotten utterly lost, and, in the process, so have we," she writes in *Psychology Today*.[17]

> **The *capacity for solitude* is a muscle that anyone can strengthen.**

"The relief provided by solitude, reverie, contemplation, alone and private times is inestimable," Buchholz urges. "Remember that love is not all there is to psychic well-being; work and creativity also sustain health."

As artists and as human beings, time alone to work, develop personal interests, and exercise creativity is imperative. The hobbies and personal passions we cultivate on our own—whether studying history, creating ink pen doodles, speculating in stocks and shares, playing the piano, or gardening—play a crucial role in shaping meaning in our lives. The creative person is constantly seeking to discover himself, to remodel his own identity, and to find meaning in the universe through what he creates. And while the artist's work may be inspired by experience and interaction with others, it is in the reflection of solitude when ideas are crystallized and insights formed. As Goethe put it, "One can be instructed in society, one is inspired only in solitude."

In a world of constant distractions and demands, solitude is particularly critical. The artist must insist upon carving out the psychic space in which to connect with the wellspring of thoughts, dreams, and memories within. On a practical level, sustained focus on an important creative task simply requires a lack of distraction from others. Not only artists and writers but also great business leaders have spoken of the need for solitude in coming up with their best ideas. As the cofounder of Apple Computer, Steve Wozniak, explained in his book *iWoz*, alone time makes innovative thinking possible. His one piece of advice to hopeful innovators? "Work alone":

Most inventors and engineers I've met are like me—
they're shy and they live in their heads. They're
almost like artists. In fact, the very best of them are
artists. And artists work best alone—best outside of
corporate environments, best where they can control
an invention's design without a lot of other people
designing it for marketing or some other committee.[18]

If you've ever tried to do creative work in an open office,
you'd probably agree. Research has shown that creative people
frequently require solitude in order to generate interesting new
ideas, and then turn to collaboration to spin those ideas into a
coherent concept or product.[19]

Your Brain on Solitude

What artists know from experience, neuroscientists have discovered in the lab: Solitary, inwardly focused reflection
employs a different brain network than outwardly focused
attention. When our mental focus is directed toward the outside world, such as when paying attention to a lecture or being
vigilant while driving on the freeway, the executive attention
network typically works in opposition to the imagination network: When one is activated, the other is suppressed.[20] This is
why our best ideas don't tend to arise when our attention is
fully engaged elsewhere.

But the bulk of our day does not require intense vigilance.
As noted earlier, the executive attention network has the capacity to flexibly shift its focus of attention from the outside world
to inner experience. It's during these moments of inner reflection that the executive attention network pulls away from the
dorsal attention network and communicates with the

imagination network. While typically at odds with each other when focusing on the outside world, the latter two networks can be quite complementary for creativity, and boosting the function of one can boost the function of the other. In fact, the brain's ability to toggle between networks and switch gears is tied to well-being and psychological health and is an essential foundation for the healthy development of cognitive control, self-regulation, emotional regulation, and can also lead to our greatest insights.[21]

But we often don't give ourselves much time for purposeful inner reflection—the pace of modern life leaves little time for seemingly unproductive activity as we face increasing distractions and demands for our attention. The mind *must* have the space to settle down if it is to come up with the insights that make for original creative work. When we're engaged in solitary reflection, the brain is able to process information, crystallize memories, make connections, reestablish a sense of identity and construct a sense of self, make meaning from our experiences, and even guide moral judgment. When we're alone relaxing and daydreaming—or simply tuning out our immediate surroundings—the brain's imagination network is activated. This gives us a sort of inner focus, a lens through which to see ourselves and others more clearly.

The most important processes within the imagination network are critical for "active, internally focused psychosocial mental processing," says Mary Helen Immordino-Yang, a neuroscientist who studies social emotion and self-awareness.[22] One key process that activates the imagination brain network is what she calls *constructive internal reflection*. It's a form of deep internal focus—that intense reflective state that many artists and philosophers describe as a prerequisite for the birth of their most original ideas—that helps us make meaning of new information and creative connections between complex thoughts. This type of reflection is facilitated by solitude and typically occurs when the mind is not engaged with anything in the environment. For this reason, creative connections often occur when we're effortlessly relaxing, too—the mind engages in this sort of internal processing while the body is occupied with mundane or habitual tasks, like showering or washing the dishes.

The ability for mental projection fostered by reflection is intimately connected with creativity. Both perspective taking and imagination recruit overlapping structures in the brain and draw on similar capacities. Constructive internal reflection also helps us reconcile our memories with our current experience and our dreams for the future. Research by Daphna Oyserman and colleagues found that an intervention focused on connecting the current school environment with a mental vision of one's future self led to better grades, higher standardized test scores, better attendance, more academic initiative, greater connection to school, and a greater concern about doing well.[23]

Solitude and the Search for Truth

Solitude and creativity have a long and storied history. Since ancient times, a solitary life has been seen as a key to unlocking the mind's highest creative, intellectual, and spiritual potential.

Philosophers dating back to ancient Greece have celebrated solitude as essential to pursuits of the mind and even to living a good life. Aristotle posited the solitary act of contemplation as the "highest good for man," which could be practiced only without the distractions and influence of others. Though Aristotle lauded the virtues of the active life of statesmanship and participating in the democracy, he also viewed the life of philosophical contemplation as a life of activity, albeit solitary activity, that is directed toward the highest good of seeking truth.[24]

Centuries later, French Renaissance philosopher and essayist Michel de Montaigne popularized the idea of solitude as a means of intellectually separating oneself from the crowd and forging a unique perspective and sense of self-reliance. (As we'll discuss in Chapter 10, Montaigne's view was an early look at the willingness to defy the crowd as a predictor of creative achievement.) He wrote in his essay "Of Solitude," "contagion is very dangerous in the crowd."[25]

To develop one's own inner wisdom and avoid adopting a lemming-like mentality, Montaigne believed, we must strike out on our own and experience both the risks and the rewards of solitude. He wrote, "We have lived enough for others; let us at least live out the small remnant of life for ourselves; let us now call in our thoughts and intentions to ourselves, and to our own ease and repose. . . . The greatest thing in the world is for a man to know that he is his own."

Inspired in many ways by the ancients, existentialist thinkers returned to this tradition of solitude, both in the content of their philosophy and in their own lives. Proust called Kierkegaard, Nietzsche, and Schopenhauer—who carried on the tradition of the solitary self in philosophy—the "lonely intellectuals."[26]

German existentialist philosopher Martin Heidegger, too, sought the answers to life's biggest questions in a remote cabin in the German mountains, where he spent the better part of a decade in solitary reflection writing his magnum opus, *Being and Time*. Heidegger left university life in the German town of Freiburg, where he worked as a professor and later a rector, for his family's remote mountain cottage in the Black Forest to devote himself to answering a single question that guided his life's work. The question was "What is being?" and the answer became *Being and Time,* a work of sweeping scope and depth that is commonly regarded as one of the most important works of contemporary European philosophy. The majority of *Being and Time*—and a number of Heidegger's other philosophical works—was written at the mountain cottage and in a rented room in a nearby farm house. The cottage, which Heidegger referred to as "die Hütte," or "the hut," was built by his wife, Elfride, as a place where her husband could work in peace and quiet. There, Heidegger said he felt "transported" into *Being and Time's* "own rhythm."[27] Philosopher Eric Sean Nelson explains that for Heidegger, "solitude is a condition not of escaping the world but of encountering it."[28] In silence, we can finally *hear* the world around us. This notion powerfully shaped both the philosopher's own creative habits and his idea of *authenticity* as a type of purposeful solitude that can be maintained even in the midst of others.

Of course, solitude is also a way to directly connect with something greater—to experience that feeling of mythical oneness and total union with God or nature. In 1845, Henry David Thoreau famously left the shackles of society behind, set out for Walden Pond, and wrote what is now perhaps the most famous text on the virtues of solitude and a life lived in tune with nature. In *Walden, or Life in the Woods*, Thoreau refers to the company of others as "weary and dissipating," while being alone, in contrast, is "wholesome" and thoroughly enjoyable. "I love to be alone," he wrote. "I never found the companion that was so companionable as solitude."[29] Thoreau lived in relative solitude for two years, two months, and two days, during which time he wrote some of his greatest work.

D. H. Lawrence, who was greatly influenced by Thoreau, also sought alone time to connect with not just the individual self, but the universal Self. As Lawrence wrote, "Be quite alone, and feel the living cosmos softly rocking."[30]

As you can see, many of the most profound creative and spiritual experiences we encounter take place internally, when we allow ourselves the time to disconnect from others and turn inward. Matthieu Ricard, the French Buddhist monk, bestselling author, photographer, and humanitarian—who has been called the "happiest man in the world"—has turned to solitude as both a spiritual and a creative practice. Ricard says that during solitary walks, he lets ideas float at the surface of his mind, "without trying to interfere with them drifting here and there." Eventually, one of these ideas crystallizes. The mind stops drifting, and says "aha!"[31] He's written about the connection he feels with the flow of life when spending time alone in nature:

> In the solitude of immaculate nature, each moment is worth its weight in gold [and] brings us closer to the ultimate nature of things. The outside silence opens the doors of the inner silence. Then, the freshness of the present moment nurtures our heart with good qualities. When silence reigns, our mind can easily stretch over the space around us and melt into it. The outside peace and the inner peace are as one.[32]

After a period of retreat into solitude, at some point these thinkers felt compelled to return to society and tell others about their experience. As we've seen, key to creativity is the balance of focus on the self and focus on others, inwardness and outwardness, deep reflection and motivated action. The ability to appropriately toggle between inner and outer worlds is one of the artist's greatest assets—for, as British psychiatrist Anthony Storr puts it, the aim of their work is to "[color] the external world with the warm hues of the imagination."[33] In the deep inwardness and reflection of solitude, the artist is able to tap into his deep stores of unconscious creativity and intuitive wisdom and then bring that deep insight to the surface of the mind and onto the paper or canvas.

5

Intuition

The intuitive mind is a sacred gift and the rational
mind a faithful servant. We have created a society
that honors the servant and has forgotten the gift.

—ALBERT EINSTEIN

A "Peculiar Presentiment"

Even after five years had passed, young chemist Albert
Hofmann still couldn't stop thinking about one seemingly
useless chemical compound that he had synthesized in the lab.

Hofmann had been attempting to isolate a compound
thought to have potential circulation- and respiration-
stimulating properties and therefore possible medical value.
Working for a Swiss chemical company, the thirty-two-year-
old scientist was tasked with synthesizing twenty-five chemical
compounds using ergot, a poisonous fungus that grows on rye
and had been used in folk medicine, particularly among mid-
wives and alchemists, for centuries. It was believed that an
active substance in the fungus (in small doses) might have
medical applications. Hofmann combined lysergic acid, the
nucleus of ergot's biologically active compounds, with other
materials, using it as the basis for a number of chemical reactions in the hopes of targeting a useful compound.

He synthesized a full twenty-five compounds using lysergic acid, but he never quite found what he was looking for. Yet there was something about the twenty-fifth combination— a reaction with the ammonia derivative diethylamine, to create a final compound, abbreviated LSD-25—that struck him, unremarkable though it seemed. The only distinctive quality of the substance was that the animals became slightly excitable when it was tested on them—an effect deemed unimportant.[1]

Hofmann continued with the research, and his work with ergot went on to inform some important pharmaceuticals. But he couldn't shake the strange feeling that compound twenty-five might possess properties that he had not been able to identify at the time. Five years later, with little more than a nagging feeling to guide him, Hofmann synthesized the compound once again.

"I could not forget the relatively uninteresting LSD-25," he wrote in his 1980 memoir. "A peculiar presentiment . . . induced me, five years after the first synthesis, to produce LSD-25 once again so that a sample could be given to the pharmacological department for further tests."[2]

This was a rather strange request on Hofmann's part. Standard practice at the lab was that experimental substances once deemed not to be of pharmacological interest were removed from the research program, never to be revisited.

The story of what occurred next has gone down in psychedelic history. In the final stage of crystallizing LSD-25, a trace amount of the substance got on Hofmann's hand, causing him to feel a bit strange and go home sick. This odd reaction piqued his curiosity and inspired a course of self-experimentation. On April 19, 1943, Hofmann ingested an "infinitesimal dose" of LSD and, while riding his bike home from the lab, experienced the first acid trip ever. (That day is forever known to LSD aficionados as "bicycle day.") Hofmann became overwhelmed by sharpened colors and patterns, lofty thoughts, and feelings of euphoria and connection with the universe. The highly altered state of consciousness he experienced that day was like nothing he had felt before, with the exception of an inexplicable mystical experience of oneness with nature that he once had while hiking through the Swiss mountains as a boy.[3] He wrote, "This self-experiment showed that LSD-25 behaved as a psychoactive substance with extraordinary properties and potency. . . . There was to my knowledge no other known substance that evoked such profound psychic effects in such extremely low doses, that caused such dramatic changes in human consciousness and our experience of the inner and outer world."[4]

Today, the discovery of the hallucinogenic drug is often labeled one of the greatest "accidents" in modern scientific history. But the discovery was far more than a lucky happenstance. Quoting French chemist Louis Pasteur, Hofmann later said, "In the realm of scientific observation, luck is granted only to those who are prepared."

While we usually think of intelligence, particularly of the scientific variety, as one's level of skill in deliberate reasoning and analysis—the sort of skill that can be measured using IQ tests—Hofmann's discovery illustrates the power of a very different, and often undervalued, type of intelligence: the power of the unconscious mind.[5] With years of experience in synthesizing chemical compounds, Hofmann had developed a deep storehouse of knowledge, and his mind had become highly attuned to subtle qualities and variations in the chemicals. Even when rational (and institutional) thinking told him that the new compound was without value, a different part of his mind told him to pay closer attention— and he was right.

Hofmann's story of almost preternatural intuition isn't unusual in the arts and sciences. Reflecting on their biggest breakthroughs, many innovators have described elusive solutions as coming to them in a sudden flash of insight, while artists often describe their best ideas arising as if out of nowhere. The unconscious mind is the governing force behind many of the myriad decisions we make each day—from the mundane (what to eat for breakfast) to the more impactful (whether to quit your job).

Gut feelings and inner knowings—those unconscious nudges that propel us to action or bring about sudden shifts in perspective—are a guiding force in our lives. This was certainly the case for Steve Jobs, who first began to explore the power of the unconscious mind when he was traveling through India after dropping out of college. Later, Jobs went so far as to call intuition "more powerful than intellect." In a 2011 essay for the *New York Times*, his biographer Walter Isaacson described intuition as being at the core of the Apple founder's genius:

> His imaginative leaps were instinctive, unexpected, and at times magical. They were sparked by intuition, not analytic rigor. Trained in Zen Buddhism, Mr. Jobs came to value experiential wisdom over empirical analysis. He didn't study data or crunch numbers but like a pathfinder, he could sniff the winds and sense what lay ahead.[6]

It's not uncommon to hear creativity described as a mystical process of inspiration from somewhere beyond the self. "What I capture in spite of myself interests me more than my own ideas," Picasso once said, explaining that he had to simply begin drawing—and stop thinking—in order to let inspiration flow from his paintbrush.[7]

Many writers have also said that in order to do their best work, they must enter a deeper state of mind, beyond everyday thoughts and emotions. E. M. Forster said that the writer, under the spell of inspiration, enters a dreamlike state. "He lets down as it were a bucket into his subconscious and draws up something which is normally beyond his reach. He mixes this thing with his normal experiences, and out of the mixture he makes a work of art."[8] Henry James, too, allotted the unconscious an important role in writing fiction, saying that he would drop good ideas into the "deep well of unconscious cerebration," in hopes that "buried treasure might come to light."[9]

Fahrenheit 451 author Ray Bradbury even insisted that a writer ought to avoid developing his rational thinking skills, for fear that they'd get in the way of his intuition. College wasn't a suitable place for writers, Bradbury said, because learning to overintellectualize things threatened to crush the intuitive mind with reason and analysis. The writer himself kept a sign above his typewriter for twenty-five years that read, "Don't think!" As Bradbury explained in a 1974 interview, "The intellect is a great danger to creativity . . . because you begin to rationalize and make up reasons for things, instead of staying with your own basic truth—who you are, what you are, what you want to be."[10]

Seeds of the tension between the creative unconscious and the rational mind can be traced all the way back to the ancient Greeks, who believed that there were nine Muses who protected the arts and offered creative inspiration to us mere mortal artists. When inspiration struck, it did not come from the mind of the artist himself, but was instead a gift from the Muses. Creative inspiration was neither rational nor embodied—so how could the human mind be responsible for ideas that it did not "think up" itself? How, in essence, does one create something from nothing? Plato explained in his dialogue *Ion*, "Epic poets who are good at all are never masters of their subject. They are inspired and possessed."[11]

The Romans, too, grappled with the question of where creative inspiration comes from—and concluded that it could not possibly arise from the mind itself. As author Elizabeth Gilbert points out in her popular TED talk on creative genius, the ancient Romans believed that one could not be a genius—rather, one *had* a genius, a sort of fickle, disembodied creative spirit that could come and go at will. "A genius was this sort of magical divine entity that is believed to literally live in the walls of an artist's studio, kind of like Dobby the house elf . . . who would come out and invisibly assist the artists with their work and shape the outcome of that work," she says.[12]

Creative inspiration remained something of a mystery into the Romantic era, when British literary critic William Hazlitt claimed that genius, by definition, acts unconsciously. "Those who have produced immortal works, have done so without knowing how or why. The greatest power operates unseen," he wrote in an essay on genius. Only when the artist deviates from the "natural bent of the mind," he argued, does she begin to feel her own incapacity, and therefore to experience obstacles.[13]

As Hazlitt suggests, insight often *does* occur when the rational mind quiets down—at least for a moment, and often unintentionally—and we open ourselves up to the more subtle processes of our unconscious thought systems. The original *Eureka!* moment famously occurred when the Greek philosopher and mathematician Archimedes discovered the calculation for measuring volume, which had long eluded him, while relaxing in the bathtub. Suddenly and without warning, he realized exactly how to calculate the amount of space occupied by a three-dimensional object. He then—so the story goes—ran naked through the streets in rapture shouting "Eureka!" Deep intuitions like Archimedes's, bolstered by high levels of scientific expertise, were also what guided famous insights such as Hofmann's discovery of LSD, Watson and Crick's discovery of the double-helix structure of DNA, and Darwin's formulation of the theory of natural selection. As Pasteur said, in science, luck is granted to those who are prepared.

Intuition tends to be overlooked or deemed unscientific because of its connections to the psychic and new age, but its power is real, and we're starting to have a better idea of what it looks like in the brain and how it might be maximized. The U.S. military is even investigating the power of the unconscious mind,[14] which has helped troops make quick judgments during combat and can end up saving lives.

We now know that intuition *is* a form of thinking—but it's a different mode of cognition than the one we use for conscious, effortful deliberation. Intuition arises from unconscious, or spontaneous, information-processing systems, and it plays an important role in how we think, reason, create, and behave socially. Over the past thirty years, cognitive scientists have made huge strides in demystifying the power of the unconscious mind.[15] The conceptualization of the unconscious as the source of suppressed and often socially inappropriate ideas, wishes, and desires—as perpetuated by Freud and other psychodynamic psychologists—has gradually been transformed into an unconscious that is recognized to serve many adaptive functions. The recognition and study of this mode of thought has given rise to *dual-process* theories of human cognition, which propose that there are two fundamental modes of information processing that constantly interact to help us think, reason, and create.

A Tale of Two Minds

Research on dual-process theories of cognition suggests that we possess one mode of thought that is fast and automatic and one that is more controlled and deliberate.[16] You might be familiar with the seminal work of Nobel Prize winners Daniel Kahneman and Amos Tversky on the ways our intuitive judgments can lead us to make erroneous decisions. In his bestselling book *Thinking, Fast and Slow*, Kahneman reviews a large body of research suggesting that cognitive illusions, or mistakes, tend to occur when our fast and automatic "System 1" is not kept in check by the rational deliberation of "System 2."

In recent years, researchers have preferred to think of different processes, rather than systems, and have gone beyond judgment and decision making to also look at the importance of a variety of processes for social cognition and creativity.[17] *Type 1* processes consist of a number of mental structures and states that can influence our thought and actions outside our conscious awareness or control.[18] Independent of input from the conscious mind, type 1 processes drive us to action, but often without our awareness[19]—this system "operates unseen," in Hazlitt's words. Like Picasso and Bradbury, many creative people describe their ideas as the product of a mode of thinking that is beyond conscious control. What they're describing is effortless and spontaneous type 1 thinking, which includes creativity-boosting processes such as intuition, emotions, implicit learning, reduced latent inhibition, cognitive shortcuts (or heuristics, as psychologists call them), automatic associations based on prior experience, and evolutionarily evolved instincts.

Type 2 processes, on the other hand, are more effortful and controlled, and they play a greater role in a number of skills that most people tend to think of as intelligence—reflection, rationality, metaphorical and analogical thought, cause-and-effect reasoning, reality monitoring (the ability to distinguish imagination from reality), metacognition (the ability to reflect on one's own mental activities), and executive functioning.[20]

While less attention has been paid to individual differences in *unconscious* information processing—unsurprising in a society that tends to value the rational and analytical over the intuitive, emotional, and imaginative—in recent decades, research on the potentially adaptive functions of type 1 processing has accumulated.[21] Researchers have suggested that the brain's implicit information-processing system can be, in fact, *very* intelligent. Nonconscious processes may indeed be faster and structurally more sophisticated than our conscious thinking systems.[22]

Scott's 2009 dual-process theory of intelligence suggests that a hierarchy of controlled and spontaneous processes act together, to a certain degree, to determine all intelligent behaviors.[23] Working in the background of consciousness, spontaneous type 1 processes help us assimilate new information into our existing knowledge structures, aiding us in complex pattern recognition. This is one of the reasons unconscious processing and acuity may be increased in a particular area of focus by acquiring expertise. The better we know something, the more able we may be to automatically and implicitly come up with a potential solution.

What's more, implicit learning, a critical type 1 process, is frequently a catalyst for moments of creative inspiration and insight. Neuroscientist Jeffrey Hawkins has found that when confronted with a new problem, we conjure up memories of similar situations and use these memories to create analogies that help us solve the problem.[24] The more abstract we are with our connections between memories and predictions, the more skilled and sophisticated our creative thinking will be. As you can imagine, abstract and broad-ranging connections tend to breed novel and unusual ideas. When our pattern-recognition system uses unusual analogies to make unconventional connections, we come up with more original ideas and solutions.

Controlled and spontaneous processes are both valuable, but at different times during the creative process.[25] Spontaneous processes play the largest role during the *generative* phase of creative thinking, when we're coming up with new ideas. Then, during the *exploratory* phase of creative cognition, we tap into the conscious, rational mind to play around with the ideas we've generated, and to uncover their uses. So when first approaching a creative problem, we tend to loosen and diffuse our attention and then consciously refocus that attention when it's time to figure out how to make those ideas fly.

Rely too heavily on intuition, and you risk certain cognitive pitfalls. In *The Invisible Gorilla*, psychologists Christopher Chabris and Daniel Simons, winners of the 2004 Ig Nobel Prize for unusual research, point out that good decisions require a capacity for both automatic and deliberate modes of thought and for a certain degree of flexibility in switching from one to the other. Chabris and Simons conclude, "The key to wise decision-making, we believe, is knowing when to trust your intuition and when to be wary of it and do the hard work of thinking things through."[26]

Finding a balance of these thinking styles is critical to achieving mastery in any creative field.[27] With the integration of intuition stemming from a deep rational focus, the master is able to gain a more holistic view of the world and to peer into a deeper side of life. "When we fuse this intuitive feel with rational processes, we expand our minds to the outer limits of our potential and are able to see into the secret core of life itself," Robert Greene writes in his book *Mastery*.

The creative process often exemplifies this delicate dance of analytical and unconscious processing. Take Henri Poincaré, the nineteenth-century French mathematician, for instance. Poincaré described instances in which he suddenly found the answer to a mathematical problem at times when his attention was directed elsewhere and he wasn't consciously deliberating on the problem. He believed that unconscious thinking was to thank for these moments of sudden creative inspiration. Insights, he said, come with "characteristics of conciseness, suddenness, and immediate certainty."[28]

Poincaré once described the experience of rationally deliberating on a particular mathematic problem for weeks, and then deciding to briefly push the question out of his mind as he ventured off on an outdoor excursion. He wrote, "Just as I put my foot on the step, the idea came to me, though nothing in my former thoughts seemed to have prepared me for it. . . . I made no verification . . . but I felt absolute certainty at once."[29]

This is a fairly accurate description of the way we toggle between these modes of thought during the creative process.[30] But

Poincaré was also prophetic in describing what we now know about sudden insights.

Flashes of Insight

"An insight is an unexpected shift in the way we understand things," decision-making expert Gary Klein said in a 2013 interview with the *Huffington Post*. "It comes without warning. It's not something that we think is going to happen and that's why it's unexpected. It feels like a gift and in fact it is."[31]

Insights have led scientists to groundbreaking revelations about the nature of the universe, or at least the galaxy. Astronomer William Wilson Morgan discovered the spiral structure of the Milky Way in a "flash inspiration . . . a creative intuitional burst" one night when he glanced up at the sky and made a casual observation about the organization of the stars. It was a breakthrough. He later substantiated the idea with data and calculations, and the new knowledge became a cornerstone of our scientific understanding of our place in the universe.

Insights *are* like gifts from the unconscious mind. Instead of sitting in front of a blinking cursor, straining to find a solution, our unconscious processing system does the heavy lifting for us. As cognitive neuroscientists John Kounios and Mark Beeman note, insights may feel sudden, but they are generally preceded by a great deal of unconscious mental activity.[32] Think about that feeling when a solution enters the very "fringes" of your conscious awareness—this crossroads between conscious perception and intuitive thinking, the moment when an observation of the stars triggers a gut feeling that you have arrived upon a realization about the fundamental structure of the galaxy.[33] These moments of illumination and clarity bubble up to the surface level of our awareness from way down in the depths of the unconscious. Research has shown that feelings of "warmth" about a solution remain at fairly stable, low levels as the solution is approached, and then spike dramatically at the moment of insight.[34]

While most tests we're given in school—such as standardized tests of achievement and IQ tests—are primarily analytical, most problems in *life* require insightful thought processes. William James, the founder of the field of psychology, referred to the ability to find a worthy problem as "sagacity."[35] Likewise, Einstein commented that "the mere formulation of a problem is far more often essential than its solution."[36]

In recent years, psychologists have begun to understand the set of skills that differentiate good analytical problem solvers from good insightful problem solvers. The key to insightful problem solving appears to be the ability to harness a mix of intuitive processes and analytical processes and the flexibility to switch between them.

Consider a study conducted by University of Minnesota psychologist Colin DeYoung and colleagues, in which they investigated the relationship between various cognitive abilities and insightful problem solving. Here's an example of one of the problems they presented to participants:

> There is an ancient invention still used in many parts
> of the world today that allows people to see through
> walls. What is it?

That was an easy one (75 percent of participants answered correctly with "window"). Now try this one:

A young boy turned off the lights in his bedroom and managed to get into bed before the room was dark. If the bed is ten feet from the light switch and the lightbulb and he used no wires, strings, or other contraptions to turn off the light, how did he do it?

If you found that one a bit trickier, don't worry—only 30 percent of the participants in the study answered it correctly! (*Spoiler*: The correct answer is that it was still daylight.) The researchers also measured *convergent thinking* through tests of vocabulary and working memory (the ability to monitor and manipulate information in consciousness) and *divergent thinking* by having participants respond to problems such as "Suppose that all humans were born with six fingers on each hand instead of five. List all the consequences or implications that you can think of."

Then, they tested the ability to "break frame" by asking participants to describe a series of playing cards they saw on the computer screen. After seeing a number of cards, participants encountered an anomalous card—a black four of hearts. Faced with this anomalous card, many participants just weren't able to break their framing of the problem (they became fixated on the idea that the task was to identify normal playing cards), so many of them attempted to preserve either the color or shape of the card, describing it as a "four of spades" or a "four of hearts." One participant was so stuck that after multiple inaccurate descriptions of the anomalous card, he proclaimed: "It looks like a black four of hearts. But that's impossible!"

Those who were adept at solving the insightful problems had a better vocabulary, working memory, imagination, and ability to break their frame on the anomalous card task. But compared to analytical problem solving (which primarily required mathematical and logical analysis), insightful problem solving was *uniquely* associated with the ability to flexibly switch categories on the divergent thinking task and the ability to break frame on the anomalous card task. These findings are consistent with a number of other studies showing that insightful problem solving doesn't solely draw on knowledge and memory, but also requires the ability to break out of habitual framing and switch perspectives or thinking strategies.[37]

Kounios and Beeman, who have studied the way that the brain generates *Aha!* moments, have shown how insights break through mental blocks or impasses. They used a variety of methodologies, including brain-imaging technology and EEG, to pin down exactly where, when, and how insights occur in the brain.[38] To capture the insight process, they administered the Remote Associates Test (RAT) to participants, a test based on Sarnoff Mednick's seminal associative theory of creativity.[39] On the RAT test, participants must find a word that connects three seemingly unrelated words (for example, *fish*, *mine*, *rush*). Doing well on this task requires conceptual restructuring because the process of arriving at the answer isn't immediately obvious. Creative people have been shown to be better able to access these distant, remote, and nonobvious associations.[40]

Kounios and Beeman found that different brain regions were active at different stages of the insight process. Before solving the problems, when their minds were at rest, insightful people displayed more *externally* focused attention (as exhibited by greater activation across the visual cortex).[41] This is consistent with the idea that creative, insightful people are naturally keen observers of their surroundings (see Chapter 7). But once told they were going to be solving an insight problem, these insightful individuals flipped their mind-set and showed increased activity inbrain regions that are critical for inner reflection and mental flexibility.[42] This suggests that when insightful people solve insight problems, their brains start preparing to flexibly switch attention to promising, nonobvious solutions coming from the unconscious mind.

After the mind has been primed for insight, a number of changes occur in the brain right before the actual flash of insight occurs. Just before the moment of insight, a short reduction of visual input occurs—activity in the visual cortex almost comes to a halt as people shut out the outside world and their minds reach for the unconsciously activated solution that's just *so close* to conscious awareness. At the moment of insight itself—when participants realized the solution to the RAT problems—the researchers found a sharp spike in neural activity in the right anterior temporal lobe.[43] According to Kounios and Beeman, this brain area in the right hemisphere "facilitates integration of information across distant lexical or semantic relations, allowing solvers to see connections that had previously eluded them."[44]

Think about it: Sometimes, when you're so close to a solution, you may even squint your eyes as you desperately search for it. This temporary shutdown of the visual cortex turns the mind's focus inward on the impending solution, which serves to reduce distraction and boost the "loudness" of the solution as it finally comes to mind. The brain areas associated with processing the external world go dark, and then suddenly there is a flash of illumination in consciousness.

While the right anterior temporal lobe appears to be conducive to insights, the left anterior temporal lobe can sometimes get in the way of insights. Indeed, some people with anterior temporal lobe dementia to the left side of their brain have been found to suddenly display creative and artistic interests and skills they had never shown before.[45] It's possible that the dementia allowed them to shed some of the conscious, language-based conceptual knowledge that was keeping their unconscious skills dormant. Other research has found that exceptional skills among savants that are typically nonverbal in nature—including musical, artistic, calendar calculating, lightning arithmetic calculating, and mechanical/visual spatial skills—are frequently associated with dysfunction of the left anterior temporal lobe.[46] Because many of these savants have below-average IQ scores, this offers further support for the incredible power of the unconscious mind operating independently of conscious reasoning.[47]

Stimulating Insight

Anecdotally, many artists and scientists report spikes in emotional intensity after the moment of insight, including a "highly positive surprise at either the content or manner of the realization," Kounios and Beeman note.[48] Einstein called his realization of the general theory of relativity "the happiest moment of my life," while Virginia Woolf once said, "Odd how the creative power brings the whole universe at once to order." Analytic solutions, on the other hand, tend not to be accompanied by such bursts of positive emotion.[49]

But what about *before* the moment of insight? The traditional view is that being in a positive mood broadens your attention and increases your likelihood of experiencing an insight.[50] Recent research, however, suggests that it may not be so simple. Some studies have suggested that it's not emotional valence (positive or negative emotions), but *motivational intensity*, that really matters.[51] Low motivational intensity broadens attention (to seek out possible goals), whereas high motivational intensity focuses attention on the object of interest regardless of whether the emotions are positive or negative. Therefore, if we want to stimulate deep insights, simply getting people in a positive mood is unlikely to do the trick.

Indeed, emerging research suggests that mixing together both positive *and* negative emotions can help facilitate creativity. In their delightful book, *The Upside of Your Dark Side*, Todd Kashdan and Robert Biswas-Diener show the benefits of being your "whole self"—harnessing both positive and negative emotions—for optimal success and fulfillment.[52] In one study that supports this idea in the realm of creativity, people who experienced intense positive and negative emotions scored higher on tests of creative potential than those who scored high in positive or negative emotions alone.[53]

Additionally, research by Christina Fong at Carnegie Mellon suggests that "emotional ambivalence"—the simultaneous experience of positive and negative emotions—increases sensitivity to unusual associations, a key attentional state that allows for insights to arise.[54] Fong uses the example of getting a promotion—you may be excited that you are advancing in your career, but also feel bittersweet because you will miss your friends and colleagues. She found that people experiencing emotional ambivalence displayed a heightened sensitivity to unusual relationships because they were more likely to perceive their environment as unusual. This recent body of research is consistent with the importance of experiencing unexpected environments for creativity (see Chapter 6), and also suggests that creative people don't just have messy minds; they also have *messy emotions*.

This may be why some people with bipolar disorder—which involves states of both hypomania, or exuberance, and depression—report heightened creativity.[55] While there needs to be more research on this possibility,[56] and bipolar disorder certainly shouldn't be romanticized, it is becoming quite clear that intense emotions—both positive and negative—can lead to creative insights.

Another way to stimulate insight may be to literally stimulate the brain. In an interesting line of research, neuroscientists have been looking at the effect of brain stimulation on insightful problem solving.[57] In one study, Australian neuroscientist Allan Snyder and colleagues administered the nine-dot problem—often referred to as the "impossible problem"—to participants. Try it yourself here:

Connect all nine of these dots with just four straight lines without lifting your finger or retracing a line:

If you had difficulty with this problem, you're not alone: The expected solution rate for this problem, based on a century of psychological research, is 0 percent.[58] Snyder and his colleagues gave twenty-eight participants this problem to solve, and before brain stimulation, as expected, none solved it correctly.

Then, the researchers used transcranial direct current stimulation (tDCS) to decrease the cortical excitability of the left anterior temporal lobe while simultaneously *increasing* the excitability of the right anterior temporal lobe. The idea here is that with the dominance of language quieted in the left anterior temporal lobe,[59] the right temporal lobe can better integrate distant relationships and ideas. After ten minutes of tDCS treatment, more than 40 percent of the participants solved the problem correctly. For a control condition, they put electrodes on the heads of eleven additional participants but turned off the electrical current after thirty seconds. None of these participants, who received the same experience as those who underwent the actual tDCS, solved the impossible problem. Combining the results their laboratory collected over a period of eight months, they estimated the probability of the findings happening by chance were less than *one in a billion*.

Why? It's possible that by reducing left hemisphere dominance and turning up the juice on the right anterior temporal lobe, the brain stimulation facilitated outside-the-box thinking, reducing the tendency to see the square with imposed rigid boundaries.

One of their participants was excluded from the study because he suffered a head injury when he was ten years old. He revealed his injury to the experimenters, however, only once he showed up to the testing session. Even though he couldn't participate in the study, he still expressed an interest in solving the impossible problem. Astoundingly, he not only breezed through that problem but also solved another difficult insight problem they gave him. Perplexed, the researchers tried to figure out how this person was able to solve a problem that no one else on this planet seems to be able to solve—that is, until they had their own *Aha!* moment, and asked the participant to send them his medical report from eleven years earlier. The researchers must have fallen off their chairs when they read in the neurologist's report that their participant suffered

multiple injuries to the left hemisphere, with a particular frac-
ture at the left temporal bone!

As you can see, insightful problem solving can't be boiled
down to any single way of thinking. Instead, it draws on a
range of thought processes. Indeed, our greatest insights occur
at that intersection between our inner and outer worlds.

Creative Insight: More Than Ten Thousand Hours

Creativity goes beyond mere knowledge and expertise; it
requires the ability not only to solve but to *find* problems,
and this calls for more than relying on tired formulas.

To be sure, expertise and knowledge are very important to the creative process and can even increase the
accuracy of intuition.[60] Famously, K. Anders Ericsson
showed that engaging in a craft through many hours of
deliberate practice—when one constantly strives to learn
from feedback and push beyond his or her limits—leads
to the formation of new mental structures that can help us
process information more quickly, hold more new information in our heads at one time, and engage in reasoning
within the field with more ease and fluidity.[61] When we've
built up a solid knowledge base, we're essentially operating on a densely connected network, and we're able to
access information in a more efficient manner.[62]

But as Ericsson's theory of expertise grew in popularity, it became generally assumed by the general public
that in many domains—from musicians to chess players
to artists to dancers to runners—the *most important difference* between masters and novices across all fields
was deliberate practice.[63]

There are a number of problems with applying the expert performance framework to understanding creative genius, however. For one, psychologists have suggested that the relationship between knowledge and creativity is best characterized by an "inverted U-shaped" curve: *Some* knowledge is good, but too much knowledge can impair flexibility.[64] What's more, a person's most creative contributions in her career typically come *before* she reaches her peak of knowledge within the field.[65] In some cases, such as creative writing, there appears to be an optimal amount of formal schooling, after which further schooling decreases the likelihood of eventually writing a masterpiece.[66]

What has become clear is that ten thousand hours is not a rule but an average.[67] People differ dramatically in how long it takes them to acquire the knowledge needed to play on the world stage,[68] and the *quality* of practice can be more important than mere quantity of practice. A recent review of a large number of studies on expert performance found that sheer amount of deliberate practice did not sufficiently explain most of the differences in expert performance.[69] And particularly relevant to creativity, the effects of deliberate practice were stronger for highly predicable activities (such as running) than for less predictable activities (like handling an aviation emergency).

Creative geniuses are not mere experts. They don't just get better and better at what they do. While it is easy to imagine how a chess player, over the course of many years, can achieve a high level of mastery in playing chess, it's more unclear how a novelist, musical composer, or painter might achieve creative greatness through sheer practice. By nature, creative domains are complex and ever changing.[70]

The goals and methods of creative fields are often shifting and evolving because new ideas must be *original*, *useful*, and *surprising* in order to be considered creative.[71] Can the expert performance approach fully explain this dynamic framework? Probably not.

6

Openness to Experience

By replacing fear of the unknown with curiosity we open ourselves up to an infinite stream of possibility. We can let fear rule our lives or we can become childlike with curiosity, pushing our boundaries, leaping out of our comfort zones, and accepting what life puts before us.

—ALAN WATTS

Around the time that his cult classic drug-culture novel, *Naked Lunch*, was released, beat writer William S. Burroughs was experimenting with a new writing strategy that he called the "cut-up technique." It's exactly what it sounds like: Burroughs would cut up random lines of text from a page and rearrange them to form new sentences, with the aim of freeing his mind and the minds of his readers from conventional and linear ways of thinking, and allow the mind to see things in a new light.

Like Burroughs, the Beat Generation as a whole sought to dismantle old belief systems and to encourage ways of looking at the world. In post-war 1950s America—when conformity was a defining characteristic of American culture and open-mindedness an act of rebellion—the Beats celebrated intellectual exploration, engagement in art and music, unconventionality, and deep spiritual questioning. As America made its way into the disruption and free-spiritedness of the 1960s counterculture, it was as if the collective consciousness had opened itself up to the new and unfamiliar.

In 1952, writer John Clellon Holmes first introduced the "beat generation" to the world, describing the movement as being characterized by "nakedness of mind, and ultimately, of soul." The Beats were a sort of reincarnation of the so-called Lost Generation of the 1920s, although, he said, "the wild boys of today are not lost." What they were instead was *curious*, a generation with "a greater facility for entertaining ideas than for believing in them."

Jack Kerouac, the Beat Generation poster boy whose novels have become manifestos for adventure and nonconformity, perfectly embodies the spirit of openness to experience. The revelations of Kerouac and other Beat writers do shed light on an essential rule of creativity: We *need* new and unusual experiences to think differently. In fact, cultivating a mind-set that is open and explorative might be the best thing we can do for our creative work. As Kerouac said, "The best teacher is experience."

**We *need* new and unusual experiences
to think differently.**

For not only artists but innovators of all stripes, new experiences provide the crucial tissue of real-world material that can be spun into original work. Openness to experience—the drive for cognitive exploration of one's inner and outer worlds—is the single strongest and most consistent personality trait that predicts creative achievement.[1] Openness to experience, one of the "Big Five" personality traits, is absolutely *essential* to creativity. Those who are high in openness tend to be imaginative, curious, perceptive, creative, artistic, thoughtful, and intellectual.[2] They are driven to explore their own inner worlds of ideas, emotions, sensations, and fantasies, and outwardly, to constantly seek out and attempt to make meaning of new information in their environment.

While openness as a personality trait hinges on engagement and exploration, it's also far more complex and multifaceted than that. Openness to experience comes in many forms, from a love of solving complex problems in math, science, and technology, to a voracious love of learning, to an inclination to ask the big questions and seek a deeper meaning in life, to exhibiting intense emotional reactions to music and art. Visionary tech entrepreneurs, world travelers, spiritual seekers, and original thinkers of all types tend to be have highly open personalities.

Research conducted by Scott for his doctoral dissertation suggests that there are at least three major forms of cognitive engagement making up the core of the openness domain.[3] *Intellectual engagement* is characterized by a searching for truth, love of problem solving, and drive to engage with ideas, whereas *affective engagement* has to do with exploration of the full depths of human emotion and is associated with a preference for using gut feeling, emotions, empathy, and compassion to make decisions. Finally, those who are high in *aesthetic engagement* exhibit a drive toward exploring fantasy and art and tend to experience emotional absorption in beauty. Scott found intellectual engagement to be associated with creative achievement in the sciences, while affective and aesthetic engagement were linked with artistic creativity.

Scott's research led him to another fascinating discovery about "open" personalities.[4] The desire to learn and discover seemed to have significantly more bearing on creative accomplishments than did cognitive ability. He found that people with high levels of cognitive engagement with imagination, emotions, and beauty were more likely to make significant artistic creative achievements than people who were high in IQ or divergent thinking ability (the ability to explore many possible solutions to a problem). Intellectual engagement was sometimes even found to be a better predictor of creative achievement than IQ.

Looking at creativity across the arts and sciences, Scott and colleagues found that openness to experience was more highly correlated with total creative achievement than other factors that had been traditionally associated with creativity, like IQ, divergent thinking, and other personality traits. Together, these findings suggest that the drive for exploration, in its many forms, may be the *single most important personal factor* predicting creative achievement.

Indeed, openness to experience speaks to our desire and motivation to engage with ideas and emotions—to seek truth and beauty, newness and novelty—and the act of exploring often provides the raw material for great artistic and scientific innovations. This engagement starts at the neurological level, with the way the brain reacts to unfamiliar situations and new information. What unites each individual form of openness to experience is an intense desire and motivation to seek new information that is rooted in the individual's neurophysiology and forms the very core of his or her personality.

The Neuromodulator of Exploration

The drive for exploration hinges on the functioning of dopamine, which is probably the most well-known of all the brain's neurotransmitters. As you may know, dopamine plays a strong role in learning and motivation. Unfortunately, there are many misconceptions about dopamine, which is commonly seen as the "sex, drugs and rock 'n' roll" neurotransmitter.[5] Despite many popular descriptions, dopamine is not necessarily associated with pleasure and satisfaction.

Instead, dopamine's primary role is to make us *want* things. We get a huge surge of dopamine coursing through our brains at the possibility of a big payoff, but there's no guarantee that we'll actually like or enjoy what we've obtained. Colin DeYoung explains that the release of dopamine "increases motivation to explore and facilitates cognitive and behavioral processes useful in exploration."[6] DeYoung has called dopamine the "neuromodulator of exploration."

At the broadest level, dopamine facilitates psychological plasticity, a tendency to explore and engage flexibly with new things, in both behavior and thinking.[7] Plasticity leads us to engage with uncertainty—whether it's pondering a new app to meet a consumer demand or questioning the next step in our own life path—exploring the unknown and finding reward in seeking its positive potential. With plasticity comes enhanced cognitive and behavioral engagement and exploration and, frequently, a commitment to personal growth. Of course, there's no guarantee that our open engagement will yield a positive outcome. However, for most creative people, the engagement itself is enough if it provides fodder for innovation. Indeed, research shows that psychological plasticity is associated with high levels of idea generation, engagement with everyday creative activities, and publicly recognized creative achievement.[8]

Plasticity consists of a blend of both extraversion and openness to experience, and dopamine is a source of exploratory motivation. It's easy to see why this might be the case evolutionarily; the drive to explore, the ability to adapt to new environments, and the ability to thrive in the face of uncertainty all provide important survival advantages.[9]

Nevertheless, there are crucial differences between extraversion and openness to experience. Extraversion, the personality trait that is most strongly associated with high sensitivity to environmental rewards, manifests in qualities like talkativeness, sociability, positive emotionality, assertiveness, and excitement seeking. Extraverts tend to be more likely to explore and pursue more primal "appetitive" rewards such as chocolate, social attention, social status, sexual partners, or drugs like cocaine. But dopamine, which is indeed important to extraversion, also has projections in the brain that are strongly linked to numerous other aspects of cognition. Individuals who are high in the openness to experience domain get energized not through the possibility of appetitive rewards but through the possibility of *discovering new information*. It's the thrill of the knowledge chase that most excites them.

This motivation for cognitive exploration engages and energizes us while influencing our drives for creative expression. We see the quality play out again and again in different realms of the arts and sciences. After all, it's difficult to imagine any great creative achievement that wasn't sparked by the drive to explore some aspect of the human experience.

Dopamine is the mother of human invention.

It's hardly a stretch to say that dopamine is the mother of invention.[10] In addition to facilitating cognitive exploration, the neurotransmitter is associated with a number of processes that facilitate creativity, including dreaming. We know that both daydreaming and dreaming at night are invaluable tools to help us access deeper realms of creativity. People who are high in openness to experience report dreaming more often and having more vivid dreams than those who are less open to experience,[11] very likely due to their higher dopamine production.

One intriguing possibility is that dopamine surges into the right hemisphere of the brain support both openness to experience and dreaming.[12] Dreaming inspires creative insights, and those who have more creative insights show more activation in the brain's right hemisphere.[13] Among people who are high in openness, the brain's dopamine systems are working day and night to inspire creative insights.[14]

Another important cognitive process associated with creativity is "latent inhibition"—a filtering mechanism in the brain that determines whether we respond to an object in our environment with wonder and novelty (known as "latent inhibition"), no matter how many times we've seen it before and mentally tagged it as being irrelevant to our current goals and needs. Eminent creative achievers at Harvard were found to be seven times more likely to have a *reduced* latent inhibition[15]—meaning that they had a harder time filtering out seemingly irrelevant information than others. But here's the thing: The information *did* turn out to be relevant! In related research, Scott found that those with a reduced latent inhibition had a greater faith in their intuitions, and their intuitions were in fact correct.[16] Reduced latent inhibition speaks directly to the concept of a "messy mind," as it reflects the tendency to tune in to greater amounts of information from our surroundings rather than automatically filtering and compartmentalizing.

The downside of this quality is that it might make creative people more prone to distraction than others. Darya Zabelina found that people with a "leaky" sensory filter—meaning that their brains don't filter out as much irrelevant information from the environment—tend to be more creative than those with stronger sensory gating.[17] Zabelina observed that highly creative people are more sensitive to noises in their environment—a clock ticking, a conversation in the distance—than less creative people. "Sensory information is leaking in. The brain is processing more information than it is in a typical person," Zabelina explains.[18]

This brain quirk was a known characteristic of many eminent creators, including Darwin, Kafka, and Proust, who each expressed a hypersensitivity to sound. Proust kept his blinds drawn and lined his bedroom with cork to filter out unwanted light and noise and wore earplugs while he wrote, while Kafka said that he needed the solitude of not a hermit but of a "dead man" in order to write.

And while it may sometimes be a hindrance to creative work, this distractibility also seems to be distinctly beneficial to creative thinking. Sensory hypersensitivity likely contributes to creativity by *widening* the brain's scope of attention and allowing individuals to take note of more subtleties in their environment. Very likely, taking in a greater volume of information increases your chances of making new and unusual connections between distantly related information.

These findings have deep implications for the mental illness–creativity debate. Dopamine production has been linked not only with reduced latent inhibition and creativity but also with mental illness. To be clear: Mental illness is neither necessary nor sufficient for creativity. Nevertheless, there does seem to be a nuanced link between the two, as having an extremely open mind makes flights of fancy more likely.[19] In support of this idea, there do appear to be variations in the expression of dopamine receptors in certain areas of the brain among both creative individuals and those with psychotic symptoms.

A Swedish study found that dopamine systems in healthy, highly creative adults are similar in certain ways to those found in the brains of people with schizophrenia. In both cases, there was a *lower* density of dopamine D_2 receptors in the thalamus— a brain area associated with sensory perception and motor function, which also plays an important role in creative thought, suggesting one possible link between creativity and psychopathology.[20]

Having fewer D_2 receptors in the thalamus probably means that the brain is filtering less incoming stimuli, leading to a higher flow of information being transmitted from the thalamus to other parts of the brain. In individuals who are not also suffering from the damaging symptoms of mental illness, this can lead to an increase in creative thinking and may very well underlie several cognitive processes that determine creative achievement.

"Thinking outside the box might be facilitated by having a somewhat less intact box," the study's lead author, Fredrik Ullén, said.[21]

An excess of dopamine may cause an influx of emotions, sensations, and fantasy, so much so that it causes substantial disruption to functions also important for creativity, such as working memory, critical thinking, and reflection. Too little dopamine, however, and there may be less motivation and inspiration to create.

Dopamine aside, research has also suggested similarities in brain activations between highly creative thinkers and people who are prone to psychosis. One study found that people scoring high in "schizotypy"—a personality continuum ranging from normal levels of openness to experience and imagination to extreme manifestations of magical thinking, apophenia (perceiving patterns that don't really exist), and psychosis—showed similar difficulty deactivating or suppressing activity in the precuneus region of the brain, an area associated with self-consciousness, a sense of self, and the retrieval of deeply personal memories.[22]

In reality, all of us lie somewhere on the schizotypy spectrum, and the existence of schizotypal characteristics does *not* indicate schizophrenia. The psychologically healthy biological relatives of people with full-blown schizophrenia tend to have unusually creative jobs and hobbies compared to the general population.[23] A recent study of more than 1.2 million Swedish people found, similarly, that the siblings of patients with autism and the first-degree relatives of patients with schizophrenia are significantly overrepresented in scientific and artistic occupations.[24]

It's possible that relatives of people with mental illness inherit creativity-boosting traits while avoiding the aspects of the mental illness that are more debilitating. In support of this, researchers have found that schizotypal characteristics—particularly the "positive" ones, such as unusual perceptual experiences and impulsive nonconformity—are related to creative personality traits like "individualistic," "insightful," "wide interests," "reflective," "resourceful," and "unconventional," as well as everyday creative achievements.[25]

Schizotypy is also related to flow states of consciousness and absorption.[26] As we've seen in earlier chapters, flow is the mental state of being completely present and fully absorbed in a task. When in a flow state, the creator and his or her world become one—outside distractions recede from consciousness and one's mind is fully open and attuned to the act of creating. This happens, for instance, when a playwright sits at her computer all night crafting a new scene without realizing that the sun is rising, or a filmmaker spends hours in front of her computer editing a rough cut.

Flow is essential to the artist's experience. In a study of a hundred artists in music, visual arts, theater, and literature, Barnaby Nelson and David Rawlings found that those who said they experienced more flow during the creative process were also higher in schizotypy and openness to experience.[27] The researchers link their findings to latent inhibition, arguing that a leaky sensory filter is a common thread running through schizotypy, openness to experience, flow, and absorption. The failure to precategorize incoming information as irrelevant, which is experienced by individuals with reduced latent inhibition, can result in "immediate experience not being shaped or determined by preceding events." In other words, an exceptionally large amount of information, far more than for those with higher levels of latent inhibition, enters their field of awareness and is explored by the mind. As Nelson and Rawlings explain, "It is precisely this newness of appreciation, and the associated sense of exploration and discovery, that stimulates the deep immersion in the creativeprocess, which itself may trigger a shift in quality of experience, generally in terms of an intensification or heightening of experience."

So what determines whether schizotypy goes the way of intense absorption and creative achievement or tips over into mental illness? This is where a number of other factors come into play. If mental illness is defined as extreme difficulty functioning effectively in the real world, then the complete inability to distinguish imagination from reality is surely going to increase the likelihood of mental illness. However, if one has an overactive imagination but *also* has the ability to distinguish reality from imagination and can harness these capacities to flourish in daily life (with the help of things like motivation, posttraumatic growth, resilience, and a supportive environment), then that is *far* from mental illness.

Mental processes on the schizotypy spectrum may interact with *protective* mental qualities like intellectual curiosity, working memory, and cognitive flexibility."[28] Indeed, one study conducted on people with no history of neurological or psychiatric illness found that the most creative thinkers were those who were able to *simultaneously* use their executive attention resources to engage in an effortful memory task while continuing to keep brain activity from their imagination network active.[29]

You never know: Some of the most seemingly irrelevant or "crazy" ideas at one point in time may be just the ingredients for a brilliant insight or connection in a different context. It bears repeating: Creativity is all about making new connections!

Achieving a balance between the intellectual, emotional, and aesthetic aspects of openness to experience may increase the chances that surprising and novel connections will arise and that creativity will not tip over into mental illness. Indeed, for the highest levels of creativity it may be especially important to achieve a balance between the *intellectual* aspects of openness to experience and the more fantasy-oriented aspects.

The benefits of achieving a healthy balance of the intellectual, imaginative, aesthetic, and emotional realms of cognitive exploration don't only pertain to creative work. Integrating the diverse realms of openness to experience may also lead to the highest forms of personal growth.

Seeing Things in a New Light

From traumatic life events that force us to rethink our most deeply ingrained beliefs about the world and our place in it to eye-opening journeys to new places and unfamiliar psychic landscapes, it's what *disrupts the familiar* that triggers new ways of seeing things (see Chapter 9).

Any life experience—whether traumatic or ecstatic—that diversifies our repertoire of experiences and pushes us outside of habitual thought patterns can lead to enhanced cognitive flexibility and creativity.[30] Psychologist Simone Ritter tested this hypothesis by putting test subjects on a walk through a virtual reality world where they experienced strange events that violated the laws of physics, like being made to feel as if they were walking faster than they actually were and seeing a bottle fall upward. Afterward, they asked the volunteers to take a test of cognitive flexibility requiring them to come up with as many answers as possible to the question "What makes sound?" (The more answers they came up with, the higher their cognitive flexibility score.) Those who were actively engaged in the weird virtual reality world scored higher in cognitive flexibility than those who engaged in a normal version of the virtual reality world (one without physics-defying experiences) and those who simply watched a film of weird and unexpected events. Their conclusion? We need to *directly* experience a violation of the way we think things are supposed to happen if we want to think in new and innovative ways.

But you don't have to go backpacking through Thailand or experience a trauma to get into a fertile creative mind-set. There are simpler ways to shake yourself out of familiarity (and maybe out of a creative rut too). Try out a new creative outlet or a totally different medium of expression (if you're a writer, learn to play a musical instrument; if you're a dancer, paint), take a new route home from work, or seek out a new group of people with different interests or values that you might learn from. Even a small rejiggering of your normal routine can reap major rewards for your creative life.

This plays out in broader cultural contexts as well—we can actually look to history to see how the unfamiliar breeds creative achievement. In a 1997 study, psychologist Dean Keith Simonton found that periods of immigration have preceded periods of extraordinary creative achievement in various cultural contexts.[31] Why? Immigrants bring fresh ideas, culture, and customs to an existing cultural infrastructure, creating more diverse experiences for *everyone* in that culture (not just the immigrants themselves) and thus triggering creative ways of thinking.

If habit and convention are the killers of creativity, then it's the unfamiliar that gives birth to great ideas and innovations. We know that habit and banality can seriously hamper creative thought (after all, how do we make new connections out of what is stale and uninspiring?) and that what's new, novel, and unusual can help us hatch our most inventive ideas. Even when it comes to expertise, too much familiarity with our preferred form of expression or area of study can keep us from flexible and innovative thinking. As research has shown, creativity benefits from an *outsider's mind-set*.

Creativity benefits from an *outsider's mind-set*.

While expertise is an important aspect of excellence in any creative discipline, one risk of being a seasoned pro is that we become so entrenched in our own point of view that we have trouble seeing other solutions. Experts may have trouble being flexible and adapting to change because they are so highly accustomed to seeing things in a particular way. For this reason, the newcomers to a field are sometimes the ones who come up with the ideas that truly innovate and shift paradigms.[32]

By opening to experience and actively choosing to see things from different perspectives, we can counter the damaging effects of familiarity and increase our cognitive flexibility. Openness to experience goes hand in hand with *integrative complexity*, the capacity and desire to recognize new patterns and find links among seemingly unrelated pieces of information. In fact, living in and adapting to foreign cultures may also enhance integrative complexity, which can give a major boost to our powers of creative thought.[33]

Author Geoff Colvin writes of the failures of expertise in his book *Talent Is Overrated*:

> Why didn't Western Union invent the telephone? Why didn't U.S. Steel invent the minimill? Why didn't IBM invent the personal computer? Over and over, the organizations that knew all there was to know about a technology or an industry failed to make the creative breakthrough that would transform the business.[34]

The greatest innovations can occur when the wisdom of one discipline is brought into another, seemingly unrelated one. Indeed, Simonton found that the most successful opera composers mix genres in their opera compositions and also create nonoperatic compositions.[35] The composers seem to avoid overtraining by engaging in cross-training. "It would be comparable to chess masters trying to improve their game by practicing checkers and go."[36]

The importance of cross-training has also been well established in the sciences. In his extensive research on scientific genius, Simonton found that the most creative scientists don't typically pursue a single research question within a single specialized area of expertise. Instead, highly creative scientists tend to engage in a large number of loosely related activities, forming a broad "network of enterprises."[37] They also tend to have creative hobbies and interests outside of the sciences.[38] A prime example is Galileo's fascination with art, literature, and music.[39] Galileo, the son of a musician, loved the arts and many say that his scientific work was deeply influenced by his exploration of the humanities.

The interests and intellectual contributions of Aristotle—perhaps the earliest known polymath—spanned ethics, medicine, mathematics, politics, law, agriculture, medicine, and theater. Aristotle truly embodied his own famous statement that all men "by nature desire knowledge." Leonardo da Vinci—a member of what English historian Edward Carr describes as the increasingly endangered species of "people who know a lot about a lot"[40]—stands to this day as the quintessential "renaissance man," having tried his hand at painting, sculpting, architecture, math, inventing, music, anatomy, cartography, botany, writing, and more.

A more modern-day example of this species is James H. Simons, who has made a fortune from his boundary-crossing explorations. An outsider's mind-set and an insatiable intellectual curiosity have been the secret behind the illustrious career of the billionaire mathematician and hedge fund manager, recently named one of the hundred richest people in the world.[41]

A dedicated philanthropist and scientific genius, Simons graduated from the Massachusetts Institute of Technology with a degree in mathematics in just three years and went on to receive his doctorate from Berkeley in another three. By his midtwenties, he was cracking codes for the National Security Agency in Washington, D.C. Simons later returned to academia, teaching math at MIT and Harvard before making his way into the business world, where he founded one of the largest and most successful hedge funds in the world, the aptly named Renaissance Technologies.

Simons's many interests, career changes, and passion projects have been key to his success in each of these endeavors. In every individual pursuit, he brings together the wisdom of other domains and areas of interest. Guided by a hungry mind and a spirit of openness—he once persuaded his father to join an investment in Colombia after a motorcycle trip through Bogota with a college friend—Simons has fueled a lifetime of mathematical, scientific, and financial innovation.

Simons used the outsider's advantage to become immensely successful in predicting global markets, which made him a fortune in the hedge fund business. As Bloomberg noted, "At the core of Renaissance's success—and the wealth Simons is creating—is his own mathematical mind-set." The math whiz looked to mathematical formulas and scientific theorems to inform his market predictions and hired great scientific minds to make sense of the financial world at Renaissance. Whatever theories, ideas, and cross-bred calculations Simons was bringing to his financial predictions (he's yet to give away his secrets), it worked: The firm has been so successful in predicting the markets that, at times, it's left every other major hedge fund in the dust. Driven by his insatiable curiosity, Simons even examined things like the influence of sunspots and lunar phases on the market.[42]

Now, the seventy-six-year-old polymath has turned his time and money to investing in the advancement of math and science for the public good. Simons told Bloomberg in 2007,[43] "I'm undoubtedly involved in too many things at the same time. But you make your life interesting."

Mindfulness

Instructions for living a life.
Pay attention.
Be astonished.
Tell about it.

—Mary Oliver

n her junior-year application to professor Anne Fadiman's first-person writing class at Yale, aspiring writer Marina Keegan described an unusual habit that was central to her creative process.

"It began in a marbled notebook but has since evolved inside the walls of my word processor. *Interesting stuff.* That's what I call it. I'll admit it's become a bit of an addiction," Keegan wrote. "I add to it in class, in the library, before bed, and on trains. It has everything from descriptions of a waiter's hand gestures, to my cab driver's eyes, to strange things that happen to me or a way to phrase something. I have 32 single-spaced pages of interesting stuff in my life."[1]

Much of this "interesting stuff" became the inspiration for the Yale student's essays and stories. Keegan's writing, which led many commentators to label her a "voice of her generation," was driven by a ravenous curiosity about human nature and the world around her. "Every aspect of her life was a way of answering that question: how do you find meaning in your life?" Fadiman wrote.

Keegan died tragically at the age of twenty-two, just days after graduating from Yale. After her death, Keegan's commencement essay for the *Yale Daily News*, "The Opposite of Loneliness," went viral, sparking an Internet sensation and an outpouring of grief for the loss of a bright young mind.

In her too-short career, the young writer made great strides in mastering a skill that defines the literary greats: the ability to observe the full spectrum of human experience—both the internal and the external—and to turn those observations into art. Keegan had become what Henry James famously advised aspiring writers to be: someone on whom "nothing is lost." In an 1884 interview with *Longman's Magazine*, James told writers that their job was to be seekers of experience and collectors of interesting things. He suggested that it is by detecting meaning and patterns in our experiences that we become artists. James explained, "The power to guess the unseen from the seen, to trace the implication of things, to judge the whole piece by the pattern, the condition of feeling life, in general, so completely that you are well on your way to knowing any particular corner of it—this cluster of gifts may almost be said to constitute experience."[2]

Generations later, Joan Didion advised young writers to carry a notebook around with them everywhere so as to record moments of inspiration in overheard conversations, passing thoughts and sights, and little slices of life. In her essay "On Keeping a Notebook," Didion explained that in her own work, the ultimate goal of this exercise in documentation was not to create an accurate log of her activities but rather to come to better know "how it felt to be me"—to find out what the observations revealed about herself as the observer. She wrote:

> I sometimes delude myself about why I keep a notebook, imagine that some thrifty virtue derives from preserving everything observed. See enough and write it down, I tell myself, and then some morning when the world seems drained of wonder, some day when I am only going through the motions of doing what I am supposed to do, which is write—on that bankrupt morning I will simply open my notebook and there it will all be, a forgotten account with accumulated interest, paid passage back to the world out there. . . . [I imagine] that the notebook is about other people. But of course it is not. . . . My stake is always, of course, in the unmentioned girl in the plaid silk dress. Remember what it was to be me: that is always the point.[3]

But it's not only writers whose craft requires being deeply attuned to life in the myriad ways it presents itself. Most meaningful artistic and scientific achievement comes from intimate interactions between the artist and some object of inquiry in his or her world. The artist's observations become a means of answering the fundamental questions of art: What does it mean to be a human being?

Actors, musicians, business innovators, and scientists, too, must take inspiration from the world around them, through the simple—and incredibly difficult—act of paying attention. Attuning our focus both to the outer world and to our own inner world of thoughts, ideas, and emotions is what inspires us. But it's easier said than done. How often do you take the time to notice the exact way a waiter animates his hand gestures? Or even to notice the sights that you pass each day on your way to the subway?

Consider the great care and attention with which painter Georgia O'Keeffe observed the tiniest details of her subjects. O'Keeffe gave an incredible amount of focus to each flower she painted, and her soulful depictions led her audience to see flowers in a completely new light. The Taos, New Mexico, painter explained:

> In a way—nobody sees a flower—really—it is so small—we haven't time—and to see takes time, like to have a friend takes time. If I could paint the flower exactly as I see it, no one would see what I see because I would paint it small like the flower is small. So I said to myself—I'll paint what I see—what the flower is to me but I'll paint it big and they will be surprised into taking time to look at it—I will make even busy New Yorkers take time to see what I see of flowers.[4]

This impulse to record and create meaning of the little details and moments of life—as O'Keeffe said, to "paint what I see"—is arguably the birthplace of art, and it starts with being awake to the moments of our lives as they are passing. It begins, in other words, with mindfulness.

As we'll see, creative observation is a skill that requires a balance of paying attention to the world around us and tuning in to our own inner landscape—a balance of mindfulness; a focused, nonjudgmental awareness of the present moment; and mind *wandering*.

The Art of Attention

There are always flowers for those who want to see
them.

—HENRI MATISSE

In a famous 2007 social experiment, Pulitzer Prize–winning journalist Gene Weingarten of the *Washington Post* offered a startling
glimpse into just how much we miss in our daily lives. Here's
what happened: An average-looking man in a baseball cap and a
white T-shirt set up next to a trash can in a Washington, D.C.,
subway station during the morning rush hour. He opened his violin case, took out the instrument, and left his open case on the
ground for passersby to drop in dollar bills. More than one thousand people passed by as he performed six classical pieces over
the course of forty-three minutes.

The man wasn't just any street performer. He was the famous
musician and former child prodigy Joshua Bell, and he was playing Bach's Chaconne—a piece that is generally regarded to be
one of the most difficult for the violin—on a $3.5 million Strad-
ivarius. A hidden camera recording revealed that over the course
of that rush-hour performance in the subway station, only *seven
people* stopped to watch his performance for at least a minute.
However, the tape revealed that every time a child walked past
Bell, they tried to stop and watch—and each time, the child was
rushed along by their parents. Days before, however, concert-
goers had paid up to a hundred dollars for a ticket to see Bell
play the same instrument at a sold-out show in Boston.[5]

While this may be an extreme example, it goes to show how
often we speed past the world around us—sometimes missing
out on great beauty. It also begs an important question: How
much more of life will we experience if we are truly present to it?

Pioneering Harvard psychologist Ellen Langer describes mindfulness as the act of *paying attention to the present moment*. Langer, who is often referred to as the "mother of mindfulness," conducted seminal research on meditation in the 1970s and was among the first to show that exercising mindful awareness could lead to measurable improvements in cognitive function. "Mindfulness is the simple process of actively noticing new things. People always think they're aware, but they're not," she explains.[6]

In her book *Mindful Creativity*, Langer suggests that doing creative work is itself a practice in mindfulness.

"In noticing new things about the topic you're considering to write photograph or paint about, you're being creative," she says. "By noticing new things about a topic, you see novel things about it. You see that the thing you thought you knew is different—everything looks different from different perspectives."[7]

Mindfulness requires a firm anchoring in the here and now, openness to novelty and surprise, and sensitivity to the environment.[8] *Mindlessness*, on the other hand, can turn us into "automatons," says Langer—rigid and habitual in our ways of thinking and fearful of uncertainty.

This is not to say that a state of pure mindfulness is always good and a state of "mindlessness" is always bad. For instance, deliberate mindfulness can interfere with the flow state of consciousness, in which we are completely absorbed in an activity and lose track of time.[9] Also, a lot of what may *appear* mindless may nevertheless still be incredibly conducive to creativity.[10] As we saw earlier, unconscious processing can facilitate insights and help us push through creative impasses.

Nevertheless, you can imagine how mindfulness in this broad sense of being attentive and observant might also be beneficial for both creative inspiration and insightful problem solving. Think about the great fictional detective Sherlock Holmes, who would retreat into deep contemplation to solve difficult problems, putting together the pieces of a case to determine what really happened. *Mastermind* author Maria Konnikova calls Holmes a "master of mindfulness."[11]

While that may not be the most obvious way to describe the detective, Konnikova explains that Holmes has mastered the art of "unitasking." When a case is first presented, he does nothing but sit in his leather chair, eyes closed, in total silence and utter concentration until he's achieved some insight on the situation. Had Holmes *not* been a keen observer of his environment, it would have been impossible for him to investigate complex problems in such depth and breadth. "His approach to thought captures the very thing that cognitive psychologists mean when they say mindfulness," Konnikova writes.[12] This approach to creative problem solving is an increasingly uncommon one. After all, in our own creative lives, how often do we take the time to sit back in the proverbial leather chair and simply mull over an idea or problem?

We don't usually think of mindfulness—now a pop culture buzzword applied to everything from parenting to work to eating to sex—in terms of observation. Popular ideas of what it means to be mindful tend to leave out what Langer calls "everyday mindfulness," the act of observing what's around us. But the capacity to deeply observe is not only a key attentional skill, it's also a distinct creative advantage.

With a robust and rapidly growing body of research on the many benefits of mindfulness, being mindful has become recently in vogue. But mindfulness is nothing new—the roots of the ancient mind-body practice can be traced back over twenty-five hundred years to early Buddhist thought. It was during the 1970s, when scientists like Langer began to put meditation under the microscope, that mindfulness became popularized in a Western scientific and medical context. In 1979, Jon Kabat-Zinn, a trail-blazing researcher in the field, founded his eight-week Mindfulness-Based Stress Reduction (MBSR) program at the University of Massachusetts Medical Center; now the program (which combines meditation, yoga, and body awareness) is the most studied form of mindfulness training. Kabat-Zinn's often-cited definition of mindfulness is "paying attention on purpose, in the present moment, and nonjudgmentally, to the unfolding of experience moment to moment."[13] While meditation is the practice most commonly used to cultivate mindfulness, Kabat-Zinn stresses that no formal meditation practice is needed in order to be mindful.

"It's not really about sitting in the full lotus," Kabat-Zinn said in a talk at the University of California, Berkeley's Greater Good Science Center.[14] "It's about living your life as if it really mattered, from moment to moment to moment."

While the capacity to observe the present moment without distraction or judgment is a vital skill for anyone who seeks joy and fulfillment in life, it's particularly important for the creative thinker to be able to bear witness to her inner and outer worlds, and meditation can be a helpful tool for cultivating this type of attention. Since Henry David Thoreau—who is often credited as being the "first yogi in the West"[15]—artists, entrepreneurs, and thinkers have turned to mindfulness as a daily practice for psychological well-being and a source of creative inspiration. In that pursuit, a meditation practice has become an important part of their creative toolkit.

The sleek Zen Buddhism–inspired design of the Beatles' *White Album*, Leonard Cohen's 2001 album, *Ten New Songs* (written at Mt. Baldy Zen Center), and perhaps most famously, David Lynch's *Mulholland Dr.,* are just a few of innumerable creations that were dreamed up with the help of a meditation practice. Steve Jobs has even said that meditation—which he studied with Zen master Shunryū Suzuki, author of *Zen Mind, Beginner's Mind*—was the main source of his creativity.

"If you just sit and observe, you will see how restless your mind is," Jobs told biographer Walter Isaacson. "If you try to calm it, it only makes things worse, but over time it does calm, and when it does, there's room to hear more subtle things— that's when your intuition starts to blossom and you start to see things more clearly and be in the present more. Your mind just slows down, and you see a tremendous expanse in the moment. You see so much more than you could see before."

Meditation, as Jobs suggests, can help us quiet racing thoughts and tap into the quiet wisdom of the creative unconscious. Psychiatrist Norman Rosenthal's research on Transcendental Meditation (TM)—a popular technique that involves the silent repetition of a personal mantra for twenty minutes twice a day—found that many new meditators reported a "flowering of creativity" after beginning their practice; "an ability to see things from some novel angle, to pursue new directions effectively, to innovate or change—either the world or themselves—in some meaningful way."[16]

After around two years of practicing meditation, Moby said that he had achieved a higher quality of life and enhanced creativity, mostly by quieting the negativity and noise in his mind. The DJ and recording artist told Rosenthal that meditation helps him get past a place of fearing failure to one of more pure creativity. A good meditation, he said, "helps you remove the fear . . . and you're left with the joy of creation.

When I meditate, I find I do things for more honest, more enjoyable and healthier reasons."[17]

A large body of research since the 1970s has associated mindfulness—as both a practice and a personality trait—with many cognitive and psychological benefits, many of which are either centrally or tangentially beneficial for creativity and insightful problem solving. These benefits include improved task concentration and sustained attention, empathy and compassion, introspection, self-regulation, enhanced memory and improved learning, and positive affect and emotional well-being as well as relief from stress, anxiety, depression, and sleeping problems . . . and the list goes on! More recently, research has linked specific types of meditation *directly* with creative thinking. There are many perks to being mindful— let's focus on some of these benefits that are most valuable for creativity.

Driven to Distraction

Perhaps the single most valuable use of meditation for the creative person is in warding off unwanted distractions. In a world of notifications and multitasking, sustaining attention has become an increasingly difficult cognitive demand. When it's a struggle to sit down and focus on an important task for long periods of time without distraction, doing meaningful creative work becomes more and more challenging. TM guru David Lynch referred to the process of dropping down into our deep wellsprings of thought and emotion in order to come up with ideas as "catching the big fish." In his 2007 book of that title, Lynch writes: "If you want to catch a little fish, you can stay in the shallow water. But if you want to catch the big fish, you've got to go deeper."[18]

Constantly grazing on texts, emails, news, and social media compromises our ability to focus on both the external present moment and our internal streams of thought, making it difficult to tap into the default mode's imaginative activity, or as Lynch said, to "go deeper." Lynch insists that meditation is the solution, the greatest tool we have for accessing our own intuitive brain power and diving into the unconscious, where creativity resides. "Down deep, the fish are powerful and more pure," he writes. "They're huge and abstract. And they're very beautiful."

We can all relate to the feeling of being stuck in the shallow water on the surface of the mind. And when we live and work in a way that causes us to become stressed-out, sleep-deprived multitaskers at the beck and call of our digital devices, those big fish are hard to find.

Neuroscientist Richard Davidson has said that the way we live today is causing a "national attention deficit,"[19] while researcher Linda Stone warns that modern life is increasingly lived within a state of "continuous partial attention." Most of us know this state all too well—we're continually having our attention pulled away from the task at hand by notifications, alerts, calls, texts, emails, and other digital stimuli. Stone explains, "In large doses, [continuous partial attention] contributes to a stressful lifestyle, to operating in crisis management mode, and to a compromised ability to reflect, to make decisions, and to think creatively. In a 24/7, always-on world, continuous partial attention used as our dominant attention mode contributes to a feeling of overwhelm, over-stimulation and to a sense of being unfulfilled."[20]

Today, Americans spend an average of eleven hours each day interacting with digital devices,[21] and the average smartphone user checks his or her device every six and a half minutes (that's 150 times a day).[22] Increasingly, our relationship with our devices has become addictive. MRI studies have shown similar brain changes in compulsive Internet users and drug addicts, and a 2011 study showed similar withdrawal effects among students who could not use technology for twenty-four hours and smokers and drug addicts quitting cold turkey.[23] Research conducted at Harvard has found that disclosing information about ourselves on Facebook activates major reward circuits in the brain, which are also activated when cocaine or other drugs are ingested.[24]

The type of feedback that the brain gets from the ping of a device is highly reinforcing. So no matter how much you'd like to stay focused on what you're doing—writing the first chapter of your novel, practicing guitar, or simply crafting an email—it can be *incredibly* difficult to ignore that little vibration. Recently, cognitive psychologists found that hearing your phone vibrate can significantly disrupt your focus.[25]

We'd do well to consider how little, everyday distractions might add up in a way that interferes with our creativity and well-being. We've seen that the brain needs downtime in order to generate diverse associations and to let ideas incubate. But as cognitive neuroscientist Daniel Levitin warns, "our brains are busier than ever before"—and it could be taking a damaging toll on the way we think, feel, and behave.[26]

Resisting the siren song of digital distractions can be incredibly difficult, but our creative capacity may depend on our ability to do so. Insofar as we succumb to distraction, our ability to access that mental space where our richest ideas and visions live is compromised—and so is our ability to connect deeply with what's *outside* of us. Multitasking, texting, tweeting, gaming, surfing, and other incessant stimulation hijacks our attentional resources and makes us less aware of what is going on in our surroundings.

This is where mindfulness is particularly valuable to the artist, and to anyone seeking to improve their quality of life. Meditation is a powerful tool that can boost executive functioning, so that we can increase our concentration abilities and exercise greater flexibility in paying attention to what's within us and around us when we need and desire.

The Mindful Brain

Being mindful alters the very structure and function of the brain, supporting executive functions like attention and self-regulation, both of which are valuable assets to creativity—especially when it comes to motivating ourselves to sit down and focus on a challenging creative task for extended periods of time.

A significant body of research has found mindfulness training to improve key executive attention skills.[27] One of its most valuable benefits is that it boosts cognitive control, the ability to focus on an important decision while avoiding distractions and impulses. A 2014 study found that mindfulness-based cognitive therapy was effective in increasing cognitive control among adults with attention-deficit hyperactivity disorder (ADHD), leading to reduced impulsivity and inattention.[28] Of course, we don't want to throw out the baby without the bathwater: People with ADHD also tend to show an overactive imagination network.[29] The key is helping them learn the crucial skills of flexible attention so that they can pay attention to the outside world when they want or need to, while also helping them put their overactive imagination to good use.[30]

Mindfulness training can lead to measurable improvements in the ability to focus and to regulate emotions and behavior even in those who do not suffer from attentional disorders. One study showed that a brief mindfulness exercise before an exam helped students identify distracting thoughts, which led to improvements in reading comprehension and working memory.[31] Overall, the exercise led to a sixteen-point average boost on the GRE, largely by reducing disruptive mind wandering.

Clearly, you don't have to be an experienced meditator to benefit from mindfulness. As little as a single, short meditation session can have a positive impact on mental functioning.

More extensive research conducted on novice meditators who completed an eight-week MBSR course and on experienced meditators who underwent a monthlong meditation retreat showed significant improvements in three aspects of attention: *alerting* (the maintenance of an alert state of mind), *orienting* (directing and limiting one's attention), and *conflict monitoring* (the ability to prioritize competing responses).[32]

So what's going on neurologically when we're sitting silently and focusing on the breath or a mantra? Scientists have begun to uncover the changes in neurobiology and brain structure underlying the cognitive improvements linked with meditation. A 2011 Harvard study identified some of the main neural correlates of the positive changes brought about by mindfulness training programs. The study found that just eight weeks of MBSR led to increased gray matter density in areas of the brain associated with executive function—specifically attention and emotion regulation.

First, the researchers saw that gray matter density increased in the anterior cingulate cortex (ACC), a brain region located in the frontal lobe that's associated with self-regulation, thinking, emotion, rational deliberation, and problem solving. (Interestingly, high levels of media multitasking have been linked with reduced density in the ACC.[33]) The research team also saw increases in gray matter in the hippocampus, a small region within the limbic system that governs memory, learning, and emotion (and plays a crucial role in the imagination network). Increased activity in the ACC and the ventromedial prefrontal cortex—which is involved in processing risk and fear as well as inhibiting emotional responses—has been implicated in the reduction of anxiety, a well-known creativity blocker.[34] Greater activation in both of these brain areas has been shown to lead to substantial feelings of anxiety relief after a twenty-minute meditation.

In another study, the same group of Harvard researchers later found that eight weeks of meditation also led to measurable changes in brain regions associated with memory, sense of self, empathy, and stress. A 2014 review of twenty-one neuroimaging studies that examined the brains of over three hundred meditators reinforced these findings, identifying eight key parts of the brain (including the ACC and the hippocampus) that were consistently affected by mindfulness training. The studies reviewed showed that meditation training consistently altered key brain areas, including the frontopolar cortex (involved in meta-awareness), the sensory cortices and insula, the hippocampus (involved in memory formation and consolidation, and learning), and the anterior and mid-cingulate and orbitofrontal cortex (involved in self- and emotion regulation).

In these brain regions, the researchers observed increased white and gray matter volume,[35] an indication that the region may have more power to impact overall brain function.[36] While the research is still in its infancy, what it suggests is that meditation produces measurable changes in brain structure, effectively *rebuilding the brain matter* in regions important for cognition and behavior.

The Middle Way Between Mindfulness and Mind Wandering

It's incredibly important for anyone to develop focus and self-control. But when it comes to creativity, there's a caveat. What about the imagination network? What about daydreaming?

Creativity requires a balance of external focus with more inner-focused, free imagination network processes like future thinking, reflection, introspection, and memory consolidation. Although focused attention can be a gateway to creative thinking, optimal creativity likely results from both mindful and mind-wandering states of mind and, importantly, in the ability to switch easily from one mode of engagement to the other as needed.

While the traditional aim of meditation is to free the mind of inner chatter in order to fully focus on the present moment, creative people tend to have a rather different goal. Positive-constructive daydreaming is often highly conducive to creative thinking, and emotions are so often both the inspiration and fuel for creative work (see Chapter 3). For this reason, some artists might shy away from meditating, for fear that it could drain their creative resources. This way of thinking is far from correct. Meditation can not only boost our attention to the external world but also help us tap into our inner worlds.

As we pointed out earlier, while focusing attention externally is a useful mode of cognition, we don't necessarily want to be mindful *all* the time. For optimum cognitive flexibility and creativity, it's best to achieve a balance of mindfulness and mind wandering. In other words, the goal is to forge a middle way.

The goal is to forge a middle way.

In Theravada Buddhism, the concept of the "middle way" is a meeting ground between opposing extremes, a balanced way of living, behaving, and treating others that was thought to be the path to the end of suffering. This middle way is often mistaken as a sort of neutrality or passivity, but really, it's a way of reconciling opposing elements for maximum harmony and effectiveness. In the pursuit of our own highest creative potential, cultivating that middle way between mindfulness and mind wandering is one way to access the open, imaginative mind that gives rise to our most original ideas and visions.

One of the main goals of meditation, in the Buddhist tradition, is to get beyond the ego, or the self. Practicing traditional mindfulness meditation can certainly help temper compulsive self-focused mental chatter (what meditators like to call the "monkey mind") by strengthening the part of the brain that turns the focus *away* from the self and regulates attention, as we've seen. We know that mindfulness meditation, which is usually practiced by sustaining focus on the breath and clearing away distracting thoughts, is associated with strengthened executive network function. But mindfulness and other types of meditation can also be accompanied by relative deactivation of the main centers of the imagination network.[37]

The imagination network is critical for self-referential thought and internal reflection. So in suppressing activity from this brain network, some types of meditation—namely, focused-attention (FA) meditation, which encompasses Zen and mindfulness meditation—may have some undesired effects on creativity. When mind wandering is suppressed in order to completely focus attention on the present moment, mindfulness may actually prevent us from reaching our highest creative potential. University of California psychologist Jonathan Schooler's research has found a correlation between increased focus on the task at hand and *lower* scores on tests of creative problem-solving.[38] Schooler showed that people who performed an undemanding task (during which their mind was presumably wandering) performed better on a subsequent test of creative thinking than those who performed a demanding task that required more focused attention.

Clearing the mind of bothersome thoughts and emotions, while positive, may have some unintended consequences. When the mind is emptied in this way, "One's experience becomes reduced to present sensory awareness, which accommodates a self as agent in the world, but not a self as a knower of its own states and contents," explains New York University mindfulness researcher Zoran Josipovic.[39]

So how can we achieve a balance between the intense focus of mindfulness and, as Schooler describes it, the "freedom of a mind untethered to the present"? For creativity, the ideal meditation practice is one that creates this balance—supporting both the mindful brain and the mind-wandering brain and strengthening both self- and other-focused modes of thought.

The important thing to consider is how a meditation practice *deals with the thoughts that inevitably arise.* Types of meditation that seek to eliminate thoughts (that is, more traditional forms like mindfulness meditation) rather than simply encouraging greater awareness of the thoughts are not the most conducive to a creative state of mind, which by definition is open, fluid, and flexible. The goal, when it comes to enhancing creativity, is not to free the mind of thoughts. The goal is *to be fully present to thoughts as they arise* and to be able to switch flexibly between idle mind wandering and out-ward-focused attention.

**The goal is to be fully present to thoughts
as they arise.**

Because different types of meditation support the development of different cognitive skills, you can actually tailor a meditation practice to the cognitive benefits you're looking to gain. Let's take a closer look at what a meditation practice for optimizing creativity might look like.

Can Meditation Boost Creativity?

Certain types of meditation can strengthen external-focused attention while also supporting the workings of the imagination network. For instance, open-monitoring meditation, which emphasizes tuning in to one's subjective experience, has been found to increase both the activation and the functional connectivity of the imagination network. Richard Davidson, a neuroscientist who studies mindfulness, describes this technique as involving "non-reactively monitoring the content of experience from moment-to-moment, primarily as a means to recognize the nature of emotional and cognitive patterns."[40] On the other hand, traditional focused-attention meditation, such as mindfulness meditation, asks the individual to focus solely on an object such as the breath, letting go of any thoughts or emotions as they arise, and has been associated with improvements in executive functioning, as we've seen.

Lorenza Colzato, a Dutch cognitive psychologist, investigated the effects of both of these types of meditation on creative thinking. Colzato hypothesized that open-monitoring meditation—during which the individual is receptive to thoughts and emotions without attending to one particular point of focus—might be a better creativity booster than focused-attention (mindfulness) meditation, which reduces mind wandering by sustaining attention on a single object, such as the breath.[41]

The people Colzato studied had around two years of experience practicing either open-monitoring or focused-attention meditation. After a meditation session, they were asked to think of as many uses as possible for a single item (such as a brick), a test used to measure divergent thinking. After a session of open-monitoring meditation, the participants who were experienced in that type of meditation performed significantly better. Meanwhile, subjects who practiced focused-attention meditation performed better on tests of *convergent* thinking (that is, coming up with the *single* correct solution to a problem), which has been associated with IQ.

This makes a lot of sense, if we look at how these two types of meditation deal with thoughts that arise. While open-monitoring explores and engages with the meditator's inner monologue—helping him to arrive at multiple creative answers to a question—focused attention helps clear away distracting thoughts so that the meditator can zero in his attention on finding one desired solution. Colzato theorized that creative thinking benefits from weaker top-down *cognitive control*—meaning the mind is able to jump from one thought to another in a "weakly guided fashion." Open-monitoring meditation, with its emphasis on subjective experience, might encourage this type of free-flowing thought, while focused attention can do just the opposite.

Another study identified a type of meditation similar to open monitoring that led to extensive activation of the imagination network. Nondirective meditation was found to be effective in activating not only broad areas of the imagination network but also brain regions associated with memory retrieval and emotional processing.[42] It is practiced with a relaxed focus of attention on the repetition of a short mantra. The meditator focuses on the mantra while allowing spontaneous thoughts, images, emotions, memories, and sensations to emerge and pass freely. This technique is at the core of several popular meditation styles, including Transcendental Meditation (TM), Acem meditation, and relaxation response meditation. The meditator focuses on the mantra, and when she becomes aware that her thoughts have wandered, she gently brings the focus back to the present moment. It's easy to see why meditating in this way, which permits some mind wandering, would result in greater imagination network activity than a concentrative practice or sitting at rest.

The data are clear: To activate your brain's imagination network, try practicing an open-monitoring or nondirective form of meditation, which allows for constructive mind wandering while also boosting attention.

Further research has suggested that, in addition to activating the imagination network and facilitating divergent thinking, one of the key ways these meditation practices boost creativity is by cultivating observational skills. Dutch psychologist Matthijs Baas and colleagues investigated the specific mindfulness skills cultivated in different types of meditation practices to determine how these skills individually predict creativity. Baas laid out the hypothesis that particular mindfulness skills—as opposed to mindfulness as a whole—are drivers of creativity. He specifically investigated four mindfulness skills: *observation* (the ability to skillfully notice and attend to both internal and external phenomena), *acting with awareness* (the ability to engage in an activity with one's undivided attention), *description* (the ability to verbally describe objects and events in a nonjudgmental way), and *accepting without judgment* (the ability to accept the circumstances of the present moment without labeling or judging).

Of these four mindful abilities, only the skill of observation—as cultivated through open-monitoring meditation—was consistently linked with heightened creativity. Description and accepting without judgment were only weakly associated with creativity, whereas acting with awareness—a skill cultivated largely through focused-attention meditation—was *inversely* correlated with creativity. Acting with awareness may be detrimental to creative idea generation because it restricts mind wandering.

People who are adept in the observation aspect of creativity, however, tend to be higher in cognitive flexibility, which allows them to move fluidly between different modes of thought and to consider multiple approaches and solutions to a problem. There are two reasons that observation is an important driver of creativity. First, it's strongly related to the openness to experience personality domain, as both are characterized by a drive for novelty and exploration (see Chapter 6). And more than other mindfulness skills, observation is associated with the ability to take note of the contents of our internal and external landscape. Baas' team concludes, "A state of conscious awareness resulting from living in the moment is not sufficient for creativity to come about. To be creative, you need to have, or be trained in, the ability to carefully observe, notice, or attend to phenomena that pass your mind's eye."[43]

Observation is an important driver of creativity.

Living with eyes wide open can certainly be a great source of creative and personal fulfillment, but of course, it can also expose us to great suffering and pain. As we'll see next, harnessing an exquisite sensitivity to our experiences—both the good and the bad—may actually be a *necessary* part of personal and creative growth.

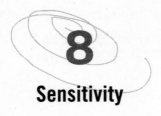

8

Sensitivity

The truly creative mind in any field is no more than this: A human creature born abnormally, inhumanly sensitive. To him . . . a touch is a blow, a sound is a noise, a misfortune is a tragedy, a joy is an ecstasy, a friend is a lover, a lover is a god, and failure is death. Add to this cruelly delicate organism the overpowering necessity to create, create, and create—so that without the creating of music or poetry or books or buildings or something of meaning, his very breath is cut off from him. He must create, must pour out creation. By some strange, unknown, inward urgency he is not really alive unless he is creating.

—PEARL S. BUCK

Recalling his recording sessions with the young Michael Jackson, producer Quincy Jones said that "Michael was so shy, he'd sit down and sing behind the couch with his back to me while I sat with my hands over my eyes—and the lights off."[1]

From watching his electrifying performances onstage, most people would never guess that Michael Jackson was a deeply shy and sensitive person. From the time he was a young boy, the King of Pop exuded energy, strength, and charisma onstage, while his personal life was characterized by crippling sensitivity, loneliness, and struggle. As Jackson heartbreakingly said, "It hurts to be me."[2]

Jackson's biographer J. Randy Taraborrelli all but gave up on trying to make sense of the many paradoxes that defined Jackson's personality. "I think that when you're talking about Michael Jackson and you try to analyze him, it's like analyzing electricity, you know?" he wrote. "It exists, but you don't have a clue as to how it works."[3]

The only thing that seemed to really make sense to Jackson himself was music. The singer opened up in an interview with Oprah Winfrey, saying, "I feel I was chosen as an instrument to give music and love and harmony to the world." By channeling his sensitivity and suffering into his work, Jackson found a sense of meaning and a way to escape from the loneliness and isolation that often overwhelmed him.

Jackson embodies a personality contradiction seen in many performers: They are both incredibly "out there" and open, and also highly sensitive. Psychologist Mihaly Csikszentmihalyi identified openness and sensitivity as oppositional personality elements that not only coexist in creative performers, but form the core of their personalities. This paradox helps explain how performers can be bold and charismatic on the one hand and emotionally fragile on the other.

"Creative people's openness and sensitivity often exposes them to suffering and pain, yet also to a great deal of enjoyment," Csikszentmihalyi wrote. "Being alone at the forefront of a discipline also leaves you exposed and vulnerable."[4]

Some of the most dynamic actors and musicians who light up the stage and screen with their presence and charisma are known to be introverted and sensitive in their off-screen lives. Audrey Hepburn, for example, was not only a beloved performer but also a highly sensitive soul. She oozed charisma in her movie roles, but she was introverted off-screen, with a certain delicacy and vulnerability that brought depth to her work and life. Director Peter Bogdanovich, who worked with Hepburn on the film *They All Laughed*, called the actress "absolutely real." In his autobiography, Bogdanovich recalls being amazed by the actress's emotional fragility. "She . . . managed to somehow take that vulnerability and sensitivity and marshal it into something she can work with and convey on the screen."

The fact that many seemingly *extraverted* performers are also highly sensitive people can also be found in the complex personalities of metal rock performers. Psychologist Jennifer O. Grimes went to three major metal rock tours, including Ozzfest, one of the largest (and wildest) in the world, where she conducted thorough interviews with twenty-one musicians from the various bands in quiet backstage rooms. What she found from these conversations was that most of the musicians exhibited the contradiction of openness and sensitivity (as well as introversion and extraversion) in their personalities.

Onstage, the musicians appear to be the prototype of extraversion: bold, loud, and wild. But backstage, Grimes saw a different side of their personalities. They required alone time to recharge and solitary activities like reading, playing their instruments, and writing to "rebalance." The musicians she spoke to reported that when they were onstage, they were "in the zone" and able to "tune out" external stimuli unrelated to their performance. Many of them reported a heightened sensitivity to their surroundings and an intensified experience of sensory input like sound, lighting, and scents. They were often prone to daydreaming and had an appreciation of fantasy, and they said that listening to or creating music allowed them to recharge when they felt overstimulated. All of the musicians also said that they experienced unusual perceptions—meaning that they had perceptually rich experiences that reflected a high level of sensory sensitivity, such as "hearing the confluence of a multitude of sounds and tonal qualities that make up a single bell chime."[5]

Taking in the world with heightened sensitivity can be both a challenge and an asset, and it often requires spending more time alone. Grimes writes, "Sometimes, individuals seek to 'block out' overwhelming stimuli, and sometimes greater intensity and focus are desired. One subject reported that his hypersensitivity to his surroundings is so powerful that he finds it effortful to associate with his environment."[6]

The subjects all described music as a way to express themselves, connect with others, and find personal fulfillment. They also tended to agree that creating art was an important way for them to bridge their inner selves and their outer worlds—pretty sensitive-sounding comments coming from hard rock musicians! Grimes's findings suggest that behind the external appearance of any highly creative person are layers of depth, complexity, and contradictions.

Not only performers but creative people of all types tend to be acutely sensitive, and conversely, sensitive people are often quite creative. It's easy to see how one trait feeds into the other: To both the highly creative and the highly sensitive mind, there's simply more to observe, take in, feel, and process from their environment. To highly sensitive people, as Pulitzer Prize–winning writer Pearl S. Buck suggested, the world may appear to be more colorful, dramatic, tragic, and beautiful. Sensitive people often pick up on the little things in the environment that others miss, see patterns where others see randomness, and find meaning and metaphor in the minutiae of everyday life. It's no wonder this type of personality would be driven to creative expression. If we think of creativity as "connecting the dots" in some way, then sensitive people experience a world in which there are both more dots and more opportunities for connection.

Research led by psychologist Elaine Aron has identified sensitivity as a fundamental dimension of human personality. Aron and others found that highly sensitive people tend to process more sensory input and to pick up on more of what's going on in both their internal and external environment.

An estimated 15 to 20 percent of people are considered to be, in Aron's terms, highly sensitive,[7] but among artists and creative thinkers, that percentage is likely much higher. High levels of sensitivity are correlated with not only creativity but also overlapping traits such as spirituality, intuition, mystical experiences, and connection to art and nature.[8]

Thanks to the pioneering work of Aron and others, psychologists now view sensitivity and responsiveness to the environment as important personality factors in humans and animals. Aron, a sensitive person herself, was inspired by the classic research of Jerome Kagan, who found that 10 to 20 percent of infants have a highly reactive nervous system that makes them more sensitive to environmental stimuli.[9] The early work of psychologist Jan Kristal, too, observed and categorized low sensitivity threshold, or sensitivity to stimuli, as one of nine basic traits distinguishing young children. Kristal observed that "slow to warm up" children were sensitive in many environments, and exhibited traits like social withdrawal.[10]

As Kristal and others have observed, sensitive people notice and respond more to subtle changes in their surroundings because of a trait known as sensory processing sensitivity (SPS), which forms the core of the Highly Sensitive personality type. Most extensively observed in individuals using the Highly Sensitive Person Scale, SPS involves a greater sensitivity to stimuli not just on an emotional but also on cognitive and physical levels. Aron theorized that this greater emotional reactivity likely results from processing things more deeply.

With this combination of reactivity and depth of processing, the individual with SPS has stronger emotional reactions, both positive and negative, which lead to observable behaviors like "pausing to check" in a new situation and using deeper strategies and taking more time to plan effective action.[11] Sensitivity is a cognitive orientation but also involves heightened immune system reactivity. On a physical level, highly sensitive people describe being more affected by caffeine, medication, and pain than others. Fundamentally, sensitivity heightens what's already in the individual's psychic and external environment. As a temperamental disposition, it can be both a blessing and a curse—sensitivity can make life more colorful and by the same token more challenging.

Mark Salzman, a friend of the great cellist Yo-Yo Ma, describes Ma as one of the most joyful people he's met. But he noted that the musician isn't always cheerful—he also experiences negative emotions as deeply as he does positive ones. "Yo-Yo is so responsive to what is going on around him. . . . If you put him in a room with people who are grieving, he will be as sad as anyone," Salzman said.[12]

This depth of feeling almost certainly explains how we feel when we hear him perform. Many audience members at Ma's concerts are left, as Salzman puts it, "excited to the core." He writes, "You find yourself paying more attention to the person you're with, more aware of the rain on the windshield on the ride home. You feel more grateful just to be alive."

When artists are able to channel this quality of deep responsivity into their work, as Ma does, it is truly a gift, making our world richer with art, literature, music, and performance.

"For [highly sensitive people], emotional experience is at such a constant intensity that it shapes their personality and their lives—job performance, social life, intimate relationships—as much as gender and race do," journalist Andrea Bartz writes in *Psychology Today*. "Those who learn to dial down the relentless swooping and cresting of emotions that is the almost invariable accompaniment to extreme sensitivity are able to transform raw perception into keen perceptiveness."[13]

Through creative work, sensitive people are able to channel their energy and emotions and create a sense of meaning out of their experiences. The keen perceptiveness of sensitive minds has been funneled into works of art that offer windows looking on the human condition. At their most powerful, these windows allow us to see ourselves and our place in the world in a new light. To the highly sensitive person, the need to express and share these insights and observations can be so strong that creating art is not simply a passion but indeed a necessity. As journalist Deborah Ward writes of her own creative process, "Creativity is the pressure valve for all that accumulated emotional and sensory data. It opens the doors and lets the energy flow out of me and into my work like electricity from Niagara Falls. And when I create, there is a peace and feeling of fulfillment that I can hardly describe. But that doesn't mean it's easy."[14]

Are You a Highly Sensitive Person?

So what exactly does it mean to be a highly sensitive person, and how do you know if you are one?

In the 1990s, Aron became curious what it *really* means when people are colloquially described as "sensitive." Along with her husband, Arthur, also a psychologist, she conducted interviews with people who self-identified as "highly sensitive." The Arons put up advertisements looking for people who were "introverted" or easily overwhelmed by things like noisy places or evocative or shocking entertainment, selecting an equal number of men and women across a wide range of ages and occupations. They then interviewed each person for three to four hours on a range of personal topics, from their childhood and personal history to current attitudes and life problems.

Many respondents expressed a connection to the arts and nature as well as an unusual sympathy for the helpless (animals, "victims of injustice"). Many also expressed their spirituality ("seeing God in everything," going on long meditation retreats) as playing an important role in their lives. The Arons were surprised to see quite a few extraverts in their sample, considering that their advertisement specifically called for introverts.

Based on these interviews, they created a sixty-item questionnaire that included items that went far beyond simply being overwhelmed by stimulation. The questions ranged from having a rich and complex inner life to intensely falling in love; to having vivid dreams; to being deeply moved by the arts and music; to being startled easily; to being heavily affected by changes in one's life; to being especially sensitive to pain, hunger, and caffeine. The final version of their scale, known as the Highly Sensitive Person (HSP), contains twenty-seven items, which were tested on a group of undergraduate psychology students as well as on a random sample of participants.

To the Arons' surprise—considering the broad range of elements—all of the items tended to clump together. In other words, those who scored high on one item tended to score high on all the other items, and those who scored low on one item tended to also score low on the others. It's also noteworthy that although their final twenty-seven-item scale refers more frequently to negative emotions, the items on their larger original scale that had to do with positive emotions ("When you are feeling happy, is the feeling sometimes really strong?") were still positively correlated with the negative-affect items. This is in line with the idea that sensitivity is associated with a wider range of emotional processing—both positive and negative.

Although the total score on the HSP Scale was associated with neuroticism, being highly sensitive appeared to be a larger personality trait than neuroticism alone. Even after taking neuroticism and negative affect into account, the scale still positively correlated with items such as "feeling love intensely" and "sometimes experiencing intense feelings of happiness." And, it's interesting to note, highly sensitive people were not all introverts. This makes sense, considering that there are plenty of highly sensitive introverts *and* extraverts. Indeed, as the metal rock performers showed, the coexistence of introverted and extraverted characteristics is one of the central paradoxes of creative people.

What's more, the HSP Scale might be capturing different aspects of personality. For instance, one study found that the scale could be broken down into three basic factors: ease of excitement, low sensory threshold, and aesthetic sensitivity.[15] Ease of excitement and a low sensory threshold are associated with a tendency toward negative emotions and anxiety, while aesthetic sensitivity is positively correlated with well-being and openness to experience.[16] Combining ease of excitement and low sensory threshold, Jonathan Cheek and colleagues found two clear factors on the HSP Scale: "temperamental sensitivity" and "rich inner life."[17]

If you're interested in getting a sense of where you stand on the two main factors, here they are:

Temperamental Sensitivity

1. Are you bothered by intense stimuli, like loud noises or chaotic scenes?
2. Do you become unpleasantly aroused when a lot is going on around you?
3. Are you made uncomfortable by loud noises?
4. Are you easily overwhelmed by things like bright lights, strong smells, coarse fabrics, or sirens close by?
5. Are you easily overwhelmed by strong sensory input?
6. Do you find it unpleasant to have a lot going on at once?
7. Do you startle easily?
8. Do you get rattled when you have a lot to do in a short amount of time?
9. Does your nervous system sometimes feel so frazzled that you just have to get off by yourself?
10. Do changes in your life shake you up?
11. Do you find yourself needing to withdraw during busy days, into bed or into a darkened room or anyplace where you can have some privacy and relief from stimulation?
12. Do you make it a high priority to arrange your life to avoid upsetting or overwhelming situations?

13. Are you annoyed when people try to get you to do too many things at once?
14. When you must compete or be observed while performing a task, do you become so nervous or shaky that you do much worse than you would otherwise?
15. Do you make a point to avoid violent movies and TV shows?
16. Do other people's moods affect you?
17. Are you particularly sensitive to the effects of caffeine?
18. Does being very hungry create a strong reaction in you, disrupting your concentration or mood?
19. Do you tend to be more sensitive to pain?

Rich Inner Life

20. Do you notice and enjoy delicate or fine scents, tastes, sounds, works of art?
21. Are you deeply moved by the arts or music?
22. Do you seem to be aware of subtleties in your environment?
23. Do you have a rich, complex inner life?
24. When people are uncomfortable in a physical environment do you tend to know what needs to be done to make it more comfortable (like changing the lighting or the seating?)

Now, researchers are also just beginning to understand the neurological basis of high sensitivity. In one recent study, eighteen students from a school in Beijing were shown a set of sixteen black-and-white photographs of natural and man-made scenes.[18] Using Photoshop, they altered each picture, making either major changes (adding an extra fence post to a prominent fence) or more subtle changes (adding half a hay bale to an existing row of hay bales). Then, the students were placed in an fMRI scanner and were shown seventy-two images with these different levels of alteration. The participants' task was to decide whether each picture was the same or different from the preceding image by pressing buttons on a box while in the scanner.

They found that the more sensitive the students, the faster they were able to detect the changes. The highly sensitive participants also showed increased brain activation in regions of the brain relating to visual attention when making finer distinctions between the pictures, suggesting that the subjects had a greater awareness of the subtle details of the scene.

Other recent fMRI data support the notion that highly sensitive people process information differently. One study found that people scoring high on the HSP Scale displayed greater reactions to photos of happy and sad faces compared to neutral faces. They also reacted more to a spouse's happy or sad facial expressions, compared to strangers with the same exact expressions.[19] In particular, they showed greater brain activation in areas associated with empathy and self-awareness.

The researchers also found significant activations in the insula—an area of the brain that plays an important role in self-awareness, self-reflection, and the regulation of our moment-to-moment emotional states to facilitate decision making.[20] Recent research suggests that larger insula cortex volume may even be associated with greater well-being, including reports of greater personal growth, self-acceptance, purpose in life, and autonomy.[21]

Orchids and Dandelions

Like all other personality dispositions, sensitivity emerges as a dynamic interaction of nature and nurture. Childhood can be instrumental in how sensitivity plays out over an individual's lifetime. In positive, supportive environments, a child's reactivity and sensitivity to stimuli can promote intellectual curiosity and excitement about learning, and contribute to more positive feelings toward teachers and mentors. But when sensitivity intersects with a negative childhood environment, it can contribute to negative emotions, depression, and inhibition of behavior.[22]

Traditionally, sensitivity has been viewed as an undesirable trait—a body of research on highly reactive phenotypes suggested that some children were particularly vulnerable to developing psychopathology when exposed to adversity (such as hostile parenting or poverty) due to their exaggerated stress response. This biological response was seen to be maladaptive—but psychologists W. Thomas Boyce and Bruce Ellis weren't buying it.

Boyce and Ellis proposed a radically different hypothesis: that reactivity is a form of enhanced biological sensitivity to context (BSC), which has been favored by natural selection because of the benefits across *many different environments*.[23] In stressful environments, sensitivity can be adaptive because it increases vigilance to threats and dangers, and in nonstressful environments it can increase openness to social resources and support. Thus natural selection would have favored a single genotype that supports a *range of expressions*, allowing for the right fit between the organism and the environment, depending on the circumstance.

Boyce and Ellis adopted the Swedish metaphor of "dandelion and orchid children," referring to *dandelion children* as those who survive and thrive in nearly any environment, just like dandelion flowers prosper regardless of soil, sun, drought, or rain. *Orchid children*, on the other hand, are those whose survival and flourishing depend heavily on their environment. Less resilient than the dandelion child, an orchid child may struggle more to grow and thrive through challenging life circumstances, but those who do can truly blossom. "In conditions of neglect, the orchid promptly declines, while in conditions of support and nurture, it is a flower of unusual delicacy and beauty," Boyce and Ellis write.

The orchid hypothesis, while something of an over-simplification, has been supported by a number of recent studies. Most strikingly, intriguing differences in genetic mutations associated with both dopamine and serotonin of dandelion versus orchid children have been revealed. While each genetic mutation explains only a small portion of the differences in behavior observed among people, and not all of the genetic effects have been replicated, this emerging research does suggest that both gene-gene interactions and gene-environment interactions are important to arrive at a complete picture of human development. The key insight here is that many of our genes don't contribute to positive or nega-tive outcomes across all environments. Instead, these genes are related to heightened sensitivity to the environment—for better *and* for worse.

Some of the same genes that are associated with psychological challenges—including depression, anxiety, and inability to focus—are also associated with resources that can help us flourish, including intellectual curiosity, positive emo-tions, and the ability to regulate our emotions.[24] As Blair and Diamond explain, human development is dynamic, nonlinear, and probabilistic—meaning that we can't predict behavior based on genes or the environment alone; we must take into account the ongoing dance between nature and nurture."[25]

What the dandelion-orchid data tells us is that sensitivity—particularly under nurturing conditions—can be a *gift*.

Feeling Alive

Our selves are constantly evolving as we learn more about the world and our own identities and seek meaning in our experiences.[26] According to Michael Piechowski, the process of inner transformation is itself a creative process, for through the process of advanced inner development, you are literally *creating* a new self.[27] Similarly, Rosa Aurora Chávez-Eakle and colleagues note that "the creative process allows self-reorganizations that makes [it] possible to experience states that seem to be pathological. . . . A highly creative individual is in constant self-actualization. . . . Creativity makes life worth living, and involves a strong sense of being alive."[28] Or as Nietzsche put it, those who actively create and re-create themselves are truly "free spirits"—artistic creators of their own lives.[29]

This sense of aliveness is beautifully captured in a seminal theory by Polish psychiatrist Kazimierz Dąbrowski. Through decades of experience with clinical and biographical studies of patients, artists, writers, spiritual teachers, and developmentally advanced children and adolescents, he became interested in understanding why some people's interactions with the world seemed to be higher in intensity than others.[30] Why do some people seem to fall in love, experience happiness and sadness, and engage with life with greater depth than others? And why is it that some children exhibit significantly higher levels of intellectual curiosity and imagination?

For Dąbrowski, the answer to these questions was *overexcitability*. He believed that "overexcitabilities"—heightened reactions to both the internal and external world—guide the self-transformation process to a higher level of development.[31] According to Piechowski (who collaborated with Dąbrowski), these overexcitabilities intensify experiences, and are "channels through which flow the colors, textures, insights, visions, currents, and energies of experience."[32] Overexcitabilities are critical to becoming an authentic and autonomous individual.

Overexcitability can lead to inner emotional tension and constructive conflict with one's environment, as well as the means to resolve these conflicts. In this way, intensity and sensitivity were believed to increase the likelihood that people would blossom into the fullest expressions of themselves—taking risks, seeking meaning, expressing themselves creatively, and seeking out opportunities for self-improvement. Of course, intensity and sensitivity do not automatically lead to personal growth. Indeed, writers and artists who concentrate on the muck of life, the ugly, and the brutal without any sign of hope or redemption aren't necessarily reaching the highest levels of personal growth. Nevertheless, for Dąbrowski, the ability to intensely experience the world was a critical part of the capacity for inner transformation.

If you've tapped into your creative side, there's a good chance that you'll see yourself in at least one of Dąbrowski's five types of overexcitability—psychomotor, sensual, intellectual, imaginational, or emotional. *Psychomotor overexcitability* involves a surplus of physical energy and expression of emotional tension, expressed in rapid speech, compulsive chattering, intense physical activity, nail biting and picking, pencil tapping, and workaholism.[33] With *sensual overexcitability* comes an appreciation of simple sensory pleasures arising from touch (feeling fabric or skin) and smell (perfumes, food, gasoline), and a delight in the aesthetic (music, color, sounds of words, writing styles, and other beautiful things). *Sensual overexcitability* can be exhibited in a tendency to overeat, attend musical concerts and art museums, and a high sexual libido. This enhanced sensitivity can also manifest itself as intense *displeasure* for overpowering smells, distasteful food, or as Cheryl Ackerman puts it, when "the seams on your socks don't line up just right."[34]

Imaginational overexcitability suggests richness of imagination and the capacity to live in a world of fantasy. This is expressed through vividness of mental images, rich associations, use of metaphor in communication, and detailed dreams or nightmares, along with an interest in fantasy, poetry, magical tales, magical thinking, and imaginary friends. An overexcitable imagination can also give rise to a fear of the unknown. In Edgar Allan Poe's short story "Imp of the Perverse," Poe expresses the way that intensified imagination can lead to great anxiety:

> We stand upon the brink of a precipice. We peer into the abyss—we grow sick and dizzy. Our first impulse is to shrink from the danger. Unaccountably we remain. By slow degrees our sickness and dizziness and horror become merged in a cloud of unnamable feeling. By gradations, still more imperceptible, this cloud assumes shape . . . far more terrible than any genius or any demon of a tale, and yet it is but a thought . . . it is merely the idea of what would be our

sensations during the sweeping precipitancy of a fall from such a height.[35]

Indeed, a heightened level of imaginational overexcitability has been linked to higher levels of insomnia, anxiety, and fear of "the ultimate unknown"—death.[36] But it also has also led to the creation of some of the greatest art, poetry, and literature.

Introspection, engagement in independent, reflective thought, and enjoyment of solving intellectual challenges are common indicators of *intellectual overexcitability*. This type of overexcitability can be expressed through curiosity, a need to search for truth and understanding, love of theory and analysis, conceptual integration, criticism, voracious reading, keen observations, and asking probing and insightful questions. Intellectual overexcitability is distinct from IQ—the latter involves general cognitive ability, while the former involves a *love* of engaging in the intellectual universe.

Finally, *emotional overexcitability* involves characteristics and behaviors that many artists embody. Intensified feelings and emotions, deep relationships, and feelings of compassion and responsibility toward self and others are hallmarks of this type of sensitivity, which can provide the fodder for great works of literature, music, and other forms of art exploring the human emotional landscape. Potential manifestations of this quality include deep and meaningful relationships, strong emotional memory, empathy and compassion for the feelings of others, shyness, depression, need for security, difficulty adjusting to new environments, critical self-evaluation, blushing, sweaty palms, and a racing heart.[37] Piechowski writes of emotional sensitivity:

> Combined with great imagination and intellectual power, [emotional sensitivity] may lead to brooding and devastating self-criticism. It may turn morbid or neurotic. Or it may mobilize one's whole psyche toward the goal of self-realization in creativity.[38]

The strongest support for these overexcitabilities comes from studies on highly creative adults,[39] who show evidence of elevated levels of multiple overexcitabilities. These studies are consistent with research showing that openness to experience is a strong and consistent predictor of everyday creativity as well as publicly recognized creative achievement.

The overexcitabilities (and the sensitivity that gives rise to them) can be important contributors to personal growth. Through the process that Dąbrowski calls *positive disintegration*, the individual's internal psychic landscape is fragmented and dismantled. This occurs when a lower-level personality (conforming and insecure) gives way to a higher-level personality (creative, passionate, and authentic).

Both positive and negative emotions play a critical role in the positive disintegration process. Even emotional experiences that we tend to think of as negative, like neurosis and inner conflict, can contribute to personality growth. These conflicts, if we engage with and learn from them, can set the stage for emotional development, creativity, and a rich inner life.

This disintegration process can occur at any age or stage of life. And when individuals bring more conscious effort and self-awareness into their personal growth, higher levels of personality development—and creativity—become possible. As we learn, grow, and transform, we can achieve higher levels of consciousness and authenticity, and live with greater agency, choice, and direction. Sensitivity, intensity, and inner conflict are required for us to transcend to greater levels of growth, self-awareness, and compassion.

At later phases of personality development, a quest to find the true self emerges.[40] The individual no longer passively accepts external authority, but starts listening to his or her inner voice and making judgments based on his or her own standards. Through the process of transcending to the "higher self," people often become aware of what Robert Greene refers to as the *false self*—"the accumulation of all the voices you have internalized from other people—parents and friends who want you to conform to their ideas of what you should be like and what you should do, as well as societal pressures to adhere to certain values."[41] Becoming intimate with these voices helps the individual to transcend them. As Joseph Campbell said, "It is by going down into the abyss that we discover the treasures of life. Where you stumble, there lies your treasure."

What lies at higher stages of this journey of personality development? Self-actualization and a desire to help others and solve problems in the world, rather than a preoccupation with one's own petty concerns. Here, people develop universal compassion, service to humanity, and the realization of timeless values.

The culmination of the most advanced phase of personality development is the achievement of a guiding "personality ideal," meaning that the ideal by which a person lives is inspired and fulfilled.[42] At this phase, there is no longer inner conflict because there is no longer a difference between "what is" and "what ought to be."[43] The notion of a personality ideal is similar to Greene's notion of the *true self*, whose "voice comes from deep within. . . . It emanates from your uniqueness, and it communicates through sensations and powerful desires that seem to transcend you."

People who achieve extraordinary inner transformation find creative ways of solving problems, coping with emotional challenges, accepting themselves and others, and giving back. They seek to constantly give new meaning to their lives and discover their true selves—the self becomes an object of ongoing discovery and creation. They also discover that one's inner world determines his or her external reality, that we each create our personal and collective reality, that our lives are interconnected, and that the choices we make shape the world toward war or peace. In other words, they discovered that "inner peace is the foundation of world peace" and that "everything we need is within us." Indeed, after his review of these extraordinary lives, Piechowski concluded, "If we accept their discovery that we create our own reality, and that all the 'material' can be found within the inner self, then we have come upon creativity in the ultimate sense."[44]

An exemplar of self-actualization is Eleanor Roosevelt because of her "striving for independence, overcoming her great fears, development of her talents as a public speaker, writer, and politician, and her unswerving dedication to goals outside of herself."[45] Roosevelt notes the importance of personal growth in her book *The Moral Basics of Democracy*: "Laws and government administration are only the result of the way people progress inwardly, and that the basis of success in a democracy is really laid down by the people. It will progress only as their own personal development goes forward."[46]

Transformation can come from nearly endless sources. Elizabeth Gilbert is often asked how people can go on a journey of self-discovery as she did, famously documented in her bestseller *Eat, Pray, Love*, in which she spent a full year journeying through Italy, India, and Indonesia. In response, she notes:

> The last thing I ever want to become is the Poster Child for "Everyone Must Leave Their Husband And Move To India In Order to Find God." . . . It was my path—that is all it ever was. I drew up my journey as a personal prescription for solving my life. Transformative journeys come in many forms, though, and often happen without people ever leaving home.[47]

Conscious personal development through the process of positive disintegration can be compared to how Swiss-American psychiatrist and grief researcher Elisabeth Kübler-Ross famously described the making of "beautiful people":

> The most beautiful people we have known are those who have known defeat, known suffering, known struggle, known loss, and have found their way out of the depths. These persons have an appreciation, a sensitivity and an understanding of life that fills them with compassion, gentleness and a deep loving concern. Beautiful people do not just happen.[48]

Knowing loss, struggle, suffering, and defeat is crucial to the positive disintegration process and acts as catalyst for personal growth, creativity, and deep transformation. Rather than something to be avoided or denied, it is the hardships and challenges—both internal and external—that make us beautiful. As Nietzsche poetically said, "One must still have chaos in oneself to be able to give birth to a dancing star."

Though living with intense sensitivity often makes life more difficult, to be sure, psychologist Sharon Lind implores us to remember that being overexcitable also "brings with it great joy, astonishment, compassion and creativity."[49] And if we can make the best out of our difficult experiences, we are in an even better position to create meaningful work and develop a more complex identity.

Turning Adversity into Advantage

An artist must be nourished by his passions and by his despairs.

—Francis Bacon

One of Frida Kahlo's most famous self-portraits depicts her in a hospital bed naked and bleeding, connected by a web of red veins to floating objects that include a snail, a flower, bones, and a fetus. *Henry Ford Hospital*, the 1932 surrealist painting, is a powerful artistic rendering of Kahlo's second miscarriage. She wrote in her diaries that the painting "carries with it the message of pain."[1] The feminist painter was truly a master of turning suffering into art—and a real understanding of her work requires some knowledge of the pain that motivated it.

Kahlo channeled the experience of multiple miscarriages, childhood polio, and a number of other misfortunes into her iconic self-portraits. She first began painting at the age of eighteen, after a near-fatal accident in which a bus collided with a streetcar and a steel handrail impaled her through the hip and out the other side, causing multiple injuries, including spine and pelvis fractures, and a lifetime of chronic pain. Kahlo completed her first self-portrait the following year while in recovery.

Painting became Kahlo's *modus operandi*—her way to make meaning out of seemingly senseless suffering. The artist's deepest darkness became the motivation and inspiration for her work, and painting offered a way through the hardships that life had thrown her way. Pain and trauma were the inspiration behind Kahlo's autobiographical works, which express, with rawness and honesty, the depths of her emotions.

Art born of adversity is an almost universal theme in the lives of many of the world's most eminent creative minds. For artists who have struggled with physical and mental illness, parental loss during childhood, social rejection, heartbreak, abandonment, abuse, and other forms of trauma, creativity often becomes an act of turning challenge into opportunity.

Much of the music we listen to, the plays we see, and the paintings we look at—among other forms of art—are attempts to find meaning in human suffering. Art seeks to make sense of everything from life's smallest moments of sadness to its most earth-shattering tragedies. We all experience and grapple with suffering. In our individual and collective quest to understand the darker sides of human life, works of art like Kahlo's self-portraits, which show us the truth of another's pain and loneliness, carry the power to move us deeply.

We're told, throughout our lives, that what doesn't kill us makes us stronger. It's difficult to think of a phrase that's more deeply ingrained in our cultural imagination than this one, first spoken by Nietzsche and since co-opted by pop culture (think Kelly Clarkson and Kanye West). Platitude though it may be, the expression has become common parlance because it expresses a fundamental truth of human psychology: Experiences of extreme adversity show us our own strength. And in the wake of trying times, many people not only return to their baseline state of functioning, but learn to truly thrive.

We all love a good story of triumph in the face of adversity—the journey through struggle to strength is the crux of what Joseph Campbell called the "Hero's Journey," and also forms the core of the all-American Horatio Alger rags-to-riches tale, in which a character rises above trying circumstances in order to achieve greatness. It's one of the most common cross-cultural story arcs. Innumerable tales in history and pop culture tell the stories of courageous individuals who overcame the odds, not only returning to a level of normal functioning but becoming better than ever before. The survivor is then able to pass on his or her new wisdom and compassion to others.

The origins of this archetype can be traced back to ancient Greek and Roman philosophers, who recognized that any conception of the good life must have a place for the inevitable struggles and challenges we all face. Stoic philosophy, in particular, focused on the question of how to deal with a capricious and inherently unpredictable world that could turn all our dreams and desires to rubble in a matter of seconds. Roman statesman Marcus Aurelius, one of the most famous proponents of Stoicism, penned *The Meditations*, the ultimate manifesto on strength after adversity, from a battle camp during a war that he was losing. As Aurelius wrote, "The impediment to action advances the action. What stands in the way becomes the way."[2]

Again in the mid-twentieth century, this idea crops up in existentialist thought as European thinkers grappled with the widespread suffering and disillusionment of the World War II era. In *Man's Search for Meaning*, Holocaust survivor Viktor Frankl laid out his theory that man's fundamental drive is to find life's "potential meaning under any conditions." Even in the midst of unimaginable suffering (several of his family members were killed in concentration camps), Frankl maintained that life's most devastating circumstances were an opportunity to find purpose and strength. Life is never made unbearable by circumstances, he said, but by lack of meaning and purpose. "When we are no longer able to change a situation, we are challenged to change ourselves," Frankl wrote.[3]

In the Buddhist tradition, there's a saying, "No mud, no lotus."[4] The symbolic lotus flower blooms out of the mud; its growth is rooted in the dirt and grime. As the metaphor goes, it is from suffering that we learn compassion, from loss that we learn understanding, and from overcoming struggles that we come to discover our own strength and beauty. These struggles, it's believed, are precisely what we need in order to grow. As Gregory David Roberts wrote in *Shantaram*, "Sometimes you break your heart in the right way, if you know what I mean."[5]

In a 1988 interview, the late actor and comedian Robin Williams opened up to *Rolling Stone* about finding gratitude for life's hardships, including his divorce and the death of his father. After one of the most difficult years of his life, Williams said that during a time of hardship, a friend advised him to find gratitude. "Someone said I should send out Buddhist thank-you cards, since Buddhists believe that anything that challenges you makes you pull yourself together," he said.[6]

This trials-to-triumph narrative is far from idealism or watered-down self-help inspiration. The idea of growth after adversity has been touted by not only ancient and modern wisdom traditions but also recent psychology research. In the past

twenty years, psychologists have begun studying this phenomenon, known in the scientific community as *posttraumatic
growth*. The term was coined in the 1990s by psychologists
Richard Tedeschi and Lawrence Calhoun to describe instances
of individuals who experienced profound transformation as
they coped with various types of trauma and challenging life
circumstances.[7] It's now been observed in more than three
hundred scientific studies, and research has found that up to 70
percent of trauma survivors report some positive psychological
growth.[8]

> **Up to 70 percent of trauma survivors report
> some positive psychological growth.**

What doesn't kill us may make us not only stronger but
also more creative. Great artistic achievements often arise out
of intense suffering. While trauma should never be glorified or
sought out as a creative tool, adversity can provide powerful
inspiration for work that strives to make sense of the artist's
inner life and emotional state. And when a piece of art suc-
ceeds in elevating suffering in some way, the results can be
breathtaking. Ray Charles once spoke of how intensely he
could experience Beethoven's darkness when he listened to the
Moonlight Sonata. Charles said in an interview with *Rolling
Stone*, "Man, you could just feel the pain this man was going
through. He was very, very lonesome when he wrote that."[9]

Out of loss, there can be creative gain. The relationship
may be twofold: People who experience adversity may be
more likely to pursue creative outlets, and it's possible that
creatively inclined people (who are likely sensitive and high

in the openness to experience personality domain) experience more adversity in their lives as a result of their tendency to be vulnerable by doing things differently than others. Psychological disorders are a somewhat common form of adversity experienced by highly creative people, which can give rise to both creative inspiration and a compulsion for self-expression. Anne Sexton once said, "Poetry led me by the hand out of madness," while Virginia Woolf wrote her novel *To the Lighthouse* as a way to cope with the loss of her mother. "In expressing it I explained it and then laid it to rest," Woolf said.

Further proof of the link between trauma and creativity is the "orphanhood effect," which has demonstrated that highly accomplished individuals experience disproportionately high rates of parental loss as compared to the general population—rates that are equal to those receiving psychiatric care for depression and suicidal symptoms.[10] It's not difficult to find examples of this among eminent artists: Truman Capote's mother had been an alcoholic since he was sixteen years old and committed suicide when he was an adult. As a boy, Jerry Garcia watched his father drown in the American River. Writers Edward Albee, Joseph Conrad, W. Somerset Maugham, Leo Tolstoy, and William Wordsworth were all orphaned in childhood—and the list goes on.

It bears repeating that trauma is neither *necessary* nor *sufficient* for creativity. Experiences of trauma in any form are tragic and psychologically devastating, no matter what type of creative growth occurs in their aftermath. These experiences can just as easily lead to long-term loss as gain. Indeed, loss and gain, suffering and growth, often co-occur. But in their attempts to cope with trauma, many artists may have found, as Frankl puts it, that "in some ways suffering ceases to be suffering at the moment it finds a meaning."[11] Creative work can be a way of exploring and giving expression to that meaning.

Creative work doesn't *require* adversity, and it's important to remember that the myth of the tortured artist is just that—a myth. The image of the highly creative person as a dark, self-destructive soul who spins his pain into art doesn't reflect the reality of creative achievement, which draws on positive as much as negative life experiences. When music journalist Paul Zollo asked Yoko Ono if all the tragedy she had experienced in her life had opened her up in some way or made her a better artist, Ono explicitly rejected the idea that great art requires adversity. "I think tragedy comes in all forms," she said. "No one should encourage artists to pursue tragedy so that they might become a good artist. You don't have to have tragedy to create, really."

Adverse events are moments that force us to reexamine our beliefs and life projects—and therein lies their power and creative potential, explains Marie Forgeard, a psychologist at McLean Hospital/Harvard Medical School, who has done extensive research into posttraumatic growth and creativity.

"We're forced to reconsider things we took for granted, and we're forced to think about new things," says Forgeard. "Adverse events can be so powerful that they force us to think about questions we never would have thought of otherwise."

Out of Loss, There Is Gain

Growth after trauma can take a number of different forms, including a greater appreciation for life, the identification of new possibilities for one's life, more satisfying interpersonal relationships, a richer spiritual life and a connection to something greater than oneself, and a sense of personal strength.[12] A battle with cancer, for instance, can result in a renewed gratitude for one's family, while a near-death experience could be a catalyst for connecting with a more spiritual side of life. Psychologists have found that experiences of trauma also commonly result in increased empathy and altruism, and a motivation to act in the interest of the good of others.[13]

So how is it that out of suffering we can come to not only return to our baseline state but to deeply improve our lives? And why are some people crushed by trauma, while others thrive? Tedeschi and Calhoun explain that posttraumatic growth, in whatever form it takes, can be "an experience of improvement that is for some persons deeply profound."[14]

The two University of North Carolina researchers created the most accepted model of posttraumatic growth to date, which holds that people naturally develop and rely on a set of beliefs and assumptions that they've formed about the world, and in order for growth to occur after a trauma, the traumatic event must deeply challenge those beliefs. By Tedeschi and Calhoun's account, the way that trauma shatters our worldviews, beliefs, and identities is like an earthquake—even our most foundational structures of thought and belief crumble to pieces from the magnitude of the impact. We are shaken, almost literally, from our ordinary perception, and left to rebuild ourselves and our worlds. The more we are shaken, the more we must let go of our former selves and assumptions, and begin again from the ground up.

"A psychologically seismic event can severely shake, threaten, or reduce to rubble many of the schematic structures that have guided understanding, decision making, and meaningfulness," they write.[15] "One's safety is challenged; one's identity and future are challenged."

The physical rebuilding of a city that takes place after an earthquake can be likened to the cognitive processing and restructuring that an individual experiences in the wake of a trauma. Once the most foundational structures of the self have been shaken, we are in a position to pursue new—and perhaps creative—opportunities.

The "rebuilding" process looks something like this: After a traumatic event, such as a serious illness or loss of a loved one, individuals intensely process the event—they're constantly thinking about what happened, and usually with strong emotional reactions. It's important to note that sadness, grief, anger, and anxiety, of course, are common responses to trauma, and growth generally occurs alongside these challenging emotions—not in place of them. The process of growth can be seen as a way to adapt to extremely adverse circumstances and to gain an understanding of both the trauma and its negative psychological impact.

Rumination—stewing over negative thoughts and emotions—naturally occurs after a traumatic event, and counterintuitive though it may seem, this kind of repetitive thinking is a crucial step toward thriving in the wake of a challenge. When we mull over a negative experience, we're working hard to make sense of it and to find a place for it in our lives that still allows us to have a strong sense of meaning and purpose. After the experience of adversity, the mind is actively dismantling old belief systems that no longer hold up and creating new structures of meaning and identity. Perhaps most fundamentally, trauma challenges our belief in a benevolent and predictable universe. The illusion of control is shattered and must be released, as it no longer accords with the individual's experience of the world, which now appears capricious, unpredictable, and seemingly beyond human control.

While rumination often begins as automatic, intrusive, and repetitive negative thinking, in time, the individual's way of thinking about the traumatic event and its impacts becomes more organized, controlled, and deliberate. It starts to act as a process of meaning making. The search for meaning is the essential element of posttraumatic growth, and particularly of creative growth.

Rebuilding can be an incredibly challenging process. As we've seen, the work of growth requires detaching from and releasing deep-seated goals, identities, and assumptions, while also building up new goals, schemas, and meanings. It can be grueling, excruciating, and exhausting. But it can open the door to a new life. The trauma survivor begins to see herself as a thriver and revises her self-definition to accommodate her new strength and wisdom. She may reconstruct herself in a way that feels more authentic and true to her inner self and to her own unique path in life.

In Finland, there's a word for what these survivors have in spades: *sisu*. Sisu refers to extraordinary determination, courage, and resoluteness in the face of extreme adversity. In recent years, Finnish social psychologist Emilia Lahti has been scientifically studying sisu. Lahti argues that sisu contributes to what she refers to as an "action mind-set," a consistent and courageous approach to challenges that enables individuals to see beyond their present limitations and into what might be.

New Possibilities

How does creative growth occur in the wake of adversity?

Forgeard has asked questions about how creativity was inspired and motivated by conflict, and how the creative act could be psychologically healing for those who had experienced trauma and extreme life challenges. One of the few researchers devoted to studying the link between posttraumatic growth and creativity, she has examined the effects of adversity on famous artists and on hundreds of everyday people.

Studying the lives of eminent creative people through history, Forgeard saw a pattern of suffering being spun into fodder for creative work—many artists seemed to struggle with adversity (including loss and mental health problems) and to use their suffering as motivation and inspiration to create. As we've noted, eminent creators, particularly in the arts, have been found to have higher levels of life challenges (early parental loss, emotional instability, social rejection, and physical illness) than the general population.[16] Forgeard suspected that the concurrence of life struggles and high levels of creativity was not accidental—for some people, she hypothesized, adversity was in fact a key to creative achievement.

Forgeard began by asking over three hundred people to describe the most stressful experience of their lives, which in most cases was a traumatic event that happened to them or to a loved one.[17] She also asked about their creative activities and whether they thought adversity may have contributed to their creativity, and found that people who perceived experiencing higher levels of distress as a result of adversity also said they experienced enhanced creativity. The data also revealed that perceived changes in creativity were more common among people who were high in openness to experience. These perceptions of increased creativity, even if they are only perceptions, constitute an important form of posttraumatic growth.

"The study showed that there seems to be a correlation between an adverse experience and creativity," says Forgeard.

"The more distressing the experience in their lives, the more posttraumatic growth they experienced, and the more posttraumatic growth they experienced, the more changes in creativity they also reported."[18]

It wasn't just overall growth that people experienced; those who reported boosts in creativity experienced higher growth in certain areas. Creative growth was linked with growth in terms of seeing new possibilities in one's life and, curiously, with both positive and negative changes in interpersonal relationships.[19]

Creativity can even become a positive coping mechanism after a difficult experience. Some people might find that the experience of adversity forces them to question their basic assumptions about the world and therefore to think more creatively. Others might find that they have a new (or renewed) motivation to spend time engaged in creative activities. And others who already had a strong interest in creative work may turn to creativity as the main way of rebuilding their lives.

Creativity truly carries healing power. It is particularly the *meaning-making aspect* of creative thinking and expression that seems to contribute to growth after trauma. For this reason, art therapy and expressive writing can be powerful tools for posttraumatic growth.[20] More recently, Forgeard and colleagues investigated how creative work facilitates healing, finding that the meaning-making aspect of creative expression may contribute substantially to growth after trauma.

Creativity can be used as a vehicle for posttraumatic growth through art therapy and expressive writing. Art therapy is often used as a way to allow people to sift through challenging thoughts and emotions in an unthreatening manner and to better express themselves. Similarly, regular expressive writing for a period of days or weeks—consisting of fifteen to twenty minutes of writing about a topic that triggers strong emotions—is thought to help individuals to better understand and express both positive and negative emotions.[22] Research has found that this type of writing can indeed improve both psychological and physical health, including lessening symptoms of posttraumatic stress disorder and depression,[23] as well as improving some cognitive functions, such as working memory. Psychologists have found that these benefits extend even to writing about positive experiences and imagined trauma.[24]

These types of creative therapy lead to growth through several underlying factors, including the facilitation of absorption (flow), distraction from the challenging situation, positive emotions, and meaning making. When we engage in creative activities, we tend to become absorbed in what we're making, entering a kind of flow state that can induce a sense of control, enjoyment, and accomplishment. Creative work can also act as a positive distraction from thoughts of the trauma, directing the individual's attention to an enjoyable activity and potentially broadening attention in a way that facilitates new modes of thought. And perhaps most significant, as we've seen, creative work can help us make meaning out of challenges and suffering that may feel senseless.

For writers (or anyone who's taken up journaling to cope with life's challenges), this orientation toward meaning making is exhibited even on the level of word choice. The beneficial effects of expressive writing are correlated with the degree to which writers use cognitive words like *know* and *understand*, which reflect new ways of conceptualizing the emotionally salient event.[25] Famous authors who suffer from depression are also more likely to use these same words, which reflect a state of rumination or repetitive thinking,[26] a mental activity associated with both depression and posttraumatic growth, particularly creative growth.[27]

"The relationship between depression and creativity may actually be accounted for by rumination," Forgeard said. "If you're someone who reflects a lot and can't stop thinking about particular things, it could both make you more vulnerable to depression and more creative."[28]

But it's important to note that creative work isn't just a tool to facilitate growth; it's also a sign that growth has occurred and an expression of healing. Posttraumatic growth often leads people to see new possibilities in their lives, and one of those new possibilities may be an artistic hobby or an entirely new career that allows them to express their creativity.

New Visions

Many painters' struggles with debilitating and life-threatening illnesses have been followed by periods of great creative achievement. Indeed, illness can lead to the emergence of new and more original work by breaking an artist's habits and thought patterns, creating a sense of disharmony, and forcing the artist to find new ways to do his work.[29]

Serious health problems have a way of forcing us to reconsider our assumptions and identities and to find new ways of engaging with ourselves and the world. For painters, a new way of seeing the world can result in highly original creative work and a greater sense of meaning in the midst of their struggles. When serious mental or physical illness shatters an artist's assumptions and worldview, it can also shake up his form, creating the opportunity for emotionally rich work that breaks free of stylistic restrictions and artistic boundaries.

Swiss painter Paul Klee of the Bauhaus art school suffered from a rare and ultimately fatal autoimmune disease that crippled his most valuable creative tool—his hands. It became challenging for Klee to even hold a pen, but he never stopped painting. In fact, he painted constantly and enjoyed a period of intense creative productivity toward the end of his life. Klee created *more than twelve hundred works* the year after his diagnosis, including some of his largest, most original pieces.

"I create—in order not to cry," he said.[30]

> ## "I create—in order not to cry."

Francisco de Goya, too, suffered from a serious illness that deeply shaped his creations. Goya's body of work can be divided into two periods—before and after his illness at age forty-six, which caused enduring weakness, malaise, right-side paralysis, loss of vision, and permanent deafness. Goya is commonly regarded as having produced his greatest works during the period following his illness, when he retreated into his imagination and turned his focus entirely to his art.

"The visual experience after the illness was heightened by the exclusion of acoustics stimuli and the artist's talent rose to the highest level," write Polish art historians S. Betlejewski and R. Ossowski.[31] "His character became more withdrawn and introspective and his entire vitality was directed to his painting."

Claude Monet's changes in vision following a bout of illness also had a drastic effect on the aesthetic of his work. The

painter suffered from cataracts,[32] which progressively deterio-
rated his eyesight. Drastic stylistic changes in his work can be
witnessed in the period after he began losing his color perception, when his paintings became more abstract and he shifted
toward muddier hues.

And of course, one of the most famous case studies in creativity and mental illness, Vincent van Gogh—the prototype
of the tortured artist—struggled with crippling anxiety, depression, and possible bipolar disorder in the years during and
leading up to some of the most creative periods of his life. In
1888, van Gogh committed himself to an asylum in Saint-
Rémy-de-Provence, where he worked feverishly, creating some
of his most iconic paintings, including *Irises* and *Starry Night*.
Some art critics have suggested that the swirling lines in the
sky of *Starry Night*, which depicts the nighttime view outside
his asylum window, are a representation of the artist's tempes-
tuous mental state.

Van Gogh's illness sometimes rendered him unable to
paint. But when he was able to work, painting gave him a
sense of peacefulness and purpose. "I am often in the greatest misery," he wrote in a letter to his brother, Theo. "But
still there is within me a calm, pure harmony and music. In
the poorest huts, in the dirtiest corner, I see drawings and
pictures."[33]

Gain Without Pain?

An experience of adversity doesn't have to be a full-blown
trauma to change the way we see the world. In fact, an event
doesn't have to be adverse *at all* for it to shift our perspective
and motivate us to create. Any event—big or small, negative or
positive—can move us to express ourselves creatively.

Inspired by the growing body of research on posttraumatic growth, University of Pennsylvania researcher Ann Marie Roepke, a colleague of Forgeard's, decided to investigate the question of creative growth after adversity in a different way, asking: Can there be gain *without pain*? Could our highest moments inspire the same sort of lasting psychological growth that psychologists observed in the wake of trauma and intense adversity?[34]

What Roepke found was that positive events can powerfully shape our character, worldview, and beliefs, a phenomenon she labeled *post-ecstatic growth*. The most uplifting and positive moments of people's lives could improve their psychological well-being by impacting personal growth, wisdom, spirituality, worldview, meaning, and purpose. Roepke observed that positive emotions seemed to build a person's psychological resources, broadening attention, inspiring new thought and behaviors, and stimulating creative thinking. Broadening attention in this way seemed to allow people to see new possibilities and goals, sometimes acting as a catalyst for seismic shifts in worldview.

The overwhelming majority of participants in Roepke's study experienced at least a small amount of personal growth following a positive event. It was positive events grounded in *meaning*—as opposed to accomplishments, relationships, or events evoking intense pleasure—that were mostly likely to lead to growth. These experiences of awe, wonder, inspiration, and connection to something greater than the self—a spiritual awakening, the gift of new life, a realization of the nature of interconnection—that led people to see the world anew and, as a result, to grow.

By moving toward new goals and ways of being, people often changed their relationships, priorities, identities, and even spiritual beliefs. "This is the growth we see in ourselves after the highest and lowest moments of our lives," Roepke says.

In fact, it seems that the more an experience leads you to conceive of new possibilities in your life, the more you may grow. This important lesson can apply not only to life's greatest triumphs and trials but to the myriad everyday experiences of meaning that open up our world just a little bit more. It could be reading a book that challenges your life philosophy, beginning a daily meditation practice, connecting with nature, befriending someone with a different background or interests from your own, or traveling to somewhere you've never been before.

So if you're looking for a creative boost, treat all of life's meaningful moments—the good and the bad—as potential sources of inspiration and motivation. The best way to do that? *Take risks and be prepared to fail.*

10

Thinking Differently

Here's to the crazy ones. The misfits. The rebels. The troublemakers. The round pegs in the square holes. The ones who see things differently.

—APPLE AD, 1997

Apple's 1997 "Think Different" campaign is often hailed as one of the most successful (and creative) in the history of advertising. Featuring black-and-white portraits of great iconoclasts through history—including Gandhi, Martha Graham, Albert Einstein, and Alfred Hitchcock—the inspiring ads helped the company bounce back from a period of bad sales to reestablish itself as a hub of innovation, with products tailored to creative types, original thinkers, and early tech adopters. And it worked.

The efforts of Steve Jobs and his team are brilliant marketing, to be sure, but they also speak to a fundamental truth of creativity and innovation. As we've seen, the one absolutely essential ingredient of any type of creative achievement is *thinking differently*. In rejecting traditional ways of thinking, successful creative work defies standards and authority, causes trouble, and ultimately paves the way for real change. "We believe that . . . people can change [this world] for the better,"

Jobs told Apple staffers at the internal meeting during which he unveiled the campaign.[1]

Think about some of the greatest creative minds and most important historical movements in art and science. The one thing they all have in common is that they challenged the status quo—and often, in this endeavor, were met with resistance and adversity. Frequently, their work was labeled a failure. But in sharing initially unpopular ideas, they also, as the Apple ad says, "push the human race forward."

Consider one of the original iconoclasts: sixteenth-century Italian philosopher, astronomer, and mathematician Giordano Bruno. Bruno's revolutionary theories were centuries ahead of his time and even anticipated major advances in modern science. He proposed the controversial theories of the infinite universe and plurality of worlds, which not only rejected traditional geocentric astronomy but also went beyond the Copernican model, suggesting that the universe was not fixed but *infinite* and that there must be life on other planets. Bruno encountered relentless opposition from established religious and scientific institutions for spreading such controversial ideas and was repeatedly forced to flee his home to avoid persecution. His theories and philosophies were so unorthodox at the time that he was declared a heretic, arrested by the Inquisition, and in 1600 was burned at the stake.

Despite the constant risks to his life, Bruno never held back from expressing what he thought to be true. As the astronomer has been widely quoted, "It is proof of a base and low mind for one to wish to think with the masses or majority, merely because the majority is the majority. Truth does not change because it is, or is not, believed by a majority of the people."[2]

In the world of contemporary art, too, the rejection of traditional forms and subject matter can be a risky undertaking—albeit one that pushes not only art but society forward. American photographer Robert Mapplethorpe has said that he chose to take up photography because it seemed like the "perfect vehicle for commenting on the madness of today's existence." In the 1970s and 1980s, Mapplethorpe fearlessly captured subjects that were considered extremely taboo at the time, most famously his explorations of gay desire and sadomasochism.

Mapplethorpe wasn't worried about offending the public or causing trouble. His fearlessness was reflected in each of his images, which captured his provocative subjects in enormous prints ("To make pictures big is to make them powerful," he said). Mapplethorpe's works and exhibitions, particularly those depicting nudes and sexual acts, were often boycotted and banned. In 1989, the prestigious Corcoran Gallery of Art in Washington, D.C. even canceled a planned retrospective of his work.[3] Looking back on Mapplethorpe's career, a French photography magazine recently called his art "some of the most shocking and indeed some of the most dangerous images in . . . the history of art."[4]

The history of creative thought and social progress is littered with similar stories of banned books, culture wars, persecuted artists, and paradigm-shifting innovations that changed the way we look at the world. Almost every innovation that truly made a difference was initially met with varying degrees of resistance, if not full-fledged condemnation. Henri Matisse, who himself earned a reputation as a rebel for pushing the art world from Impressionism and Postimpressionism into modernity, put it this way: "Creativity takes courage."

"Creativity takes courage."

These iconoclasts are true *nonconformists*, people whom psychologist Robert J. Sternberg defined as being "willing to generate and promote ideas that are novel and even strange and out of fashion."[5] In 1985, Sternberg and colleagues conducted a study in which they asked people about the essential aspects of a highly creative person. Some of the key attributes they listed are as follows: "Tries to do what others think is impossible," "Is a non-conformist," "Is unorthodox," "Questions societal norms, truisms, and assumptions," and "Is willing to take a stand." Sternberg found that artists who answered this question often said that a creative person is one who takes risks and is willing to follow through on the consequences of those risks. Businesspeople, meanwhile, responded that a creative person in the business world is one who steers clear of the pitfalls of conventional ways of thinking. Philosophers insisted that creative minds never automatically accepted the "accepted," and physicists emphasized the importance of questioning the basic assumptions upon which we operate.

Creative people are united by their unwillingness to abide by conventional ways of thinking and doing things. The common strand in all the answers was the idea that creative people reject popular, conventional ways of thinking and instead support new and fresh ideas.

The creative act itself is one of breaking from tradition and routine in order to create new patterns, ask new questions, and seek new answers. Creative people march to the beat of a different drummer—themselves! In choosing to do things differently, they accept the possibility of failure—but it is precisely this risk that opens up the possibility of true innovation.

Defying the crowd takes courage, and there's no doubt that it's easier and more comfortable to follow popular opinion. But risk and failure are essential components of meaningful creative achievement and, really, of *any* creative work.[6] Breaking from traditional ways of thinking—within a creative field, the society or culture, or one's *own mind*—is necessary for establishing novel, previously unthought-of connections. As Sternberg explains, the most original contributions in any field are unlikely to result from efforts to please the crowd.

To generate and share original ideas in a world that is distrustful of creativity requires a certain bravado. To not only generate but to *share* nontraditional ideas, one must be willing to be a bit of a troublemaker and risk being labeled an outsider. As Isaac Asimov, the prolific author and biochemist, writes, "A person willing to fly in the face of reason, authority, and common sense must be a person of considerable self-assurance. Since he occurs only rarely, he must seem eccentric (in at least that respect) to the rest of us."[7]

Those who ask the "impertinent question" must be prepared to be ostracized and to stand by their ideas when they are rejected and criticized. The proposition that the Earth was round (not flat) and Copernicus's theory that the Earth revolved around the sun (rather than the opposite) were widely decried and viewed as heretical for many years before they were accepted. Galileo lamented in a letter to fellow astronomer Johannes Kepler that he was deterred by the fate of Copernicus, who, "although he had won immortal fame with a few, was ridiculed and condemned by countless people (for very great is the number of the stupid)."[8]

Creativity is often the natural result of risk taking. Stern-berg's "propulsion theory" suggests that creative contributions in a particular field can be measured based on the extent to which a new idea shifts that field away from current paradigms and toward a new way of thinking. By this model, the most creative works are the ones that are most successful in propel-ling existing ideas forward. A truly creative contribution to any field requires leadership and vision insofar as it moves the field to an entirely new place.

Consider an initially failed propulsion in the field of medi-cine. In the mid-nineteenth century, Hungarian obstetrician Ignaz Semmelweis hypothesized that disease could be spread in hospitals through small particles on physicians' hands. Semmelweis came to believe that many lives could be saved if medical professionals followed a hand-washing protocol, so he implemented antiseptic procedures in the obstetrical clinic of the Vienna hospital where he worked. Semmelweis found that washing hands with a chlorinated lime solution significantly reduced mortality rates. It was a fairly contentious idea at the time—and, like many radical ideas, the proposition was not accepted by his colleagues. Semmelweis was ridiculed and dis-missed from his position at the hospital. This caused him a great deal of distress, and he was later committed to an insane asylum. It wasn't until years later, when Louis Pasteur developed the germ theory of disease, that Semmelweis's pioneering work on antiseptic procedures finally gained widespread acceptance.[9]

Many Nobel laureates have similar stories. In a 2009 paper, Juan Miguel Campanario investigated a number of instances in which leading researchers encountered resistance from the scientific community and science journal editors in reference to manuscripts that would later earn them the Nobel Prize.[10] The journal *Physical Review Letters* rejected a key paper on the landmark discovery of superfluid helium, which later earned its authors the 1996 Nobel Prize in Physics, while the prestigious journal *Nature* rejected the groundbreaking paper that first detailed magnetic resonance imaging (MRI) technology. It wasn't until thirty years after the landmark discovery of MRI technology that physicist Paul Lauterbur won the 2003 Nobel Prize in Medicine. Today, ten million patients each year undergo MRI examinations.[11] Lauterbur later recalled, "Many said it couldn't be done, even when I was doing it!"[12]

Despite the fact that open-mindedness is the institutional norm in science—and, as we've seen, intellectual curiosity is the best predictor of scientific creativity—Campanario's research revealed a systemic skepticism toward new theories that challenged existing scientific paradigms. And beyond Nobel Prize winners, many scientists and commentators have suggested that the scientific peer-review system is designed in a way that discourages innovation and instead rewards research that reinforces existing paradigms.

The worlds of art, music, and performance can be similarly unwelcoming to new ideas—jazz being perhaps the most famous example in the music world. The new musical genre, which was defined by improvisation and free expression, broke all the rules of music and, predictably, and was met with criticism and ire. In fact, early jazz was widely rejected in twentieth-century America. In visual art, both critics and the public were hostile to avant-garde visual art movements like Impressionism and modernism, which broke free from old values and stylistic norms in order to create new forms and modes of expression. By definition, any work that is considered avant-garde is initially rejected, until it earns critical approval, becomes mainstream, and in is in turn eventually uprooted by something new.

The Bias Against Creativity

Creativity is the greatest rebellion in existence.

—Osho

As Asimov declared in his famous 1959 essay on creativity and idea generation, "The world in general disapproves of creativity."

"The world in general disapproves of creativity."

The idea that both current and past cultures tend to disapprove of creativity might initially seem counterintuitive. After all, don't we all aspire to be more creative? In popular culture, creativity is often held up as a virtue—we celebrate the lives of history's great artists and iconoclasts and search for secrets to creative brilliance. But as Asimov explains, the fact that we celebrate new and original ideas *after* they've become widely accepted doesn't mean that we truly embrace creativity. In fact, the opposite may be true. Unconventional ideas that break from tradition or challenge our existing ways of thinking, which nearly any important creative achievements do, often push us out of our psychological comfort zone. As a general rule, we don't like things that challenge our habitual ways of thinking, which makes creative work a dangerous endeavor.

Why are paradigm-shifting ideas throughout history consistently, and predictably, ridiculed and rejected? It's because, as a culture and as individuals, we're deeply biased against creativity. This creativity bias makes sense if we look at the way our brains our wired. By nature, human beings are highly risk averse. And when there is a motivation to reduce uncertainty, creativity biases are activated on both individual and institutional levels. Across the board, people (not to mention institutions and decision makers) deny creative ideas, even when they explicitly cite creativity as being among their goals or values. Research conducted by organizational psychologists at Cornell University found that this implicit creativity bias causes us to take a negative view of creative ideas and projects, relative to those that are more practical.[13] The study, conducted by psychologist Jennifer Mueller and colleagues, showed that the creativity bias interfered with participants' ability to recognize an original idea. This bias indicates a fascinating paradox at the heart of our common attitudes toward creativity: At the same time that we desire creativity, we also fear it. This widespread bias then acts as a "concealed barrier" that innovators must be prepared to confront when attempting to gain acceptance for novel ideas.[14]

The Cornell psychologists noted that regardless of how open-minded people are in general, they *still* seek to reduce uncertainty in their lives. Most people prefer what is safe and conventional, and may unconsciously shy away from creative ideas because they are new, novel, and potentially uncomfortable. However, because the bias is not overt, we're typically unable to recognize it in ourselves. The study found that while most people *say* they feel positively toward creativity, when asked to judge the desirability of various ideas, they overwhelmingly reveal an implicit bias toward the practical over the novel.

The researchers note a deep irony here: It is often uncertainty that stimulates the search for and generation of creative ideas, but it is also our fear of uncertainty that renders us *less* able to recognize creative ideas.

It's usually only *after* an idea has gained acceptance and recognition that we applaud the idea and its creator. According to Berkeley business professor Barry Staw, an expert on creativity and organization innovation, when it comes to creativity, we tend to "celebrate the victor."[15] When a creative work earns the approval of cultural gatekeepers and is integrated into the mainstream, *then* we applaud the ingenuity of its creator. Think about it: We study history's great creative minds and the brilliant ideas they contributed to the world, but how often do we pause to consider the resistance they encountered and the enormous sacrifices they made to achieve creative success? Even less often do we consider the failed creative projects that paved the way for those successes.

Our cultural disapproval of creativity tends to show through when we look at creative paths that *don't* lead to mainstream success. There's a high price to pay for being creative—tireless work, solitude and isolation, failure, and the risk of ridicule and rejection. The reality of creative work is that most artists will never sell their pieces, most actors and musicians will never make it big, most writers will never pen best sellers, most start-ups will end in failure, and most scientists will never make earth-shattering discoveries. As Staw points out, it's a price that most of us don't actually want to pay.[16]

Culture of Conformity

Conformity, of course, tends to get in the way of creativity. People by nature are highly influenced by the opinions and behaviors of others, and conformity occurs when we change the way we think or act to imitate others. The behavior can be largely unconscious and almost automatic.[17] To some extent, conformity is adaptive; it helps us get along with one another, cooperate, and reach consensus on important matters. It also facilitates social approval and helps us protect ourselves from rejection. Research has found that this desire to conform to the crowd is often motivated by a self-protective goal.[18]

Inspired by Stanley Milgram's classic experiments on obedience to authority, pioneering social psychologist Solomon Asch conducted a series of studies in the 1950s to test how much the average person was willing to disregard what they knew to be true in order to conform to the group. Asch's subjects were asked to make judgments about some unambiguous questions (assessing the lengths of several lines) after hearing others in the group (who were paid by the experimenter) make clearly incorrect estimates as to how long the lines were. Only 25 percent of the subjects guessed the correct length after hearing the others' false estimates, as compared to 95 percent who were correct without the group.[19] However, in his seminal study of creative geniuses (mentioned in our introduction), Frank Barron found that the creators he studied were *less* likely to conform in an Asch-type setup. In the words of E. Paul Torrance, they were more likely to be comfortable as a "minority of one."

Asch's experiment showed that it's not uncommon for most people to follow the majority even if it means abandoning what they know to be true and even changing their judgments to fit in with a group. To some extent, this is wired in our brains. Studies conducted by neuroscientist Gregory Berns have found that the human brain is willing to disregard its own visual input in favor of the opinions of others. The view of the majority can truly influence our thinking on a perceptual level. Berns's research used brain scanning to find that conformity and nonconformity use different areas in the brain. In a task used to judge conformity, Berns found that those who conformed to an incorrect group opinion showed brain activity in areas related to perception, suggesting that their perceptions had changed; whereas nonconformity showed brain activity in areas related to conscious decision making.[20]

Still, conformity isn't inevitable. In fact, most children are natural *non*conformists. Unfortunately, either at home or in school (or both), many children grow up in environments that devalue independent and creative thought and instead reward imitation, memorization, and rote learning. The suppression of free thinking and imagination often starts in the educational system. Many people can recall an experience during childhood—probably in elementary school—when they were punished for thinking differently from everyone else. These experiences can lead children to suppress their natural inquisitive and creative instincts.

Research by psychologists Daphna Buchsbaum and Alison Gopnik found that common teaching methods that emphasize direct instruction—those in which the child is shown what to do rather than given the opportunity to figure it out for herself—can hamper the child's ability to solve problems independently and creatively and may instead encourage mindless imitation.[21] While this method may allow the student to acquire the information more quickly, she won't be learning the important real-world skills of asking questions and sleuthing out new information about a problem.

"Perhaps direct instruction can help children learn specific facts and skills, but what about curiosity and creativity— abilities that are even more important for learning in the long run?" Gopnik, a professor of psychology at the University of

California, Berkeley, wrote in *Slate*.[22] As she points out, learning to imitate sometimes means learning to generate the less
intelligent response. This is the response that most students
give, because of both the way they are instructed and the fact
that they may be punished for presenting the more creative
answer.

In fact, teachers have been found to display a clear preference for students who show *less* creativity. Research has shown
that creative students tend not to be favored by teachers. Judgments of a teacher's favorite student were negatively correlated
with creativity, and judgments of a teacher's least favorite student were positively correlated with creativity. While teachers
said that they liked creative students, they (somewhat bafflingly)
defined creativity using terms like *well behaved* and *conforming*. When given adjectives more typically used to describe
creative people, the teachers said that they disliked these kinds
of students.[23]

But when students are encouraged to exercise their creativity and to engage imaginatively with the materials, the results
can be impressive. Research by Robert Sternberg and others
shows that students who are taught using creative methods
learn more and engage with information more actively.[24]

In what is now the most-watched TED talk of all time,
Sir Ken Robinson argues that the problem is that from an
early age, kids are being taught to fear making mistakes, but
without learning to play with different solutions and ways of
thinking (which will inevitably lead to incorrect answers),
they won't be prepared for the uncertainty and the new challenges of the changing world. As Robinson puts it, "If you're
not prepared to be wrong, you'll never come up with anything original."[25]

The Perks of Being an Outsider

Children learn from an early age that a failure to conform can lead to disapproval from teachers and peers, which may motivate them to try to be like everyone else. As an old Japanese proverb says, "The nail that sticks up will be hammered down." In schools, the workplace, and society in general, failure to conform can lead to social rejection. But rejection, as painful as it can be, has a silver lining when it comes to creativity.

British writer Colin Wilson described the creative soul who risks rejection in order to be true to himself or herself in *The Outsider*, his 1956 manifesto on nonconformity. The book drew a deep connection between creativity and alienation. Wilson, who at the time was part of a group of antiestablishment writers labeled "angry young men," theorized that great minds stood apart from the rest of society. Though they lived within cultures of conformity, "men of vision"—like Kafka, Nietzsche, and van Gogh—played by their own rules. While most men went along with the crowd, accepting life's miseries "like a cow standing in the rain," Wilson said that eminent creators used their imagination "not to escape reality but to create it."[26]

Wilson (who himself was something of an eccentric) was the first to present the hypothesis that social rejection may be not only the result of creativity but indeed the force that fuels it. As Wilson asserted, inspiration was to be found in defying the crowd. Now, research suggests that he was onto something. The need for uniqueness and individuality is a basic human motivation, as is the need for belonging. For the most part, we seek to achieve some level of balance between being an individual and being part of a group. Creative people, however, may have a greater need for uniqueness. This drive to separate from the group has been associated with both non-conformity and creativity.[27]

Of course, rejection is no fun, and it's been found to carry some negative psychological effects. Experiences of rejection can hinder cognitive performance, particularly when it comes to self-regulation and other tasks requiring executive control. But it seems that the extent to which we experience the negative effects of rejection depends on the extent to which we view ourselves as unique and independent individuals.

When you experience rejection, it's natural to take certain measures in order to preserve your self-esteem, like trying to fit in with a social group and gain their approval. However, research has shown that people who view themselves as independent may be somewhat immune to the negative effects of rejection, and may even use social rejection as creative fuel.

This phenomenon has been observed in the lab.[28] A Johns Hopkins University study asked a group of students to create drawings of a creature from a planet "unlike earth." The drawings were then rated for originality and creative merit. Before the task, some of the participants had been primed with a task that put them into an independent mind-set, while others were primed with a group mind-set. The students who were primed with the independent mind-set generated more original illustrations after being told that they were rejected from a group, as compared to those who were included in the group.

Sharon Kim and her colleagues, who conducted the study, hypothesized that these boosts in creativity were fueled by a *differentiation mind-set*, or as they put it, "salient feelings of being different from others." Independent people not only may be resistant to the negative consequences of rejection but indeed may be strengthened by experiences that reaffirm their sense of independence. As Kim puts it, "Independent selves are motivated to remain distinctly separate from others." This motivation may, in turn, trigger psychological processes that boost creative thinking.[29]

Rejection is not just a catalyst for creativity—it can also be a *by-product* of it. As the study's authors write, "The very traits that distinguish highly creative people, such as unconventionality, make them easy targets for rejection."

A Numbers Game

As much as they risk disapproval from others, creative people also risk failure on their own terms. It's a great myth that creative geniuses consistently produce great works. They don't. In fact, systematic analyses of the career trajectories of people labeled geniuses show that their output tends to be highly uneven, with a few good ideas mixed in with many more false starts.[30] While consistency may be the key to expertise, the secret to creative greatness appears to be doing things differently—even when that means failing.[31]

According to Dean Keith Simonton, true innovation requires that creators engage in a sort of Darwinian process in which they try out many possibilities without fully knowing what their eventual public reception will be.[32] Especially during the idea-generation stage, trial and error is essential for innovation. Simonton's theory does *not* mean that creators are working completely in the dark; ideas are not generated in complete ignorance of their ultimate value to society. Instead, new ideas just aren't *guaranteed* to be fruitful.

So how are creative masterminds so successful, if they don't really know what they're doing? Simonton's extensive analysis of geniuses found two major factors to be critical in explaining the creative process of geniuses. First, creative geniuses simultaneously immerse themselves in many diverse ideas and projects. Second, and perhaps even more important, they also have extraordinary *productivity*. Creators create. Again and again and again. In fact, Simonton has found that the quality of creative ideas is a positive function of quantity: The more ideas creators generate (regardless of the quality of each idea), the greater the chances they would produce an eventual masterpiece.[33]

Creators create. Again and again and again.

Thomas Edison—one of the greatest inventors of all time—had roughly a one-third rejection rate for all the patents he filed.[34] Even among the 1,093 patents he did get accepted, most went nowhere. In fact, the number of truly extraordinary creative feats he achieved can probably be counted on one hand. As Simonton points out, a look at Edison's entire body of patents might not reflect his creative genius as much as his creative failures.[35]

During the peak years of Edison's career, between the ages of thirty-five and thirty-nine, the inventor was working on the electric light and power distribution system. As part of this process, he attempted to develop fuel cells to power the lightbulbs.[36] However, these efforts faced repeated difficulties, including one experiment in which the windows were blown out of his lab.[37]

Edison *was* unlucky—he failed to invent fuel cells. The first commercially successful fuel cells were developed in the mid-twentieth century, long after Edison moved on to pursuing other ideas. Edison accepted the inevitable frustrations of the creative process and turned his attention to other projects that would eventually lead to the invention of the electric lightbulb—the source of his recognition as a genius today.

Such frequent shifts among projects may have primed Edison's mind to consider options he might have otherwise ignored.[38] By taking on a range of projects, Simonton notes, "Edison always had somewhere to channel his efforts whenever he ran into temporary obstacles—especially any long series of trials followed only by consecutive errors." Despite having failed more than he succeeded, Edison's few successes were so great that they surpassed all of the other inventors in the history of technology.

A very similar pattern can be found within Shakespeare's creative output.[39] The variability in quality of his large body of work is in itself impressive! Simonton computed a popularity score for each of Shakespeare's thirty-seven plays and found that the most popular plays were created around mid-career (age thirty-eight). At this time, he composed his masterpiece *Hamlet*, which received a popularity rating of 100 percent.

However, right before and after *Hamlet*, Shakespeare produced a few duds. For instance, soon after *Hamlet,* the Bard wrote *Troilus and Cressida*, which has a popularity rating of just 23 percent. But after *Troilus and Cressida*, he produced his three greatest tragedies since *Hamlet—Othello* (rating of 74 percent), *Lear* (rating of 78 percent), and *Macbeth* (rating of 83 percent). Then, once again, he fell well below expectations with *Timon of Athens* (rating of 3 percent) and *Pericles* (rating of 8 percent).

Even Beethoven left a trail of musical failures in his wake. While none of Beethoven's compositions could be considered worthless, they aren't all masterpieces either.[40] Beethoven sometimes composed inferior works around the same time he was working on a major masterpiece. One analysis found that even a computer could tell that his even-numbered symphonies were of a markedly different quality than his odd-numbered symphonies.[41] Beethoven himself recognized this, referring to some of his nine symphonies as "little."

One reason for variable quality is the need to innovate. All creators—whether inventors, actors, or choreographers—are under constant pressure to avoid doing things the exact same way.[42] In this quest for originality, creative geniuses fail and fail often. Indeed, the creative act is often described as a process of failing repeatedly until something sticks, and highly creative people learn to see failure as simply a stepping-stone to success. Doing things differently sometimes involves doing things badly or wrong.

Even today's most successful innovators—including Steve Jobs, who was fired from his own company at age thirty—tend to have as many stories of failure as they do of success. Or take J. K. Rowling—likely one of the only authors who holds a claim to making billions as an author—who has become an outspoken advocate for the importance of creative failure. As many *Harry Potter* fans know, the first book in Rowling's series was rejected by twelve publishers before being accepted by Bloomsbury— and only then because the chairman's eight-year-old daughter insisted on it. Rowling later said, "Some failure in life is inevitable. It is impossible to live without failing at something, unless you live so cautiously that you might as well not have lived at all—in which case, you fail by default."

Daring to Resist Conformity

You don't have to seek out social rejection or court failure in order to experience a creative boost. Cultivating a spirit of everyday nonconformity can foster the development of personality traits and thinking habits that are important to creative achievement.

Anything that challenges traditional ways of thinking can also prime the mind for unconventional thinking. Cross-cultural experiences, for instance, can be a great way to foster creativity. One study found that studying abroad increased measures of creative thinking among students.[43] It could even be something as small as taking a different route to work, listening to a new genre of music, or checking out an exhibit from an art style you're not familiar with—anything that keeps the mind flexible and open to new ideas will start to create new pathways in the brain. These types of changes in routine can help us overcome what's known in Gestalt psychology as "functional fixedness," a cognitive bias that limits the way we use an object to what it was originally intended for and keeps us from seeking new usages. Andy Zynga—CEO of Nine-Sigma, a global innovation services provider—called this bias, which renders us unable to think differently, "the hobgoblin of uncreative minds."[44]

Evidence of nonconformity can even be seen on the neurological level. If we look at the brains of nonconformists and compare them to those of average people, two main differences emerge: their *perceptions*, and their *fear responses*. Iconoclasts, as neuroscientist Gregory Berns calls these free thinkers, perceive things differently from other people. They create new connections and generate ideas that are radically outside the norm. In order to do this, the brain of the iconoclast must create new categories and make new connections, which start at the level of perception.[45]

Perception, and therefore imagination, is limited by the categories that we've learned from our past experiences. For this reason, the nonconformist may seek out changes in the environment as a way to sharpen their perception. To break free from traditional ways of thinking and labeling, one must "bombard the brain with new experiences," which forces a reevaluation of existing categories and a creation of new connections. Changing perception is critical for the generative stage of creativity, when the artist is seeking out new ideas. When it comes time to share his ideas, the nonconformist must then be able to control the fear response triggered by the possibility of failure and social isolation. He tempers this response, turning it into a more constructive emotion, like anger or pride, which can be fueled into creative work.

When the fear response has been tempered, the artist is able to overcome risk aversion and embrace novelty. Of course, this is easier said than done. As human beings, we're wired to seek out categories, labels, and clean conclusions. Because of our natural aversion to uncertainty, there are very few things in life that we enjoy more than a sure thing or a tidy solution! But in order to think differently, the fear of uncertainty has to go. The nonconformist embraces the unknown and learns to play in life's gray areas—asking impertinent questions and engaging with numerous solutions to a single problem. Those murky, ambiguous places, as highly imaginative people well know, are quite often where the creative magic happens.

While most people go to great lengths to avoid ambiguity, people who have overcome the fear of uncertainty tend to have a much higher tolerance for the ambiguous questions and circumstances that launch most creative projects. In his interviews discussing the creative process with forty MacArthur geniuses, Denise Shekerjian found that most of them practice something she calls "staying loose," or embracing the questions and the uncertainty of the creative process, often without regard for practicality or efficiency. This "looseness"—a sort of free play with one's material—is particularly important at the start of a project, as it allows the imagination to lead the individual to the best solution.

A sense of play, even in the face of fear, is an important asset when generating new and different ideas. Thinking differently doesn't have to be scary or overwhelming; just making the conscious effort to see things in a new light can yield results. The key to generating original ideas is a willingness to think in unconventional ways and to explore ideas that may be radical or unpopular, a task that many find taxing. Up to 80 percent of adults said that the task of "thinking differently" is uncomfortable or even exhausting, according to research conducted at Harvard.[46] But making an effort to think unconventionally can help us connect the dots in new and innovative ways by increasing associational thinking.

In a study of more than three thousand entrepreneurs and business executives, business professors Jeff Dyer and Hal Gregersen found that noninnovators don't make as much of an effort to think differently as innovators do. The study found that innovators spend 50 percent more time *trying* to think differently and that those who consistently tried to think in new ways and make new connections *did succeed* in thinking differently—all it required was the effort.[47]

The innovators who spent more time consciously thinking differently were far more likely to engage in associational thinking, reporting that they solved creative problems by drawing on diverse knowledge. These people were more likely to actually create innovative products. And when those unconventional thinkers become leaders, real creative achievement in the workplace becomes possible. A 2003 study found that unconventional behavior on the part of group leaders (such as hanging ideas on a clothesline or standing on furniture) facilitates more creative group output.[48] Creativity is infectious.

Creativity is infectious.

Living Creatively

When the artist is alive in any person, whatever his kind of work may be, he becomes an inventive, searching, daring, self-expressive creature. He becomes interesting to other people. He disturbs, upsets, enlightens, and opens ways for better understanding. Where those who are not artists are trying to close the book, he opens it and shows there are still more pages possible.

—AMERICAN PAINTER ROBERT HENRI

As we've seen, creativity works in mysterious and often paradoxical ways. We human beings are messy creatures, to be sure, and creativity is a process that reflects our fundamentally chaotic and multifaceted nature. It is both deliberate and uncontrollable, mindful and mindless, work and play. It is both the realm of a select group of geniuses through history, and the domain of every human being.

When we embrace our own messiness—engaging with the world with our own unique imagination and artistry—we give others permission to do the same. We help create a world that is more welcoming of the creative spirit and, it is hoped, make it possible to find a greater connection with ourselves and others in the process.

In his analysis of creative achievement, psychiatrist Arnold Ludwig came up with a "template for greatness"—a set of thirty variables that strongly predicted the highest levels of creative excellence.[49] Many of the elements—such as contrariness, the capacity for solitude, psychological unease, and resilience in the face of life's obstacles—have already been discussed throughout this book. But included in Ludwig's template was also having "a personal seal." As he notes, "Individuals are not likely to assume the mantle of true greatness unless their works and achievements bear their personal seals or distinctive signatures."

Not only in our creative work but in our own lives can we bear these distinctive signatures. Recognizing ourselves as creators and fostering creativity in our everyday lives brings us to life and connects us to who we are. Creativity isn't just about innovating or making art—it's about *living* creatively. We can approach any situation in life with a creative spirit. We all have the capacity to dream, explore, discover, build, ask questions, and seek answers—in other words, to be creators. Creative self-expression opens us up to who we are and invites us to explore and express our own unique set of qualities and experiences, to play with ambiguities, and to connect the dots in a way that they've never been connected before.

In embracing a creative way of living, we bloom into the expansiveness of our own being and our beautiful human complexity. We give ourselves permission to embody those glorious multitudes that Whitman spoke of. So go ahead—contradict yourself! Be serious and playful, practical and romantic, sensitive and strong, a dreamer and a doer. As Whitman said, we exist as we are, and that is "enough."[50]

Acknowledgments

There are so many people who helped make this book possible.

Many thanks are owed to Giles Andersen, our fearless agent, whose dedication and hard work brought this book from an idea to a hardcover reality. Thank you for believing in this idea from the very beginning.

Thanks to Marian Lizzi, whose editorial expertise took the manuscript to another level and ultimately helped it become something that we are both deeply proud of.

To Shannon Dailey and Taylor Kreiss, you guys are lifesavers and we're so grateful for the time and energy you dedicated to this project.

Thanks also to Anne Marie Roepke, Marie Forgeard, Sandra Russ, Dean Keith Simonton, Jennifer Grimes, Jonathan Cheek, Adam Grant, Susan Cain, Bo Stjerne Thomsen, and Michael Piechowski for valuable insights and suggestions on earlier drafts of the manuscript.

Scott would like to thank Martin Seligman, Angela Duckworth, Marie Forgeard, Amy Walker, the Templeton

Foundation, and the National Philanthropic Trust for their invaluable support of his research at the Imagination Institute. He would also like to show his gratitude for all of the terrific collaborators he has had the privilege of working with over the years, many of whom are mentioned throughout this book. This list includes generous mentors who have taught him so much, including Herbert A. Simon, Anne L. Fay, Randy F. Pausch, James C. Kaufman, Jerome L. Singer, Robert J. Sternberg, Nicholas J. Mackintosh, Jeremy R. Gray, Colin G. DeYoung, and Rex E. Jung. Finally, thanks to Elliot Samuel Paul for being such an encouraging and reflective best friend, and his parents, Michael and Barbara Kaufman, for accepting, supporting, and guiding such a messy mind.

Likewise, Carolyn would like to thank Arianna Huffington and her colleagues at the *Huffington Post* for being supportive of this project from the very beginning. Thanks to her friends, far too many to name here, who have reached out with love and support in many ways throughout this process. Specifically, thanks to Christof, the most supportive partner she could have asked for, to Josh and Eliza for bringing her to Maine and Colorado for vacation/"writer's retreats," to Caroline for being there through it all, and to Rachel for her helpful comments on the post traumatic growth chapter. And to her family, she is grateful for the constant cheerleading.

Notes

PREFACE

1. https://vimeo.com/32790071.

2. DeYoung, C. G., Quilty, L. C., & Peterson, J. B. (2007). Between facets and domains: 10 aspects of the big five. *Journal of Personality and Social Psychology, 93*, 880–896.

3. Simonton, D. K. (2007). The creative process in Picasso's *Guernica* sketches: Monotonic improvements versus nonmonotonic variants. *Creativity Research Journal, 19*(4), 329–344.

4. Simonton, The creative process in Picasso's *Guernica* sketches.

5. Mellow, J. R. (1976, July 4). *Picasso: A Biography,* by P. O'Brian. [Review.] *New York Times.* nytimes.com/books/98/10/18/specials/obrian-picasso.html.

6. Huffington, A. S. (1996). *Picasso: Creator and Destroyer.* New York: HarperCollins.

7. *Cahiers d'Art* (1935), *10*(10), 173–178. Reprinted in: Barr H. A., Jr. (1946). *Picasso, Fifty Years of His Art* (p. 272). New York: Museum of Modern Art.

INTRODUCTION: MESSY MINDS

1. Stevens, V. (2014). To think without thinking: The implications of combinatory play and the creative process for neuroethics. *The American*

Journal of Play, 7(1), 99–119. Hadamard, J. (1996). *The Mathematician's Mind: The Psychology of Invention in the Mathematical Field.* Princeton, NJ: Princeton University Press.

2. Popova, M. (2013, August 28). *The Art of Thought*: Graham Wallas on the four stages of creativity, 1926. [Review.] *Brain Pickings.* brainpickings.org/2013/08/28/the-art-of-thought-graham-wallas-stages. Wallas, G. (2014). *Art of Thought.* Kent, UK: Solis Press.

3. Lubart, T. I. (2001). Models of the creative process: Past, present and future. *Creativity Research Journal, 13*(3–4), 295–308. Mumford, M. D., Reiter-Palmon, R., & Redmond, M. R. (1994). Problem construction and cognition: Applying problem representations in ill-defined domains. In M. A. Runco (Ed.), *Problem Finding, Problem Solving, and Creativity* (pp. 3–39). Westport, CT: Ablex Publishing.

4. Guilford, J. P. (1950). Creativity. *American Psychologist, 5*, 444–454.

5. Eindhoven, J. E., & Vinacke, W. E. (1952). Creative processes in painting. *Journal of General Psychology, 47,* 165–179. Getzels, J., & Csikszentmihalyi, M. (1976). *The Creative Vision: A Longitudinal Study of Problem Finding in Art.* New York: Wiley Interscience, p. 90. Israeli, N. (1962). Creative processes in painting. *Journal of General Psychology, 67,* 251–263. Israeli, N. (1981). Decision in painting and sculpture. *Academic Psychology Bulletin, 3,* 61–74. Calwelti, S., Rappaport, A., & Wood, B. (1992). Modeling artistic creativity: An empirical study. *Journal of Creative Behavior, 26,* 83–94.

6. Doyle, C. L. (1998). The writer tells: The creative process in the writing of literary fiction. *Creativity Research Journal, 11,* 29–37.

7. Ghiselin, B. (1956). The creative process and its relation to the identification of creative talent. In C. W. Taylor (Ed.), *The 1955 University of Utah Research Conference on the Identification of Creative Scientific Talent* (pp. 195–203). Salt Lake City: University of Utah Press. Ghiselin, B. (1963). Automatism, intention, and autonomy in the novelist's production. *Daedalus, 92*(2), 297–311.

8. Watterson, B. (1990). Kenyon College commencement address. Retrieved from http://www.brainpickings.org/2013/05/20/bill-watterson-1990-kenyon-speech/ July 6, 2015.

9. Simonton, D. K. (2014). Thomas Edison's creative career: The multilayered trajectory of trials, errors, failures, and triumphs. *Psychology of Aesthetics, Creativity, and the Arts, 9,* 2–14.

10. Kaufman, S. B. (2014, December 24). The messy minds of creative people. [Blog post.] *Scientific American*. blogs.scientificamerican. com/beautiful-minds/2014/12/24/the-messy-minds-of-creative-people.

11. Csikszentmihalyi, M. (1996). *Creativity: The Work and Lives of 91 Eminent People*. New York: HarperCollins.

12. Sowinska, A. (2005) *Dialectics of the Banana Skirt: The Ambiguities of Josephine Baker's Self-Representation*. Ann Arbor, MI: MPublishing, University of Michigan Library, http://quod.lib.umich. edu/cgi/t/text/text-idx?cc=mfsfront;c=mfs;c=mfsfront;idno= ark5583.0019.003;rgn=main;view=text;xc=1;g=mfsg.

13. Quoted in Been, E. (2012, September 6). David Foster Wallace: Genius, fabulist, would-be murderer. *The Atlantic*. http://www.the-atlantic.com/entertainment/archive/2012/09/david-foster-wallace-genius-fabulist-would-be-murderer/261997/.

14. Barron, F. (1963). *Creativity and Psychological Health*. Oxford, UK: Van Nostrand. Barron, F. (1968). *Creativity and Personal Freedom*. Oxford, UK: Van Nostrand.

15. Richards, R. (2006). Frank Barron and the study of creativity: A voice that lives on. *Journal of Humanistic Psychology, 46*(3), 352–370.

16. Richards, Frank Barron and the study of creativity.

17. Arons, M., & Richards, R. (2001). Two noble insurgencies: Creativity and humanistic psychology. In K. J. Schenider, J. F. T. Bugental, & J. F. Pierson (Eds.), *Handbook of Humanistic Psychology* (pp. 127–142). Thousand Oaks, CA: Sage. Barron, F. (1969). *Creative Person and Creative Process*. New York: Holt, Rinehart & Winston.

18. Cox, C. M. (1926). *Genetic Studies of Genius*. Vol. 2. *The Early Mental Traits of Three Hundred Geniuses*. Stanford, CA: Stanford University Press. Terman, L. M., & Oden, M. H. (1959). *Genetic Studies of Genius*. Vol. 5. *The Gifted Child Grows Up*. Palo Alto, CA: Stanford University Press.

19. Richards, Frank Barron and the study of creativity.

20. Barron, *Creative Person and Creative Process*. Piirto, J. (2009). The personalities of creative writers. In S. B. Kaufman & J. C. Kaufman (Eds.), *The Psychology of Creative Writing* (pp. 3–22). Cambridge, UK: Cambridge University Press.

21. Barron, F. (1953). An ego-strength scale which predicts response to psychotherapy. *Journal of Consulting Psychology, 17*, 327–333.

22. Richards, Frank Barron and the study of creativity.

23. Sternberg, R. J. (2006). The nature of creativity. *Creativity Research Journal, 18*(1), 87–98. Csikszentmihalyi, M. (1988). Society, culture, and person: A systems view of creativity. In R. J. Sternberg (Ed.), *The Nature of Creativity* (pp. 325–339). New York: Cambridge University Press. Amabile, T. M. (1983). *The Social Psychology of Creativity.* New York: Springer. Amabile, T. M. (1983). The social psychology of creativity: A componential conceptualization. *Journal of Personality and Social Psychology, 45*(2), 357–376. Gardner, H. (1993). *Creating Minds.* New York: Basic Books.

24. Simonton, D. K. (1999). Talent and its development: An emergenic and epigenetic model. *Psychological Review, 106*, 435–457.

25. Papierno, P. B., Ceci, S. J., Makel, M. C., & Williams, W. M. (2005). The nature and nurture of talent: A bioecological perspective on the ontogeny of exceptional abilities. *Journal for the Education of the Gifted, 28*(3–4), 213–322.

26. Fürst, G., Ghisletta, P., & Lubart, T. (2014). Toward an integrative model of creativity and personality: Theoretical suggestions and preliminary empirical testing. *Journal of Creative Behavior.* doi: 10.1002/jocb.71.

27. DeYoung, C. G., Peterson, J. B., & Higgins, D. M. (2002). Higher-order factors of the big five predict conformity: Are there neuroses of health? *Personality and Individual Differences, 33*, 533–552.

28. Csikszentmihalyi, M. (1999). Implications of a systems perspective for the study of creativity. In R. J. Sternberg (Ed.), *Handbook of Creativity* (pp. 313–336). Cambridge, UK: Cambridge University Press.

29. Bressler, S. L., & Menon, V. (2010). Large-scale brain networks in cognition: Emerging methods and principles. *Trends in Cognitive Science, 14*(6), 277–290.

30. Kaufman, S. B. (2013, August 19). The real neuroscience of creativity. [Blog post.] *Scientific American.* blogs.scientificamerican.com/beautiful-minds/2013/08/19/the-real-neuroscience-of-creativity.

31. Buckner, R. L. (2012). The serendipitous discovery of the brain's default mode network. *NeuroImage, 62*, 1137–1145.

32. Buckner, The serendipitous discovery of the brain's default mode network.

33. Christoff, K. (2012). Undirected thought: Neural determinants and correlates. *Brain Research, 1428*, 51–59.

34. Immordino-Yang, M. H., Christodoulou, J. A., Singh, V. (2012). Rest is not idleness: Implications of the brain's default mode for human development and education. *Perspectives on Psychological Science, 7*, 352–365. De Brigard, F., Spreng, N. R., Mitchell, J. P., & Schacter, D. L. (2015). Neural activity associated with self, other, and object-based counterfactual thinking. *NeuroImage, 109*, 12–26. Jack, A. I., Dawson, A. J., Begany, K. L., Leckie, R. L., Barry, K. P., Ciccia, A. H., & Snyder, A. Z. (2013). fMRI reveals reciprocal inhibition between social and physical cognitive domains. *NeuroImage, 66*, 385–401. Boyatzis, R. E., Rochford, K., & Jack, A. I. (2014). Antagonistic neural networks underlying differentiated leadership roles. *Frontiers in Human Neuroscience, 8*(14).

35. Otherwise known as the "core" subsystem, the "medial temporal" subsystem, and the "dorsal medial" subsystem. See Andrews-Hanna et al., The default network and self-generated thought.

36. Andrews-Hanna et al., The default network and self-generated thought. Buckner, R. L., Andrews-Hanna, J. R., & Schacter, D. L. (2008). The brain's default network: Anatomy, function, and relevance to disease. *Annals of the New York Academy of Sciences, 1124*(1), 1–38. Schacter, D. L., & Addis, D. R. (2007). The cognitive neuroscience of constructive memory: Remembering the past and imagining the future. *Philosophical Transactions of the Royal Society B: Biological Sciences, 362*(1481), 773–786. Hassabis, D., Kumaran, D., Vann, S. D., & Maguire, E. A. (2007). Patients with hippocampal amnesia cannot imagine new experiences. *Proceedings of the National Academy of Sciences, 104*(5), 1726–1731. Spreng, R. N., Mar, R. A., & Kim, A. S. N. (2009). The common neural basis of autobiographical memory, prospection, navigation, theory of mind, and the default mode: A quantitative meta-analysis. *Journal of Cognitive Neuroscience, 21*(3), 489–510. Mitchell, J. P., Banaji, M. R., & Macrae, C. N. (2005). The link between social cognition and self-referential thought in the medial prefrontal cortex. *Journal of Cognitive Neuroscience, 17*(8), 1306–1315. Mar, R. A. (2011). The neural bases of social cognition and story comprehension. *Annual Review of Psychology, 62*(1), 103–134.

37. Andrews-Hanna et al., The default network and self-generated thought. Immordino-Yang et al., Rest is not idleness.

38. Jung, R. E., Mead, B. S., Carrasco, J., & Flores, R. A. (2013). The structure of creative cognition in the human brain. *Frontiers in Human Neuroscience, 7*(330).

39. Vartanian, O., Bristol, A. S., & Kaufman, J. C. (Eds.). (2013). *Neuroscience of Creativity*. Cambridge, MA: MIT Press.

40. Beaty, R. E., & Silvia, P. J. (2012). Why do ideas get more creative across time? An executive interpretation of the serial order effect in divergent thinking tasks. *Psychology of Aesthetics, Creativity, and the Arts, 6*(4), 309–319. Benedek, M., Franz, F., Heene, M., & Neubauer, A. C. (2012). Differential effects of cognitive inhibition and intelligence on creativity. *Personality and Individual Differences, 53*(4), 480–485. Jauk, E., Benedek, M., & Neubauer, A. C. (2014). The road to creative achievement: A latent variable model of ability and personality predictors. *European Journal of Personality, 28*(1), 95–105. Gilhooly, K. J., Fioratou, E., Anthony, S. H., & Wynn, V. (2007). Divergent thinking: Strategies and executive involvement in generating novel uses for familiar objects. *British Journal of Psychology, 98*(4), 611–625. Nusbaum, E. C., & Silvia, P. J. (2011). Are intelligence and creativity really so different? Fluid intelligence, executive processes, and strategy use in divergent thinking. *Intelligence, 39*(1), 36–45. Silvia, P. J., Beaty, R. E., & Nusbaum, E. C. (2013). Verbal fluency and creativity: General and specific contributions of broad retrieval ability (Gr) factors to divergent thinking. *Intelligence, 41*(5), 328–340.

41. Beaty, R. E., Benedek, M., Kaufman, S. B., & Silvia, P. J. (2015). Default and executive network coupling supports creative idea production, *Scientific Reports, 5*(10964). Christoff, K., Gordon, A. M., Smallwood, J., Smith, R., & Schooler, J. W. (2009). Experience sampling during fMRI reveals default network and executive system contributions to mind wandering. *Proceedings of the National Academy of Sciences, 106*(21), 8719–8724. Ellamil, M., Dobson, C., Beeman, M., & Christoff, K. (2012). Evaluative and generative modes of thought during the creative process. *NeuroImage, 59*(2), 1783–1794. Gao, W., Gilmore, J. H., Shen, D., Smith, J. K., Zhu, H., & Lin, W. (2013). The synchronization within and interaction between the default and dorsal attention networks in early infancy. *Cerebral Cortex, 23*(3), 594–603. Gerlach, K. D., Spreng, R. N., Gilmore, A. W., & Schacter, D. L. (2011). Solving future problems: Default network and executive activity associated with goal-directed mental simulations. *NeuroImage, 55*(4), 1816–1824. Gerlach, K. D., Spreng, R. N., Madore, K. P., & Schacter, D. L. (2014). Future planning: Default network activity couples with frontoparietal control network and reward-processing regions during process and outcome simulations. *Social Cognitive and Affective Neuroscience, 9*(12), 1942–1951. Immordino-Yang et al., Rest is not idleness. McMillan, R. L., Kaufman, S. B., & Singer, J. L. (2013). Ode to positive

constructive daydreaming. *Frontiers in Psychology*, *4*(626). Meyer, M. L., Spunt, R. P., Berkman, E. T., Taylor, S. E., & Lieberman, M. D. (2012). Evidence for social working memory from a parametric functional MRI study. *Proceedings of the National Academy of Sciences, 109*(6), 1883–1888. Meyer, M. L., & Lieberman, M. D. (2012). Social working memory: Neurocognitive networks and directions for future research. *Frontiers in Psychology*, *3*(571). Spreng, R. N., & Grady, C. L. (2010). Patterns of brain activity supporting autobiographical memory, prospection, and theory of mind, and their relationship to the default mode network. *Journal of Cognitive Neuroscience, 22*(6), 1112–1123. Smallwood, J., Brown, K., Baird, B., & Schooler, J. W. (2012). Cooperation between the default mode network and the frontal-parietal network in the production of an internal train of thought. *Brain Research, 1428*, 60–70; Andrews-Hanna, J. R., Smallwood, J., & Spreng, R. N. (2014). The default network and self-generated thought: Component processes, dynamic control, and clinical relevance. *Annals of the New York Academy of Sciences, 1316*(1), 29–52.

42. Beaty et al., Default and executive network coupling supports creative idea production. Limb, C. J., & Braun, A. R. (2008). Neural substrates of spontaneous musical performance: An fMRI study of jazz improvisation. *PLoS ONE, 3*(2). Liu, S., Chow, H. M., Xu, Y., Erkkinen, M. G., Swett, K. E. et al. (2012). Neural correlates of lyrical improvisation: An fMRI study of freestyle rap. *Scientific Reports, 2: 834*. Beaty, R. E. (2015). The neuroscience of musical improvisation. *Neuroscience & Biobehavioral Reviews, 51, 108–11*. Mayseless, N., Eran, A., & Shamay-Tsoory, S. G. (2015). Generating original ideas: The neural underpinning of originality. *NeuroImage, 116*, 232–239. Liu, S., Erkkinen, M. G., Healey, M. L., Xu, Y., Swett, K. E., Chow, H. M., & Braun, A. R. (2015). Brain activity and connectivity during poetry composition: Toward a multidimensional model of the creative process. *Human Brain Mapping*. doi: 10.1002/hbm.22849.

43. Ellamil et al., Evaluative and generative modes of thought during the creative process.

44. Sternberg, R. (2007). Creativity as a habit. In A. G. Tan (Ed.), *Creativity: A Handbook for Teachers* (pp. 3–25). Hackensack, NJ: World Scientific.

45. Kaufman, J., & Beghetto, R. (2009). Beyond big and little: The four C model of creativity. *Review of General Psychology, 13*, 1–12.

46. Howe, M. J. A. (2001). *Genius Explained*. Cambridge, UK: Cambridge University Press. Weisberg, R. W. (1993). *Creativity:*

Beyond the Myth of Genius. New York: W. H. Freeman. Simon, H. A., & Newell, A. (1972). *Human Problem Solving.* Englewood Cliffs, NJ: Prentice-Hall.

47. Ivcevic, Z., & Mayer, J. D. (2009). Mapping dimensions of creativity in the life-space. *Creativity Research Journal, 21*, 152–165; Ivcevic, Z. (2007). Artistic and everyday creativity: An act-frequency approach. *Journal of Creative Behavior, 41*, 271–290; Ivcevic, Z., & Mayer, J. D. (2006). Creative types and personality. *Imagination, Cognition, and Personality, 26*, 65–86.

48. Ceci, M. W., & Kumar, V. K. (2015). A correlational study of creativity, happiness, motivation, and stress from creative pursuits. *Journal of Happiness Studies*, doi: 10.1007/s10902-015-9615-y.

49. Mackey, A. P., Miller Singley, A. T., & Bunge, S. A. (2013). Intensive reasoning training alters patterns of brain connectivity at rest. *Journal of Neuroscience, 33*(11), 4796–4803. Mackey, A. P., Whitaker, K. J., & Bunge, S. A. (2012). Experience-dependent plasticity in white matter microstructure: Reasoning training alters structural connectivity. *Frontiers in Neuroanatomy, 6.* Guerra-Carrillo, B., Mackey, A. P., & Bunge, S. A. (2014). Resting-state fMRI: A window into human brain plasticity. *The Neuroscientist, 20*(5), 522–533. Stevenson, C. E., Kleibeuker, S. W., de Dreu, C. K. W., & Crone, E. A. (2014). Training creative cognition: Adolescence as a flexible period for improving creativity. *Frontiers in Human Neuroscience, 8*(827).

50. Christenson, S. L., Reschly, A. L., & Wylie, C. (Eds.) (2013). *Handbook of Research on Student Engagement.* New York: Springer. Cordova, D. I., & Lepper, M. R. (1996). Intrinsic motivation and the process of learning: Beneficial effects of contextualization, personalization, and choice. *Journal of Educational Psychology, 88*, 715–730. Damon, W. (2009). *The Path to Purpose: How Young People Find Their Calling in Life.* New York: Free Press. Fredricks, J. A., Alfeld-Liro, C. J., Hruda, L. Z., Eccles, J. S., Patrick, H., & Ryan, A. M. (2002). A qualitative exploration of adolescents' commitment to athletics and the arts. *Journal of Adolescent Research, 17*, 68–97. Fredricks, J. A., Alfeld, C., & Eccles, J. (2010). Developing and fostering passion in academic and nonacademic domains. *Gifted Child Quarterly, 54*, 18–30. Kaufman, S. B. (2013). *Ungifted: Intelligence Redefined.* New York: Basic Books. Ryan, R. M., & Deci, E. L. (2000). Self-determination theory and the facilitation of intrinsic motivation, social development, and well-being. *American Psychologist, 55,* 68–78. Oyserman, D.,

Terry, K., & Bybee, D. (2002). A possible selves intervention to enhance school involvement. *Journal of Adolescence, 25,* 313–326. Oyserman, D., Bybee, D., & Terry, K. (2006). Possible selves and academic outcomes: How and when possible selves impel action. *Journal of Personality and Social Psychology, 91,* 188–204. Shernoff, D. J. (2013). *Optimal Learning Environments to Promote Student Engagement.* New York: Springer. Vanseteenkiste, M., Simons, J., Lens, W., Deci, E. L., & Sheldon, K. M. (2004). Motivating learning, performance, and persistence: The synergistic effects of intrinsic goal contents and autonomy-supportive contexts. *Journal of Personality and Social Psychology, 87,* 246–260; Yeager, D. S., Bundick, M. J., & Johnson, R. (2012). The role of future work goal motives in adolescent identity development: A longitudinal mixed-methods investigation. *Contemporary Educational Psychology, 37,* 206–217. Yeager, D. S., Paunesku, D., D'Mello, S., Spitzer, B. J., & Duckworth, A. L. (2014). Boring but important: A self-transcendent purpose for learning fosters academic self-regulation. *Journal of Personality and Social Psychology, 107,* 559–580.

51. Root-Bernstein, M. (2014). *Inventing Imaginary Worlds: From Childhood Play to Adult Creativity Across the Arts and Sciences.* Lanham, MD: Rowman & Littlefield Education.

52. Feist, G. J., & Runco, M. A. (1993). Trends in the creativity literature: An analysis of research in the *Journal of Creative Behavior* (1967–1989). *Creativity Research Journal, 6,* 271–286.

53. Kaufman & Beghetto, Beyond big and little. Kaufman, J. C., & Sternberg, R. J. (2007). Resource review: Creativity. *Change, 39,* 55–58.

54. Plucker, J. A., & Makel, M. C. (2010). Assessment of creativity. In J. C. Kaufman & R. J. Sternberg (Eds.), *The Cambridge Handbook of Creativity* (pp. 48–73). Cambridge, UK: Cambridge University Press. http://www.div10.org; http://www.div10.org/division-10-journal; http://onlinelibrary.wiley.com/journal/10.1002/(ISSN)2162-6057; http://www.tandfonline.com/toc/hcrj20/current; http://www.journals.elsevier.com/thinking-skills-and-creativity/; https://www.baywood.com/journals/previewjournals.asp?Id=0276-2366.

55. Seligman, M. E. P. (1998, January). Building human strength: Psychology's forgotten mission. *APA Monitor, 29*(1). Senter for Kognitiv Praksis. senterforkognitivpraksis.no/artikler/building-human-strength-m-seligman.html?Itemid=. Seligman, M. E. P., & Csikszentmihalyi, M. (2000). Positive psychology: An introduction. *American*

Psychologist, 55, 5–14. Seligman, M. E. P. (2012). *Flourish: A Visionary New Understanding of Happiness*. New York: Atna Books.

56. Frankl, V. (1959). *Man's Search for Meaning*. Boston: Beacon Press. Maslow, A. H. (1954). *Motivation and Personality*. New York: Harper and Row. Maslow, A. H. (1968). *Toward a Psychology of Being* (2nd ed.). New York: Van Nostrand. Moss, D. (2001). The roots and genealogy of humanistic psychology. In K. J. Schneider, J. F. T. Bugental, & J. F. Pierson (Eds.), *The Handbook of Humanistic Psychology: Leading Edges in Theory, Research, and Practice* (pp. 5–20). Thousand Oaks, CA: Sage Publications. Shaffer, J. B. P. (1978). *Humanistic Psychology*. Englewood Cliffs, NJ: Prentice-Hall.

57. Gregoire, C. (2014, March 4). 18 things highly creative people do differently. *Huffington Post*. http://www.huffingtonpost.com/2014/03/04/creativity-habits_n_4859769.html.

1. IMAGINATIVE PLAY

1. Paumgarten, N. (2010, December 20). Master of play: The many worlds of a video-game artist. *The New Yorker*. http://www.newyorker.com/magazine/2010/12/20/master-of-play.

2. Paumgarten, Master of play.

3. Paumgarten, Master of play.

4. Russ, S. W. (2013). *Pretend Play in Childhood: Foundation of Adult Creativity*. Washington, DC: American Psychological Association. Shavinina, L. V. (Ed.). (2003). *The International Handbook on Innovation*. Boston: Elsevier Science.

5. Shavinina, L. V. (2009). On entrepreneurial giftedness. In L. V. Shavinina (Ed.), *International Handbook on Giftedness* (Vol. 1). New York: Springer.

6. Shavinina, On entrepreneurial giftedness, p. 267.

7. Ackermann, E., Gauntlett, D., & Weckstrom, C. (2009). *Defining Systematic Creativity*. The LEGO Foundation. http://www.lego-foundation.com/en-us/research-and-learning/foundation-research.

8. Kaufman, S. B., Singer, J. L., & Singer, D. G. (2013, November 11). The need for pretend play in child development. [Blog post.] *Scientific American*. blogs.scientificamerican.com/beautiful-minds/2013/11/11/

the-need-for-pretend-play-in-child-development. Ashiabi, G. S. (2007). Play in the preschool classroom: Its socioemotional significance and the teacher's role in play. *Early Childhood Education Journal, 35,* 199–207; Singer, J. L., & Lythcott, M. A. (2004). Fostering school achievement and creativity through sociodramatic play in the classroom. In E. F. Zigler, D. G. Singer, & S. J. Bishop-Joseph (Eds.), *Children's Play: The Roots of Reading* (pp. 77–93). Washington, DC: Zero to Three Press. Clements, D. H., & Sarama. J. (2009). *Learning and Teaching Early Math: The Learning Trajectories Approach.* New York: Routledge. Ginsburg, H. P. (2006). Mathematical play and playful mathematics: A guide for early education. In D. Singer, R. M. Golinkoff, & K. Hirsh-Pasek (Eds.), *Play = Learning: How Play Motivates and Enhances Children's Cognitive and Social-Emotional Growth* (pp. 145–168). New York: Oxford University Press.

9. Boyd, B. (2010). *On the Origin of Stories: Evolution, Cognition, and Fiction.* Cambridge, MA: Belknap Press of Harvard University Press.

10. Kunitz, S. (2005). *The Wild Braid.* New York: W. W. Norton. p. 103.

11. Russ, *Pretend Play in Childhood*; Root-Bernstein, M. (2014). *Inventing Imaginary Worlds: From Childhood Play to Adult Creativity Across the Arts and Sciences.* Lanham, MD: Rowman & Littlefield Education.

12. King, S. (2001). *On Writing: A Memoir of the Craft.* New York: Pocket Books.

13. Powers, R. (2006). *Mark Twain: A Life.* New York: Simon & Schuster.

14. Root-Bernstein, *Inventing Imaginary Worlds.*

15. Root-Bernstein, *Inventing Imaginary Worlds.*

16. Updike, J. (2006, July 10). The writer in the winter. *AARP.* http://www.aarp.org/entertainment/books/info-10-2008/john_updike_writer_in_winter.html.

17. Russ, *Pretend Play in Childhood.* Root-Bernstein, *Inventing Imaginary Worlds.*

18. Russ, S. Personal communication, August 14, 2014.

19. Russ, *Pretend Play in Childhood.*

20. Root-Bernstein, *Inventing Imaginary Worlds*.

21. Russ, personal communication.

22. Fein, G. G. (1987). Pretend play: Creativity and consciousness. In D. Gorlitz & J. F. Wohlwill (Eds.), *Curiosity, Imagination, and Play: On the Development of Spontaneous Cognitive Motivational Processes* (pp. 281–304). Hillsdale, NJ: Lawrence Erlbaum Associates.

23. Singer, D. G., & Singer, J. L. (1990). *The House of Make-Believe: Children's Play and the Developing Imagination.* Cambridge, MA: Harvard University Press.

24. MacPherson, Karen. (2002, October 1). Development experts say children suffer due to lack of unstructured fun. *Post-Gazette Now* (*Pittsburgh Post-Gazette*). old.post-gazette.com/lifestyle/ 20021001childsplay1001fnp3.asp.

25. Barker J. E., Semenov, A. D., Michaelson L., Provan, L. S., Snyder, H. R., and Munakata, Y. (2014). Less-structured time in children's daily lives predicts self-directed executive functioning. *Frontiers in Psychology, 5,* 593. Russ, *Pretend Play in Childhood*. Root-Bernstein, *Inventing Imaginary Worlds*. Russ, S., & Grossman-McKee, A. (1990). Affective expression in children's fantasy play, primary process thinking on the Rorschach, and divergent thinking. *Journal of Personality Assessment*, *54*(3–4), 756–771. Kaugars, A. S., & Russ, S. (2009). Assessing pre-school children's pretend play: Preliminary validation of the Affect in Play Scale-Preschool Version. *Early Education and Development*, *20*(5), 733–755. Hoffman, J., & Russ, S. (2012). Pretend play, creativity, and emotion regulation in children. *Psychology of Aesthetics, Creativity, and the Arts*, *6*(2), 175–184. Russ, S., & Schafer, E. D. (2006). Affect in fantasy play, emotion in memories, and divergent thinking. *Creativity Research Journal*, *18*(3), 347–354. Lillard, A. S., Lerner, M. D., Hopkins, E. J., Dore, R. A., Smith, E. D., & Palmquist, C. M. (2013). The impact of pretend play on children's development: A review of the evidence. *Psychological Bulletin*, *139*(1), 1–34. Russ, S., Robins, A. L., & Christiano, B. A. (1999). Pretend play: Longitudinal prediction of creativity and affect in fantasy in children. *Creativity Research Journal*, *12*(2), 129–139. White, R. E. (2012). *The Power of Play: A Research Summary on Play and Learning.* Saint Paul: Minnesota Children's Museum. Bergen, D. (2009). Play as the learning medium for future scientists, mathematicians, and engineers. *American Journal of Play, 1,* 413–428. Ginsberg, H. P. (2006). Mathematical play and playful

mathematics: A guide for early education. In D. G. Singer, R. Golinkoff, & K. Hirsh-Pasek (Eds.), *Play = Learning: How Play Motivates and Enhances Children's Cognitive and Social-Emotional Growth* (pp. 145–165). New York: Oxford University Press. Fisher, K., Hirsch-Pasek, K., Golinkoff, R. M., & Singer, D. G. (2011). Playing around in school: Implications for learning and educational policy. In A. Pellegrini (Ed.), *The Oxford Handbook of the Development of Play* (pp. 341–362). New York: Oxford University Press. Tepperman, J. (Ed.). (2007). *Play in the Early Years: Key to School Success.* [Policy brief.] El Cerito, CA: Bay Area Early Childhood Funders. Ginsburg, H. P., Pappas, S., & Seo, K.-H. (2001). Everyday mathematical knowledge: Asking young children what is developmentally appropriate. In S. L. Golbeck (Ed.), *Psychological Perspectives on Early Childhood Education: Reframing Dilemmas in Research and Practice* (pp. 181–219). Mahwah, NJ: Lawrence Erlbaum Associates. Henniger, M. L. (1995). Play: Antidote for childhood stress. *Early Child Development and Care, 105,* 7–12.

26. Louv, R. (2006). *Last Child in the Woods: Saving Our Children from Nature-Deficit Disorder.* Chapel Hill, NC: Algonquin Books of Chapel Hill. Gray, P. (2013, September 18). The play deficit. *Aeon.* aeon.co/magazine/culture/children-today-are-suffering-a-severe-deficit-of-play. Gray, P. (2013). *Free to Learn: Why Unleashing the Instinct to Play Will Make Our Children Happier, More Self-Reliant, and Better Students for Life.* New York: Basic Books. Brown, S. (2008, May). Play *Is More Than Just Fun.* [Video.] TED. ted.com/talks/stuart_brown_says_play_is_more_than_fun_it_s_vital. U.N. General Assembly. (1989, November 20). *Convention on the Rights of the Child. United Nations, Treaty Series, 1577,* 3. refworld.org/docid/3ae6b38f0.html.

27. Gopnik, A. (2011, March 16). Why preschool shouldn't be like school. *Slate.* slate.com/articles/double_x/doublex/2011/03/why_preschool_shouldnt_be_like_school.html?wpsrc=sh_all_dt_tw_top.

28. Suggate, S. P., Schaughency, E. A., & Reese, E. (2013). Children learning to read later catch up to children reading earlier. *Early Childhood Research Quarterly, 28*(1), 33–48.

29. Bazelon, E. (2013, December 3). Into the woods. *Slate.* slate.com/articles/double_x/doublex/2013/12/forest_kindergarten_watch_kids_in_switzerland_go_to_school_outside_in_school.html. Suggate et al., Children learning to read later catch up to children reading earlier.

30. Hughes, F. P. (2010). *Children, Play, and Development* (4th ed.). Los Angeles: Sage.

31. McGonigal, J. (2011). *Reality Is Broken: Why Games Make Us Better and How They Can Change the World.* New York: Penguin Books; McGonigal, J. (2015). *SuperBetter: A Revolutionary Approach to Getting Stronger, Happier, Braver and More Resilient.* New York: Penguin Books.

32. Zabelina, D. L., & Robinson, M. D. (2010). Child's play: Facilitating the originality of creative output by a priming manipulation. *Psychology of Aesthetics, Creativity, and the Arts, 4*(1), 57–65.

33. Magnuson, C. D., & Barnett, L. A. (2013). The playful advantage: How playfulness enhances coping with stress. *Leisure Sciences, 35*(2), 129–144. Proyer, R. T. (2012). Development and initial assessment of a short measure for adult playfulness: The SMAP. *Personality and Individual Differences, 53*(8), 989–994. Proyer, R. T., & Ruch, W. (2011). The virtuousness of adult playfulness: The relation of playfulness with strengths of character. *Psychology of Well-Being: Theory, Research and Practice, 1*(1), 4.

34. Root-Bernstein, *Inventing Imaginary Worlds.*

35. Root-Bernstein, *Inventing Imaginary Worlds.*

36. The British Library. (2011, May 11). The Brontës' secret science fiction stories. [Press release.] bl.uk/press-releases/2011/may/the-bronts-secret-science-fiction-stories.

37. They estimated that the real value among the fellows was somewhere between 5 and 26 percent, and 3 and 12 percent among the students.

2. PASSION

1. Wilson, E. (2013). *Jacqueline du Pré: Her Life, Her Music, Her Legend.* New York: Arcade.

2. Wilson, *Jacqueline du Pré.*

3. Yo-Yo Ma. (2004). *Encyclopedia of World Biography.* encyclopedia.com/topic/Yo-Yo_Ma.aspx. Ma, M., & Rallo, J. A. (1996). *My Son, Yo-Yo.* The Chinese University Press.

4. Olmstead, M. (2006). *Yo-Yo Ma.* Chicago: Raintree.

5. Craig, D. (n.d.). Thom Yorke. *Interview Magazine.* http://www. interviewmagazine.com/music/thom-yorke.

6. Yorke, T. (2013, April 1). Thom Yorke. [Radio interview.] wnyc. org/story/278417-thom-yorke.

7. Waitzkin, J. (2008). *The Art of Learning: A Journey in the Pursuit of Excellence.* London: Simon & Schuster. Also see: Morelock, M. (2013). Prodigies, passion, persistence, and pretunement: Musings on the biological bases of talent. In S. B. Kaufman (Ed.), *The Complexity of Greatness: Beyond Talent or Practice* (pp. 83–102). New York: Oxford University Press.

8. Waitzkin, F. (1990). *Searching for Bobby Fischer: The Father of a Prodigy Observes the World of Chess.* London: Penguin Books.

9. Kaufman, S. B. (2008, November 1). Confessions of a late bloomer. *Psychology Today.* psychologytoday.com/articles/200810/ confessions-late-bloomer.

10. Quoted in Kaufman, Confessions of a late bloomer.

11. Walters, J., & Gardner, H. (2001). The crystallizing experience: Discovering an intellectual gift. In R. S. Albert (Ed.), *Genius and Eminence* (pp. 135–155). New York: Psychology Press.

12. Armstrong, T. (2009). *Multiple Intelligences in the Classroom* (3rd ed.). Alexandria, VA: Association for Supervision and Curriculum Development, p. 29.

13. Winner, E. (1996). *Gifted Children: Myths and Realities.* New York: Basic Books, p. 293.

14. Winner, E., & Drake, J. (2013). The rage to master: The decisive role of talent in the visual arts. In S. B. Kaufman (Ed.), *The Complexity of Greatness: Beyond Talent or Practice.* New York: Oxford University Press.

15. Csikszentmihalyi, M. (1991). *Flow: The Psychology of Optimal Experience.* New York: Harper Perennial.

16. Csikszentmihalyi, *Flow.*

17. bNjOrDaN. (2007, August 22). *Michael Jordan 1992 NBA Finals Against Portland.* [Video.] youtube.com/watch?v= G8OqJqOIdb4.

18. Kaufman, S. B. (2008, June 7). On innate talent. *Psychology Today.* psychologytoday.com/blog/beautiful-minds/200806/innate-talent.

19. Feldman, D. H., & Goldsmith, L. T. (1986). *Nature's Gambit: Child Prodigies and the Development of Human Potential.* New York: Basic Books. Feldman, D. H., & Morelock, M. J. (2011). Prodigies and savants. In R. J. Sternberg and S. B. Kaufman (Eds.), *The Cambridge Handbook of Intelligence* (pp. 210–234). New York: Cambridge University Press. Morelock, Prodigies, passion, persistence, and pretunement.

20. Bloom, B. S., & Sosniak, L. A. (Eds.). (1985). *Developing Talent in Young People.* New York: Ballantine Books.

21. Bloom & Sosniak, *Developing Talent in Young People*; Winner & Drake, The rage to master.

22. Torrance, E. P. (1983). The importance of falling in love with something. *Creative Child and Adult Quarterly*, 8(2), 72–78.

23. Torrance, The importance of falling in love with something.

24. Torrance, The importance of falling in love with something.

25. Quoted in Walker, A. (2010). *The World Has Changed: Conversations with Alice Walker.* New York: The New Press.

26. Torrance, The importance of falling in love with something.

27. Newport, C. (2012). *So Good They Can't Ignore You: Why Skills Trump Passion in the Quest for Work You Love.* New York: Grand Central.

28. Vallerand, R. J., Blanchard, C., Mageau, G.A., Koestner, R., Ratelle, C., Léonard, M., Gagné, M., & Marsolais, J. (2003). Les passions de l'ame: On obsessive and harmonious passion. *Journal of Personality and Social Psychology, 85,* 756–767. Vallerand, R. J. (2015). *The Psychology of Passion: A Dualistic Model.* New York: Oxford University Press.

29. Vallerand, R. J., Salvy, S.-J., Mageau, G. A., Elliot, A. J., Denis, P. L., Grouzet, F. M. E., & Blanchard, C. (2007). On the role of passion in performance. *Journal of Personality*, 75(3), 505–534.

30. Vallerand et al., On the role of passion in performance. Vallerand, R. J., Mageau, G. A., Elliot, A. J., Dumais, A., Demers, M.-A., & Rousseau, F. (2008). Passion and performance attainment in sport. *Psychology of Sport and Exercise*, 9(3), 373–392. Bonneville-Roussy, A., Lavigne, G. L., & Vallerand, R. J. (2011). When passion leads to excellence: The case of musicians. *Psychology of Music*, 39(1), 123–138.

31. Thrash, T. M., & Elliot, A. J. (2003). Inspiration as a psychological construct. *Journal of Personality and Social Psychology*, *84*(4), 871–889.

32. Kaufman, S. B. (2011, November 8). Why inspiration matters. *Harvard Business Review*. hbr.org/2011/11/why-inspiration-matters.

33. Thrash, T. M., Maruskin, L. A., Cassidy, S. E., Fryer, J. W., & Ryan, R. M. (2010). Mediating between the muse and the masses: Inspiration and the actualization of creative ideas. *Journal of Personality and Social Psychology, 98,* 469–487.

34. Thrash & Elliot, Inspiration as a psychological construct.

35. Thrash, T. M., Elliot, A. J., Maruskin, L. A., & Cassidy, S. E. (2010). Inspiration and the promotion of well-being: Tests of causality and mediation. *Journal of Personality and Social Psychology, 98*(3), 488–506.

36. Thrash & Elliot, Inspiration as a psychological construct.

37. Thrash et al., Mediating between the muse and the masses.

38. O'Keefe, P. A., & Linnenbrink-Garcia, L. (2014). The role of interest in optimizing performance and self-regulation. *Journal of Experimental Social Psychology, 53,* 70–78.

39. Clear, J. (n.d.). How to stay focused when you get bored working toward your goals. James Clear. jamesclear.com/stay-focused?—vid=130f18305a450132c9d022000b2a88d7.

40. Gielnik, M. M., Spitzmuller, M., Schmitt, A., Klemann, D. K., & Frese, M. (2014). I put in effort, therefore I am passionate: Investigating the path from effort to passion in entrepreneurship. *Academy of Management*, amj.2011.0727. Newport, *So Good They Can't Ignore You.*

41. Duckworth, A. L., Peterson, C., Matthews, M. D., & Kelly, D. R. (2007). Grit: Perseverance and passion for long-term goals. *Journal of Personality and Social Psychology, 92*(6), 1087–1101.

42. Snyder, C. R., Harris, C., Anderson, J. R., Holleran, S. A., Irving, L. M. et al. (1991). The will and the ways: Development and validation of an individual-differences measure of hope. *Journal of Personality and Social Psychology, 60,* 570–585.

43. Elliot, A. J., & Church, M. A. (1997). A hierarchical model of approach and avoidance achievement motivation. *Journal of Personality and Social Psychology, 72*, 218–232. Also see: Dweck, C. (2006).

Mindset: The New Psychology of Success. New York: Ballantine Books. Grant-Halvorson, H., & Higgins, E. T. (2014). *Focus: Use Different Ways of Seeing the World for Success and Influence.* New York: Plume.

44. Lopez, S. J. (2013). *Making Hope Happen: Create the Future You Want for Yourself and Others.* New York: Atria Books. Rand, K. L., Martin, A. D., & Shea, A. M. (2011). Hope, but not optimism, predicts academic performance of law students beyond previous academic achievement. *Journal of Research in Personality, 45,* 683–686. Magaletta, P. R., & Oliver, J. M. (1999). The hope construct, will, and ways: Their relations with self-efficacy, optimism, and general well-being. *Journal of Clinical Psychology, 55,* 539–551. Görres, R. (2011). Situational hope facilitates creative problem-solving. [Bachelor's thesis.] Utrecht, The Netherlands: University College Utrecht. Day, L., Hanson, K., Maltby, J., Proctor, C., & Wood, A. (2010). Hope uniquely predicts objective academic achievement above intelligence, personality, and previous academic achievement. *Journal of Research in Personality, 44,* 550–553. Curry, L. A., Snyder, C. R., Cook, D. L., Ruby, B. C., & Rehm, M. (1997). Role of hope in academic and sport achievement. *Journal of Personality and Social Psychology, 73,* 1257–1267. Snyder, C. R., Shorey, H. S., Cheavens, J., Pulvers, K. M., Adams, V. H. III, & Wiklund, C. (2002). Hope and academic success in college. *Journal of Educational Psychology, 94,* 820–826.

45. Oettingen, G. (2014). *Rethinking Positive Thinking: Inside the New Science of Motivation.* New York: Current.

46. Gregoire, C. (2014, October 2). The surprising downside of looking on the bright side. *Huffington Post.* huffingtonpost.com/2014/10/02/downside-of-looking-on-the-bright-side_n_5901162.html.

47. Oettingen, G., Marquardt, M. K., & Gollwitzer, P. M. (2012). Mental contrasting turns positive feedback on creative potential into successful performance. *Journal of Experimental Social Psychology, 48*(5), 990–996.

3. DAYDREAMING

1. Didion, J. (2007). *The Year of Magical Thinking.* New York: Knopf Doubleday, p. 162.

2. McMillan, R. L., Kaufman, S. B., & Singer, J. L. (2013). Ode to positive constructive daydreaming. *Frontiers in Psychology, 4*(626).

3. Killingsworth, M. A., & Gilbert, D. T. (2010). A wandering mind is an unhappy mind. *Science, 330*(6006), 932.

4. Smallwood, J., & Andrews-Hanna, J. (2013). Not all minds that wander are lost: The importance of a balanced perspective on the mind-wandering state. *Frontiers in Psychology, 4*(441).

5. Singer, J. L. (1974). Daydreaming and the stream of thought. *American Scientist, 62,* 417–425.

6. Singer, J. L. (1975). Navigating the stream of consciousness: Research in daydreaming and related inner experience. *American Psychologist, 30,* 727–738.

7. Singer, J. (1964). Exploring man's imaginative world. *The Teachers College Record, 66,* 165–179. Singer, J. L. (1966). *Daydreaming: An Introduction to the Experimental Study of Inner Experience.* New York: Random House. Singer, Daydreaming and the stream of thought. Singer, Navigating the stream of consciousness. Singer, J. L. (2009). Researching imaginative play and adult consciousness: Implications for daily and literary creativity. *Psychology of Aesthetics, Creativity, and the Arts, 3*(4), 190–199. Antrobus, J. S. (1999). Toward a neurocognitive processing model of imaginal thought. In J. A. Singer & P. Salovey (Eds.), *At Play in the Fields of Consciousness: Essays in the Honour of Jerome L. Singer* (pp. 3–28). Mahwah, NJ: Lawrence Erlbaum.

8. Singer, J. L. (1955). Delayed gratification and ego development: Implications for clinical and experimental research. *Journal of Consulting Psychology, 19,* 259–266. Singer, J. L. (1961). Imagination and waiting ability in young children. *Journal of Personality, 29,* 396–413. Singer, *Daydreaming.* Singer, J. L., & Schonbar, R. A. (1961). Correlates of daydreaming: A dimension of self-awareness. *Journal of Consulting Psychology, 25,* 1–6. Singer, J. L., & Antrobus, J. S. (1963). A factor-analytic study of daydreaming and conceptually-related cognitive and personality variables. *Perceptual and Motor Skills, 17,* 187–209.

9. Teasdale, J. D., Dritschel, B. H., Taylor, M. J., Proctor, L., Lloyd, C. A., Nimmo-Smith, I., & Baddeley, A. D. (1995). Stimulus-independent thought depends on central executive resources. *Memory & Cognition, 23*(5), 551–559. Smallwood, J., Obonsawin, M., & Heim, D. (2003). Task unrelated thought: The role of distributed processing. *Consciousness and Cognition, 12*(2), 169–189. Smallwood, J., Fishman, D. J., & Schooler, J. W. (2007). Counting the cost of an absent mind: Mind wandering as an underrecognized influence on educational performance.

Psychonomic Bulletin & Review, 14(2), 230–236. Smallwood, J., McSpadden, M., & Schooler, J. W. (2007). The lights are on but no one's home: Meta-awareness and the decoupling of attention when the mind wanders. *Psychonomic Bulletin & Review, 14*(3), 527–533. Smallwood, J., O'Connor, R. C., Sudbery, M. V., & Obonsawin, M. (2007). Mind wandering in dysphoria. *Cognition and Emotion, 21*(4), 816–842. Smallwood, J., Beach, E., Schooler, J. W., & Handy, T. C. (2008). Going AWOL in the brain: Mind wandering reduces cortical analysis of external events. *Journal of Cognitive Neuroscience, 20*(3), 458–469. Smallwood, J., McSpadden, M., & Schooler, J. W. (2008). When attention matters: The curious incident of the wandering mind. *Memory & Cognition, 36*(6), 1144–1150. Smallwood, J., Fitzgerald, A., Miles, L. K., & Phillips, L. H. (2009). Shifting moods, wandering minds: Negative moods lead the mind to wander. *Emotion, 9*(2), 271. Smallwood, J., Nind, L., & O'Connor, R. C. (2009). When is your head at? An exploration of the factors associated with the temporal focus of the wandering mind. *Consciousness & Cognition, 18*(1), 118–125. Schooler, J. W., Reichle, E. D., & Halpern, D. V. (2004). Zoning out while reading: Evidence for dissociations between experience and metaconsciousness. In W. Jonathan, E. D. Reichle, & D. V. Halpern (Eds.), *Thinking and Seeing: Visual Metacognition in Adults and Children* (pp. 203–226). Cambridge, MA: MIT Press. Kane, M. J., Brown, L. H., McVay, J. C., Silvia, P. J., Myin-Germeys, I., & Kwapil, T. R. (2007). For whom the mind wanders, and when: An experience-sampling study of working memory and executive control in daily life. *Psychological Science, 18*(7), 614–621. McVay, J. C., & Kane, M. J. (2009). Conducting the train of thought: Working memory capacity, goal neglect, and mind wandering in an executive-control task. *Journal of Experimental Psychology: Learning, Memory, and Cognition, 35*(1), 196–204. McVay, J. C., & Kane, M. J. (2010). Does mind wandering reflect executive function or executive failure? Comment on Smallwood and Schooler (2006) and Watkins (2008). *Psychological Bulletin, 136*(2), 188–189. McVay, J. C., & Kane, M. J. (2012). Why does working memory capacity predict variation in reading comprehension? On the influence of mind wandering and executive attention. *Journal of Experimental Psychology: General, 141*(2), 302–320. McVay, J. C., & Kane, M. J. (2012). Drifting from slow to "d'oh!": Working memory capacity and mind wandering predict extreme reaction times and executive control errors. *Journal of Experimental Psychology: Learning, Memory, and Cognition, 38*(3), 525–549. McVay, J. C., Kane, M. J., and Kwapil, T. R. (2009). Tracking the train of thought from the laboratory into everyday life: An experience-sampling study of mind wandering across controlled and ecological contexts. *Psychonomic Bulletin & Review, 16*(5), 857–863. Reichle, E. D., Reineberg, A. E., & Schooler, J. W. (2010). Eye movements during mindless reading. *Psychological Science, 21*(9), 1300–1310. Smallwood, J., & O'Connor, R. C. (2011). Imprisoned by the past: Unhappy moods lead to a retrospective bias to mind wandering. *Cognition & Emotion, 25*(8), 1481–1490. Mrazek, M. D., Franklin, M. S., Phillips, D. T., Baird, B., & Schooler, J. W. (2013). Mindfulness training improves working memory capacity and GRE performance while reducing mind wandering. *Psychological Science, 24*(5), 776–781. Mooneyham, B. W., & Schooler, J. W. (2013). The costs and benefits of mind-wandering: A review. *Canadian Journal of Experimental Psychology, 67*(1), 11–18.

10. McMillan et al., Ode to positive constructive daydreaming.

11. McMillan et al., Ode to positive constructive daydreaming.

12. Baird, B., Smallwood, J., Mrazek, M. D., Kam, J. W. Y., Franklin, M. S., & Schooler, J. W. (2012). Inspired by distraction: Mind wandering facilitates creative incubation. *Psychological Science, 23*(10), 1117–1122.

13. Baird et al., Inspired by distraction.

14. Seligman, M.E.P., Railton, P., Baumeister, R. F., & Sripada, C. (2013). Navigating into the future or driven by the past. *Perspectives on Psychological Science, 8*, 119–141.

15. Baird, B., Smallwood, J., & Schooler, J. W. (2011). Back to the future: Autobiographical planning and the functionality of mind-wandering. *Consciousness and Cognition, 20*(4), 1604–1611. Smallwood, J., Schooler, J. W., Turk, D. J., Cunningham, S. J., Burns, P., & Macrae, C. N. (2011). Self-reflection and the temporal focus of the wandering mind. *Consciousness and Cognition, 20*(4), 1120–1126.

16. Klinger, E. (1999). Thought flow: Properties and mechanisms underlying shifts in content. In J. A. Singer & P. Salovey (Eds.), *At Play in the Fields of Consciousness: Essays in the Honour of Jerome L. Singer* (pp. 29–50). Mahwah, NJ: Lawrence Erlbaum.

17. Immordino-Yang, M. H., Christodoulou, J. A., & Singh, V. (2012). Rest is not idleness: Implications of the brain's default mode for human development and education. *Perspectives on Psychological Science, 7*, 352–365.

18. Jung C. G., Chodorow, J. (Ed.). (1997). *Jung on Active Imagination*. Princeton, NJ: Princeton University Press.

19. Miller, Jeffrey C. (2004). *The Transcendent Function: Jung's Model of Psychological Growth Through Dialogue with the Unconscious*. Albany: State University of New York Press.

20. Poe, E. A. (1850). *Eleonora.*

21. Lennon, J., McCartney, P., Harrison, G., & Starr, R. (2000). *The Beatles Anthology*. San Francisco, CA: Chronicle Books.

22. Poe, E. A. (1839, August). An opinion on dreams. *Burton's Gentleman Magazine*, 105.

23. Shower for the freshest thinking. (2014). Hansgrohe. http://www1.hansgrohe.com/assets/at--de/1404_Hansgrohe_Select_ConsumerSurvey_EN.pdf.

24. Carson, S. (2010). *Your Creative Brain: Seven Steps to Maximize Imagination, Productivity, and Innovation in Your Life*. San Francisco: Jossey-Bass.

25. Brogan, J. (2012, February 27). When being distracted is a good thing. *Boston Globe*. bostonglobe.com/lifestyle/health-wellness/2012/02/27/when-being-distracted-good-thing/1AYWPlDplqluMEPrWHe5sL/story.html.

26. Fussman, C. (2013, August 8). Woody Allen: What I've learned. *Esquire*. esquire.com/features/what-ive-learned/woody-allen-0913.

27. Immanuel Kant. (2015). *Encyclopaedia Britannica*. academic.eb.com/EBchecked/topic/311398/Immanuel-Kant. Note: While this is a common account, there are various historical accounts of Kant's daily walk, some contradictory.

28. De Quincy, T. (1827). The last days of Immanuel Kant. Published online by eBooks@Adelaide, https://ebooks.adelaide.edu.au/d/de_quincey/thomas/last-days-of-immanuel-kant/.

29. Young, D. (2014). *How to Think About Exercise*. London: Macmillan.

30. Solnit, R. (2001). The legs of William Wordsworth. In *Wanderlust: A History of Walking* (pp. 105–117). New York: Penguin.

31. Thoreau, H. D. (1862, June 1). Walking. *The Atlantic.*

32. Huffington, A. (2013, August 29). Hemingway, Thoreau, Jefferson and the virtues of a good long walk. *Huffington Post.*

huffingtonpost.com/arianna-huffington/hemingway-thoreau-jeffers_
b_3837002.html.

33. Thoreau, Walking.

34. Huffington, Hemingway, Thoreau, Jefferson and the virtues of a good long walk. Loehle, C. (1990). A guide to increased creativity in research: Inspiration or perspiration? *Bioscience, 40*(2), 123–129. Oppezzo, M., & Schwartz, D. L. (2014). Give your ideas some legs: The positive effect of walking on creative thinking. *Journal of Experimental Psychology: Learning, Memory, and Cognition, 40*(4), 1142–1152. Aspinall, P., Mavros, P., Coyne, R., & Roe, J. (2013). The urban brain: Analysing outdoor physical activity with mobile EEG. *British Journal of Sports Medicine, 49*, 272–276. How does nature impact our wellbeing? (n.d.) University of Minnesota. takingcharge.csh.umn.edu /enhance-your-wellbeing/environment/nature-and-us/how-does-nature-impact-our-wellbeing.

35. Berntsen, D., & Jacobsen, A. S. (2008). Involuntary (spontaneous) mental time travel into the past and future. *Consciousness and Cognition, 17*(4), 1093–1104.

36. Schooler, J. W., Mrazek, M. D., Franklin, M. S., Baird, B., Mooneyham, B. W., Zedelius, C., & Broadway, J. M. (2014). The middle way: Finding the balance between mindfulness and mind-wandering. *Psychology of Learning and Motivation, 60*, 1–33.

37. Andrews-Hanna, J. R., Kaiser, R. H., Turner, A. E. J., Reineberg, A. E., Godinez, D., Dimidjian, S., & Banich, M. T. (2013). A penny for your thoughts: Dimensions of self-generated thought content and relationships with individual differences in emotional wellbeing. *Frontiers in Psychology, 4*(900).

38. Singer, *Daydreaming.*

4. SOLITUDE

1. Pergament, D. (2007, October 7). The enchanted island that Bergman called home. *New York Times.* nytimes.com/2007/10/07/ travel/07cultured.html?pagewanted=all&_r=0.

2. Bergman, I. (2007). *Images: My Life in Film.* New York: Arcade.

3. Currey, M. (2013) *Daily Rituals: How Artists Work.* New York: Knopf.

4. Skillion, A. (Ed.). (2001). *The New York Public Library Literature Companion*. New York: Free Press.

5. Smith, Z. (2010, February 22). Rules for writers. *Guardian*. theguardian.com/books/2010/feb/22/zadie-smith-rules-for-writers.

6. Currey, *Daily Rituals*.

7. Kear, J. (2007). Une chambre mentale: Proust's solitude. In H. Hendrix (Ed.), *Writers' Houses and the Making of Memory* (pp. 221–235). New York: Routledge.

8. Kear, Une chambre mentale.

9. Kear, Une chambre mentale.

10. Grosz, S. (2013). *The Examined Life: How We Lose and Find Ourselves*. New York: Norton.

11. Sawyer, R. K. (2007). *Group Genius: The Creative Power of Collaboration*. New York: Basic Books. Shenk, J. W. (2014). *Powers of Two: Finding the Essence of Innovation in Creative Pairs*. New York: Eamon Dolan/Houghton Mifflin Harcourt.

12. Asimov, I. (2014, October 20). Isaac Asimov asks, "How do people get new ideas?" *MIT Technology Review*. technologyreview.com/view/531911/isaac-asimov-asks-how-do-people-get-new-ideas.

13. Cain, S. (2013). *Quiet: The Power of Introverts in a World That Can't Stop Talking*. New York: Broadway Paperbacks.

14. http://www.quietrev.com.

15. Cain, S. Personal communication, January 2015.

16. Winnicott, D. W. (1958). The capacity to be alone. *The International Journal of Psychoanalysis, 39,* 416–420.

17. Buchholz, E. (1998, January 1). The call of solitude. *Psychology Today*. psychologytoday.com/articles/199802/the-call-solitude.

18. Wozniak, S., & Smith, G. (2007). *iWoz: Computer Geek to Cult Icon*. New York: Norton.

19. Congdon, C., Flynn, D., & Redman, M. (2014, October). Balancing "we" and "me": The best collaborative spaces also support solitude. *HarvardBusinessReview.*https://hbr.org/2014/10/balancing-we-and-me-the-best-collaborative-spaces-also-support-solitude.

20. Fox, M. D., Snyder, A. Z., Vincent, J. L., Corbetta, M., Van Essen, D. C., & Raichle, M. E. (2005). The human brain is

intrinsically organized into dynamic, anticorrelated functional networks. *Proceedings of the National Academy of Sciences USA*, *102*(27), 9673–9678. Andrews-Hanna, J. R., Smallwood, J., & Spreng, R. N. (2014). The default network and self-generated thought: Component processes, dynamic control, and clinical relevance. *Annals of the New York Academy of Sciences*, *1316*(1), 29–52.

21. Immordino-Yang, M. H., Christodoulou, J. A., & Singh, V. (2012). Rest is not idleness: Implications of the brain's default mode for human development and education. *Perspectives on Psychological Science, 7*, 352–364. Cocchi, L., Zalesky, A., Fornito, A., & Mattingley, J. B. (2013). Dynamic cooperation and competition between brain systems during cognitive control. *Trends in Cognitive Sciences, 17*(10), 493–501. Dwyer, D. B., Harrison, B. J., Yucel, M., Whittle, S., Zalesky, A. et al. (2014). Large-scale brain network dynamics supporting adolescent cognitive control. *Journal of Neuroscience, 34*(42), 14096–14107. Spreng, R. N., DuPre, E., Selarka, D., Garcia, J., Gojkovic, S. et al. (2014). Goal-congruent default network activity facilitates cognitive control. *Journal of Neuroscience*, *34*(42), 14108–14114.

22. Immordino-Yang et al. Rest is not idleness.

23. Oyserman, D., Bybee, D., & Terry, K. (2006). Possible selves and academic outcomes: How and when possible selves impel action. *Journal of Personality and Social Psychology, 91*(1), 188–204. Oyserman, D., Bybee, D., Terry, K., & Hart-Johnson, T. (2004). Possible selves as roadmaps. *Journal of Research in Personality, 38*(2), 130–149.

24. Aristotle. (350 B.C.E.) *Nicomachean Ethics*, Book X.

25. Montaigne, M. (1877). Of solitude. In *The Essays of Montaigne, Complete*, published online by Project Gutenberg, https://www.gutenberg.org/files/3600/3600-h/3600-h.htm.

26. Hammond, J. (Ed.). (2002). Selections from Proust. http://www.ljhammond.com/proust.htm.

27. Sharr, A. (2006). *Heidegger's Hut*. Cambridge, MA: MIT Press.

28. Nealson, E. (2008). *Rethinking Facticity*. Albany: State University of New York Press, p. 131.

29. Thoreau, H. (1854). *Walden; Or, Life in the Woods*. New York: Dover, 1995.

30. Lawrence, D. H. "Lonely, Lonesome, Lonely—O!" in *The Works of D.H. Lawrence: With an Introduction and Bibliography* (1994). Hertfordshire: Wordsworth Editions, p. 538.

31. Ricard, M. Personal communication, July 17, 2015.

32. Ricard, M., & Munier, V. (2013). *Solitudes I.* Brantigny, France: Koballan.

33. Storr, *Solitude.*

5. INTUITION

1. Hofmann, A. (1980). *LSD, My Problem Child.* New York: McGraw-Hill.

2. Hofmann, *LSD.*

3. Smith, C. S. (2008, April 30). Albert Hofmann, the father of LSD, dies at 102. *New York Times.* http://www.nytimes.com/2008/04/30/world/europe/30hofmann.html.

4. Hofmann, *LSD.*

5. Kaufman, S. B. (2011). Intelligence and the cognitive unconscious. In R. J. Sternberg & S. B. Kaufman (Eds.), *The Cambridge Handbook of Intelligence* (pp. 442–467). Cambridge, UK: Cambridge University Press. Kihlstrom, J. F. (1987). The cognitive unconscious. *Science, 237*(4821), 1445–1452. Hassin, R. R., Uleman, J. S., & Bargh, J. A. (Eds.). (2007). *The New Unconscious.* Oxford: Oxford University Press. Wilson, T. D. (2002). *Strangers to Ourselves: Discovering the Adaptive Unconscious.* Cambridge, MA: Belknap Press. Gigerenzer, G. (2008). *Gut Feelings: The Intelligence of the Unconscious.* London: Penguin Books.

6. Isaacson, W. (2011, October 29). The genius of Jobs. *New York Times.* http://www.nytimes.com/2011/10/30/opinion/sunday/steve-jobss-genius.html.

7. Brassaï. (2002). *Conversations with Picasso.* Chicago: University of Chicago Press.

8. Forster, E. M. (1947, July). On criticism in the arts, especially music. *Harper's Magazine,* 9–17.

9. Ghiselin, B. (1963). Automatism, intention, and autonomy in the novelist's production. *Daedalus, 92*(2), 297–311.

10. Bradbury, R. (1974, January 21). *Day at Night: Ray Bradbury.* [Video.] youtube.com/watch?v=tTXckvj7KL4&.

11. Plato. (1997). "Ion." In John M. Cooper (Ed.), *Plato: Complete Works.* New York: Hackett.

12. Gilbert, E. (2009, February). *Your Elusive Creative Genius.* [Video.] TED. ted.com/talks/elizabeth_gilbert_on_genius.

13. Hazlitt, W. (1889). Genius and its powers. In *Essays of William Hazlitt.* London: Walter Scott Publishing.

14. Joseph, C. (2012, March 27). U.S. Navy program to study how troops use intuition. [Blog post.] *New York Times.* atwar.blogs. nytimes.com/2012/03/27/navy-program-to-study-how-troops-use-intuition.

15. Kaufman, Intelligence and the cognitive unconscious. Kihlstrom, The cognitive unconscious. Hassin et al. (Eds.). *The New Unconscious.* Wilson, *Strangers to Ourselves.* Gigerenzer, *Gut Feelings.*

16. Epstein, S. (1994). Integration of the cognitive and the psychodynamic unconscious. *American Psychologist, 49*(8), 709–724. Epstein, S. (2014). *Cognitive-Experiential Theory: An Integrative Theory of Personality.* Oxford: Oxford University Press. Evans, J. S. B. T. (2008). Dual-processing accounts of reasoning, judgment, and social cognition. *Annual Review of Psychology, 59*(1), 255–278. Kaufman, Intelligence and the cognitive unconscious. Kahneman, D. (2013). *Thinking, Fast and Slow.* New York: Farrar, Straus, & Giroux. Evans, J. S. B. T., & Frankish, K. (Eds.). (2009). *In Two Minds: Dual Processes and Beyond.* New York: Oxford University Press. Evans, J. S. B. T., & Stanovich, K. E. (2013). Dual-process theories of higher cognition: Advancing the debate. *Perspectives on Psychological Science, 8*(3), 223–241.

17. Kaufman, Intelligence and the cognitive unconscious. Gabora, L. (2000). The beer can theory of creativity. In P. Bentley & D. Corne (Eds.), *Creative Evolutionary Systems* (pp. 147–161). San Francisco: Morgan Kauffman. Gabora, L. (2010). Revenge of the "neurds": Characterizing creative thought in terms of the structure and dynamics of human memory. *Creativity Research Journal, 22*(1), 1–13. Gabora, L. (2003). Contextual focus: A cognitive explanation for the cultural transition of the Middle/Upper Paleolithic. In R. Alterman & D. Hirsch (Eds.), *Proceedings of the 25th Annual Meeting of the Cognitive Science Society* (pp. 432–437). Boston: Erlbaum. Gabora, L. (2008).

Mind. In H. D. G. Maschner & C. Chippindate (Eds.), *Handbook of Archeological Theories* (pp. 283–296). Walnut Creek, CA: Altamira Press. Gabora, L., & Kaufman, S. B. (2010). Evolutionary approaches to creativity. In Kaufman, J., & Sternberg, R. (Eds.), *The Cambridge Handbook of Creativity* (pp. 279–300). Lin, W. L., & Lien, Y. W. (2013). The different role of working memory in open-ended versus closed-ended creative problem solving: A dual-process theory account. *Creativity Research Journal, 25*(1), 85–96.

18. Evans, Dual-processing accounts of reasoning, judgment, and social cognition. Kaufman, Intelligence and the cognitive unconscious. Gabora, The beer can theory of creativity. Gabora, Revenge of the "neurds." Gabora, Contextual focus. Gabora, Mind. Gabora & Kaufman, Evolutionary approaches to creativity. Lin & Lien, The different role of working memory in open-ended versus closed-ended creative problem solving.

19. Stanovich, K. E., West, R. F., & Toplak, M. E. (2012). Intelligence and rationality. In R. Sternberg & S. B. Kaufman (Eds.), *The Cambridge Handbook of Intelligence* (3rd ed.), (pp. 784–826). Cambridge, UK: Cambridge University Press.

20. Bowdle, B. F., & Gentner, D. (2005). The career of metaphor. *Psychological Review, 112*(1), 193–216. Costello, F. (2000). Efficient creativity: Constraint-guided conceptual combination. *Cognitive Science, 24*(2), 299–349. Green, A. E., Kraemer, D. J. M., Fugelsang, J. A., Gray, J. R., & Dunbar, K. N. (2010). Connecting long distance: Semantic distance in analogical reasoning modulates frontopolar cortex activity. *Cerebral Cortex, 20*(1), 70–76. Holyoak, K. J., & Thagard, P. (1997). The analogical mind. *American Psychologist, 52*(1), 35–44. Sternberg, R. J. (1977). Component processes in analogical reasoning. *Psychological Review, 84*(4), 353–378. Beaty, R. E., & Silvia, P. J. (2013). Metaphorically speaking: Cognitive abilities and the production of figurative language. *Memory & Cognition, 41*(2), 255–267. Silvia, P. J., & Beaty, R. E. (2012). Making creative metaphors: The importance of fluid intelligence for creative thought. *Intelligence, 40*(4), 343–351. Green, A. E., Kraemer, D. J. M., Fugelsang, J. A., Gray, J. R., & Dunbar, K. N. (2012). Neural correlates of creativity in analogical reasoning. *Journal of Experimental Psychology: Learning, Memory, and Cognition, 38*(2), 264–272. Woolgar, A., Parr, A., Cusack, R., Thompson, R., Nimmo-Smith, I. et al. (2010). Fluid intelligence loss linked to restricted regions of damage within frontal and parietal cortex. *Proceedings of the*

National Academy of Sciences USA, 107(33), 14899–14902. Gläscher, J., Rudrauf, D., Colom, R., Paul, L. K., Tranel, D., Damasio, H., & Adolphs, R. (2010). Distributed neural system for general intelligence revealed by lesion mapping. *Proceedings of the National Academy of Sciences USA, 107*(10), 4705–4709. Ramnani, N., & Owen, A. M. (2004). Anterior prefrontal cortex: Insights into function from anatomy and neuroimaging. *Nature Reviews Neuroscience, 5*(3), 184–194. Buda, M., Fornito, A., Bergstrom, Z. M., & Simons, J. S. (2011). A specific brain structural basis for individual differences in reality monitoring. *Journal of Neuroscience, 31*(40), 14308–14313. Fleming, S. M., & Dolan, R. J. (2012). The neural basis of metacognitive ability. *Philosophical Transactions of the Royal Society B: Biological Sciences, 367*(1594), 1338–1349. Green, A. E., Fugelsang, J. A., Kraemer, D. J. M., Shamosh, N. A., & Dunbar, K. N. (2006). Frontopolar cortex mediates abstract integration in analogy. *Brain Research, 1096*(1), 125–137. Ellamil, M., Dobson, C., Beeman, M., & Christoff, K. (2012). Evaluative and generative modes of thought during the creative process. *NeuroImage, 59*(2), 1783–1794. Kroger, J. K., Sabb, F. W., Fales, C. L., Bookheimer, S. Y., Cohen, M. S., & Holyoak, K. J. (2002). Recruitment of anterior dorsolateral prefrontal cortex in human reasoning: A parametric study of relational complexity. *Cerebral Cortex, 12*(5), 477–485. Hampshire, A., Thompson, R., Duncan, J., & Owen, A. M. (2011). Lateral prefrontal cortex subregions make dissociable contributions during fluid reasoning. *Cerebral Cortex, 21*(1), 1–10. Greene, J. D., Nystrom, L. E., Engell, A. D., Darley, J. M., & Cohen, J. D. (2004). The neural bases of cognitive conflict and control in moral judgment. *Neuron, 44*(2), 389–400. Burgess, P. W., Dumontheil, I., & Gilbert, S. J. (2007). The gateway hypothesis of rostral prefrontal cortex (area 10) function. *Trends in Cognitive Sciences, 11,* 290–298. Fleming, S. M., Huijgen, J., & Dolan, R. J. (2012). Prefrontal contributions to metacognition in perceptual decision making. *Journal of Neuroscience 32,* 6117–6125. Stankov, L., Lee, J., Luo, W., & Hogan, D. J. (2012). Confidence: A better predictor of academic achievement than self-efficacy, self-concept and anxiety? *Learning and Individual Differences, 22*(6), 747–758. Christoff, K., & Gabriele, J. D. E. (2000). The frontopolar cortex and human cognition: Evidence for a rostrocaudal hierarchical organization within the human prefrontal cortex. *Psychobiology, 28,* 168–186. Burgess, P. W., Simons, J. S., Dumontheil, I., & Gilbert, S. J. (2005). The gateway hypothesis of the rostral prefrontal cortex (area 10) function. In J. Duncan, L. Phillips, & P. McLeod (Eds.), *Measuring the*

Mind: Speed, Control, and Age (pp. 217–248). Oxford: Oxford University Press. Ramnani & Owen, Anterior prefrontal cortex. Kim, C., Johnson, N. F., Cilles, S. E., & Gold, B. T. (2011). Common and distinct mechanisms of cognitive flexibility in prefrontal cortex. *Journal of Neuroscience, 31*(13), 4771–4779. Beaty, R. E., Silvia, P. J., Nusbaum, E. C., Jauk, E., & Benedek, M. (2014). The roles of associative and executive processes in creative cognition. *Memory & Cognition, 42*(7), 1186–1197.

21. Kaufman, Intelligence and the cognitive unconscious.

22. Lewicki, P., Hill, T., & Czyzewska, M. (1992). Non-conscious acquisition of information. *American Psychologist, 47*(6), 796–801.

23. Kaufman, S. B. (2009). Beyond general intelligence: The dual-process theory of human intelligence. [Doctoral dissertation.] New Haven, CT: Yale University. Kaufman, S. B. (2011). Intelligence and the cognitive unconscious. In R. J. Sternberg & S. B. Kaufman (Eds.), *The Cambridge Handbook of Intelligence* (pp. 442–467). Cambridge, UK: Cambridge University Press. Kaufman, J. C., Kaufman, S. B., & Plucker, J. A. (2013). Contemporary theories of intelligence. In J. Reisberg (Ed.), *The Oxford Handbook of Cognitive Psychology* (pp. 811–822). New York: Oxford University Press.

24. Hawkins, J., & Blakeslee, S. (2005). *On Intelligence*. New York: Henry Holt.

25. Gabora, The beer can theory of creativity. Gabora, Revenge of the "neurds." Gabora, Contextual focus. Gabora, Mind. Gabora & Kaufman, Evolutionary approaches to creativity.

26. Chabris, C. F., & Simons, D. J. (2010). *The Invisible Gorilla: How Our Intuitions Deceive Us*. New York: Broadway Paperbacks.

27. Kaufman, S. B. (2011, June 11). How Renaissance people think: The thinking style of polymaths. *Psychology Today.* psychologytoday. com/blog/beautiful-minds/201106/how-renaissance-people-think.

28. Topolinski, S., & Reber, R. (2010). Gaining insight into the "aha" experience. *Current Directions in Psychological Science, 19*(6), 402–405.

29. Poincaré, H. (1930). *Science and Method*. Trans. F. Maitland. London: Thomas Nelson. (Original work published in 1908.)

30. Vartanian, O. (2009). Variable attention facilitates creative problem solving. *Psychology of Aesthetics, Creativity, and the Arts, 3*,

57–59. Vartanian, O., Martindale, C., & Kwiatkowski, J. (2003). Creativity and inductive reasoning: The relationship between divergent thinking and performance on Wason's 2–4–6 task. *Quarterly Journal of Experimental Psychology, 34*, 1370–1380. Vartanian, O., Martindale, C., & Kwiatkowski, J. (2007). Creative potential, attention, and speed of information processing. *Personality and Individual Differences, 43*, 1470–1480. Vartanian, O., Martindale, C., & Matthews, J. (2009). Divergent thinking ability is related to faster relatedness judgments. *Psychology of Aesthetics, Creativity, and the Arts, 3*, 99–103.

31. Gregoire, C. (2013, August 25). How to train your brain to see what others don't. *Huffington Post*. huffingtonpost.com/2013/08/25/insights-brain_n_3795229.html.

32. Kounios, J., & Beeman, M. (2014). The cognitive neuroscience of insight. *Annual Review of Psychology, 65*(1), 71–93. Kounios, J., & Beeman, M. (2015). *The Eureka Factor: Aha Moments, Creative Insight, and the Brain*. New York: Random House.

33. Reber, R., Wurtz, P., & Zimmermann, T. D. (2004). Exploring "fringe" consciousness: The subjective experience of perceptual fluency and its objective bases. *Consciousness and Cognition, 13*(1), 47–60. Mangan, B. (2007). Cognition, fringe consciousness, and the legacy of William James. In M. Velmans & S. Schneider (Eds.), *The Blackwell Companion to Consciousness* (pp. 671–685). Malden, MA: Blackwell. Norman, E., Price, M. C., & Duff, S. C. (2010). Fringe consciousness: A useful framework for clarifying the nature of experience-based metacognitive feelings. In A. Efklides & P. Misailidi (Eds.), *Trends and Prospects in Metacognition Research* (pp. 63–80). New York: Springer.

34. Metcalfe & Wiebe (1987), as cited in Topolinski, S., & Reber, R. (2010). Gaining insight into the "aha" experience. *Current Directions in Psychological Science, 19*(6), 402–405.

35. James, W. (1890). *The Principles of Psychology* (Vol. 2). New York: Dover. Metcalfe, J., & Wiebe, D. (1987). Intuition in insight and noninsight problem solving. *Memory & Cognition, 15*, 238–246.

36. Einstein, A., & Infeld, L. (1938). *The Evolution of Physics*. New York: Simon & Schuster.

37. Ash, I. K., & Wiley, J. (2006). The nature of restructuring in insight: An individual-differences approach. *Psychonomic Bulletin and Review, 13*, 66–73. Fleck, J. I. (2008). Working memory demands

in insight versus analytic problem solving. *European Journal of Cognitive Psychology, 2,* 139–176. Gilhooly, K. J., & Murphy, P. (2005). Differentiating insight from non-insight problems. *Thinking and Reasoning, 11,* 279–302. Fioratou, E., & Gilhooly, K. J. (2011). Executive functions in insight versus non-insight problem solving: An individual differences approach. *Thinking and Reasoning, 15*(4), 355–376. Lavric, A., Forstmeier, S., & Rippon, G. (2000). Differences in working memory involvement in analytical and creative tasks: An ERP study. *Neuroreport, 11,* 1613–1618.

38. Kounios, J., & Beeman, M. (2014). The cognitive neuroscience of insight. *Annual Review of Psychology, 65*(1), 71–93. Kounios, J., & Beeman, M. (2015). *The Eureka Factor: Aha Moments, Creative Insight, and the Brain.* New York: Random House.

39. Mednick, S. (1962). The associative basis of the creative process. *Psychological Review, 69*(3), 220–232.

40. Kenett, Y. N., Anaki, D., & Faust, M. (2014). Investigating the structure of semantic networks in low and high creative persons. *Frontiers in Human Neuroscience, 8*(407). Beaty et al., The roles of associative and executive processes in creative cognition. Prabhakaran, R., Green, A. E., & Gray, J. R. (2014). Thin slices of creativity: Using single-word utterances to assess creative cognition. *Behavior Research Methods, 46*(3), 641–659.

41. Kounios, J., & Beeman, M. (2009). The aha! moment: The cognitive neuroscience of insight. *Current Directions in Psychological Science, 18*(4), 210–216.

42. Kounios, J., Frymiare, J. L., Bowden, E. M., Fleck, J. I., Subramaniam, K., Parrish, T. B., & Jung-Beeman, M. (2006). The prepared mind: Neural activity prior to problem presentation predicts subsequent solution by sudden insight. *Psychological Science, 17*(10), 882–890.

43. Jung-Beeman, M., Bowden, E. M., Haberman, J., Frymiare, J. L., Arambel-Liu, S. et al. (2004). Neural activity when people solve verbal problems with insight. *PLOS Biology, 2*(4).

44. Jung-Beeman et al. Neural activity when people solve verbal problems with insight.

45. Miller, B. L., Cummings, J., Mishkin, F., Boone, K., Prince, F., Ponton, M., & Cotman, C. (1998). Emergence of artistic talent in frontotemporal dementia. *Neurology, 51*(4), 978–982.

46. Treffert, D. A. (2010). *Islands of Genius: The Bountiful Mind of the Autistic, Acquired, and Sudden Savant.* London: Jessica Kingsley.

47. Kaufman, S. B. (2013). *Ungifted: Intelligence Redefined.* New York: Basic Books.

48. Kounios & Beeman, The cognitive neuroscience of insight.

49. Kounios & Beeman, The cognitive neuroscience of insight.

50. Kounios & Beeman, The cognitive neuroscience of insight. Ashby, F. G., Isen, A. M., & Turken, A. U. (1999). A neuropsychological theory of positive affect and its influence on cognition. *Psychological Review, 106*(3), 529–550. Isen, A. M., Daubman, K. A., & Nowicki, G. P. (1987). Positive affect facilitates creative problem solving. *Journal of Personality and Social Psychology, 52*(6), 1122–1131. Fox, E. (2008). *Emotion Science: Cognitive and Neuroscientific Approaches to Understanding Human Emotions.* New York: Palgrave Macmillan. Fredrickson, B. L. (2001). The role of positive emotions in positive psychology: The broaden and build theory of positive emotions. *American Psychologist, 56*, 218–226. Fredrickson, B. L. (2005). Positive emotions broaden the scope of attention and thought-action repertoires. *Cognition & Emotion, 19*, 313–332.

51. Harmon-Jones, E., Gable, P. A., & Price, T. F. (2013). Does negative affect always narrow and positive affect always broaden the mind? Considering the influence of motivational intensity on cognitive scope. *Current Directions in Psychological Science, 22*, 301–307.

52. Kashdan, T., & Biswas-Diener, R. (2014). *The Upside of Your Dark Side: Why Being Your Whole Self—Not Just Your "Good" Self—Drives Success and Fulfillment.* New York: Hudson Street Press.

53. Ceci, M. W., & Kumar, V. K. (2015). A correlational study of creativity, happiness, motivation, and stress from creative pursuits. *Journal of Happiness Studies*, doi: 10.1007/s10902-015-9615-y.

54. Fong, C. T. (2006). The effects of emotional ambivalence on creativity. *Academy of Management Journal, 49*, 1016–1030.

55. Jamison, K. R. (1996). *Touched with Fire: Manic-Depressive Illness and the Artistic Temperament.* New York: Free Press. Jamison, K. R. (2005). *Exuberance: The Passion for Life.* New York: Vintage. Richards, R., Kinney, D. K., Dennis, K., Lunde, I., Benet, M., & Merzel, A. P. C. (1988). Creativity in manic-depressives, cyclothymes, their normal relatives, and control subjects. *Journal of Abnormal Psychology, 97,*

281–288. Zabelina, D. L., Condon, D., & Beeman, M. (2014). Do dimensional psychopathology measures relate to divergent thinking or creative achievement? *Frontiers in Psychology, 5,* 1–11. Furnham, A., Batey, M., Arnand, K., & Manfield, J. (2008). Personality, hypomania, intelligence and creativity. *Personality and Individual Differences, 44,* 1060–1069. Johnson, S. L., Murray, G., Frederickson, B., Youngstrom, E. A., Hinshaw, S. et al. (2012). Creativity and bipolar disorder: Touched by fire or burning with questions? *Clinical Psychology Review, 32,* 1–12.

56. Johnson et al., Creativity and bipolar disorder.

57. Chi, R. P., & Snyder, A. W. (2012). Brain stimulation enables the solution of an inherently difficult problem. *Neuroscience Letters, 515*(2), 121–124. For replications of this work, see: Goel, V., Eimontaite, I., Goel, A., & Schindler, I. (2015). Differential modulation of performance in insight and divergent thinking tasks with tDCS. *The Journal of Problem Solving, 8: 1.* Mayseless, N., & Shamay-Tsoory, S. G. (2015). Enhancing verbal creativity: Modulating creativity by altering the balance between right and left inferior frontal gyrus with tDCS. *Neuroscience, 291,* 167–176. For the use of tDCS to improve cognitive flexibility, see: Chrysikou, E. G., Hamilton, R.H., Coslett, H. B., Datta, A., Bikson, M., & Thompson-Schill, S. L. (2013). Noninvasive transcranial direct current stimulation over the left prefrontal cortex facilitates cognitive flexibility in tool use. *Cognitive Neuroscience, 4,* 81–89.

58. Kershaw, T. C., & Ohlsson, S. (2004). Multiple causes of difficulty in insight: The case of the nine-dot problem. *Journal of Experimental Psychology: Learning, Memory, and Cognition, 30*(1), 3–13.

59. Rice, G. E., Lambon Ralph, M. A., & Hoffman, P. (2015). The role of left versus right anterior temporal lobes in conceptual knowledge: An ALE meta-analysis of 97 functional neuroimaging studies. *Cerebral Cortex,* doi: 10.1093/cercor/bhv024.

60. Klein, G. A. (1999). *Sources of Power: How People Make Decisions.* Cambridge, MA: MIT Press.

61. Ericsson, K. A., Chase, W. G., & Faloon, S. (1980). Acquisition of a memory skill. *Science, 208,* 1181–1182. Ericsson, K. A., & Chase, W. G. (1982). Exceptional memory. *American Scientist, 70,* 607–615. Ericsson, K. A., & Kintsch, E. (1995). Long-term working memory. *Psychological Review, 102,* 211–245. Bedard, J., & Chi, T. H. (1992). Expertise. *Current Directions in Psychological Science, 1,* 178–183. Ericsson, K. A., Charness, N., Feltovich, P. J., & Hoffman, R. R. (Eds.).

(2006). *The Cambridge Handbook of Expertise and Expert Performance*. Cambridge, UK: Cambridge University Press. Ericsson, K. A., & Smith, J. (1991). *Toward a General Theory of Expertise: Prospects and Limits*. New York: Cambridge University Press. Ericsson, K. A. (1985). Memory skill. *Canadian Journal of Psychology, 39,* 188–231. Ericsson, K. A., Krampe, R. T., & Tesch-Römer, C. (1993). The role of deliberate practice in the acquisition of expert performance. *Psychological Review, 100,* 363–406.

62. Kaufman, *Ungifted.*

63. Colvin, G. (2010). *Talent Is Overrated*. New York: Portfolio Trade. Shenk, D. (2011). *The Genius in All of Us: New Insights into Genetics, Talent and IQ*. New York: Anchor Books. Gladwell, M. (2008). *Outliers: The Story of Success*. New York: Back Bay Books.

64. Frensch, P. A., & Sternberg, R. J. (1989). Expertise and intelligent thinking: When is it worse to know better? In R. J. Sternberg (Ed.), *Advances in the Psychology of Human Intelligence* (Vol. 5, pp. 157–158). Hillsdale, NJ: Erlbaum.

65. Simonton, D. K. (1994). *Greatness: Who Makes History and Why*. New York: Guilford.

66. Simonton, *Greatness.*

67. Kaufman, S. B. (Ed.). (2013). *The Complexity of Greatness: Beyond Talent or Practice*. New York: Oxford University Press. Kaufman, S. B. (2014). A proposed integration of the expert performance and individual differences approaches to the study of elite performance. *Frontiers in Psychology, 5*(707). Epstein, D. J. (2014). *The Sports Gene: Inside the Science of Extraordinary Athletic Performance*. New York: Penguin Group. Ericsson, K. A. (2013). Training history, deliberate practice and elite sports performance: An analysis in response to Tucker and Collins review—What makes champions? *British Journal of Sports Medicine, 47*(9), 533–535. Gladwell, M. (2013). Complexity and the ten-thousand-hour rule. *The New Yorker*. http://www.newyorker.com/the-sporting-scene/complexity-and-the-ten-thousand-hour-rule.

68. Simonton, D. K. (1991). Career landmarks in science: Individual differences and interdisciplinary contrasts. *Developmental Psychology, 27,* 119–130. Simonton, D. K. (1991). Emergence and realization of genius: The lives and works of 120 classical composers. *Journal of Personality and Social Psychology, 61,* 829–840. Simonton, D. K. (1992). Leaders of American psychology, 1879–1967: Career

development, creative output, and professional achievement. *Journal of Personality and Social Psychology, 62,* 5–17. Simonton, D. K. (1997). Creative productivity: A predictive and explanatory model of career trajectories and landmarks. *Psychological Review, 104,* 66–89. Simonton, D. K. (1999). Talent and its development: An emergenic and epigenetic model. *Psychological Review, 106,* 435–457.

69. Macnamara, B. N., Hambrick, D. Z., & Oswald, F. L. (2014). Deliberate practice and performance in music, games, sports, education, and professions: A meta-analysis. *Psychological Science, 25*(8), 1608–1618.

70. Simonton, D. K. (2014). Creative performance, expertise acquisition, individual differences, and developmental antecedents: An integrative research agenda. *Intelligence, 45,* 66–73.

71. Simonton, D. K. (2012). Taking the U.S. Patent Office criteria seriously: A quantitative three-criterion creativity definition and its implications. *Creativity Research Journal, 24*(2–3), 97–106.

6. OPENNESS TO EXPERIENCE

1. Kaufman, S. B. (2013). Opening up openness to experience: A four-factor model and relations to creative achievement in the arts and sciences. *The Journal of Creative Behavior, 47*(4), 233–255. Kaufman, S. B., Quilty, L. C., Grazioplene, R. G., Hirsh, J. B., Gray, J. R., Peterson, J. B., & DeYoung, C. G. (2015). Openness to experience and intellect differentially predict creative achievement in the arts and sciences. *Journal of Personality.* doi: 10.1111/jopy.12156. Batey, M., & Furnham, A. (2006). Creativity, intelligence, and personality: A critical review of the scattered literature. *Genetic, Social, and General Psychology Monographs, 132,* 355–429. Feist, G. J. (1998). A meta-analysis of personality in scientific and artistic creativity. *Personality and Social Psychology Review, 2,* 290–309. Silvia, P. J., Kaufman, J. C., & Pretz, J. E. (2009). Is creativity domain-specific? Latent class models of creative accomplishments and creative self-descriptions. *Psychology of Aesthetics, Creativity, and the Arts, 3,* 139–148.

2. DeYoung, C. G. (2013). The neuromodulator of exploration: A unifying theory of the role of dopamine in personality. *Frontiers in Human Neuroscience, 7*(762).

3. Kaufman, Opening up openness to experience. Kaufman, S. B. (2009). Beyond general intelligence: The dual-process theory of human intelligence. [Doctoral dissertation.] New Haven, CT: Yale University.

4. Kaufman, Opening up openness to experience.

5. Brookshire, B. (2013, July 3). Dopamine is _____. *Slate.* slate.com/articles/health_and_science/science/2013/07/what_is_dopamine_love_lust_sex_addiction_gambling_motivation_reward.html.

6. DeYoung, The neuromodulator of exploration.

7. DeYoung, C. G. (2006). Higher-order factors of the Big Five in a multi-informant sample. *Journal of Personality and Social Psychology, 91*(6), 1138–1151.

8. Silvia, P. J., Nusbaum, E. C., Berg, C., Martin, C., & O'Connor, A. (2009). Openness to experience, plasticity, and creativity: Exploring lower-order, high-order, and interactive effects. *Journal of Research in Personality, 43*(6), 1087–1090. Fürst, G., Ghisletta, P., & Lubart, T. (2014). Toward an integrative model of creativity and personality: Theoretical suggestions and preliminary empirical testing. *Journal of Creative Behavior.* doi: 10.1002/jocb.71.

9. DeYoung, The neuromodulator of exploration.

10. Previc, F. H. (2011). *Dopaminergic Mind in Human Evolution and History.* Cambridge, UK: Cambridge University Press.

11. Watson, D. (2003). To dream, perchance to remember: Individual differences in dream recall. *Personality and Individual Differences, 34,* 1271–1286.

12. Mohr, C., Bracha, H. S., & Brugger, P. (2003). Magical ideation modulates spatial behavior. *Journal of Neuropsychiatry and Clinical Neuroscience, 15,* 168–174.

13. Wagner, U., Gais, S., Haider, H., Verleger, R., & Born, J. (2004). Sleep inspires insight. *Nature, 427,* 352–355.

14. DeYoung, C. G., Grazioplene, R. G., & Peterson, J. B. (2012). From madness to genius: The openness/intellect trait domain as a paradoxical simplex. *Journal of Research in Personality, 46*(1), 63–78.

15. Carson, S. H., Peterson, J. B., & Higgins, D. M. (2003). Decreased latent inhibition is associated with increased creative achievement in high-functioning individuals. *Journal of Personality and Social Psychology, 85*(3), 499–506.

16. Kaufman, S. B. (2009). Faith in intuition is associated with decreased latent inhibition in a sample of high-achieving adolescents. *Psychology of Aesthetics, Creativity, and the Arts, 3*(1), 28–34.

17. Zabelina, D. L., O'Leary, D., Pornpattananangkul, N., Nusslock, R., & Beeman, M. (2015). Creativity and sensory gating indexed by the P50: Selective versus leaky sensory gating in divergent thinkers and creative achievers. *Neuropsychologia, 69,* 77–84.

18. Gregoire, C. (2015, March 10). Easily distracted by noise? You might just be a creative genius. *Huffington Post.* huffingtonpost.com/2015/03/10/creative-genius-brain_n_6831248.html.

19. Abraham, A. (2015). Editorial: Madness and creativity—Yes, no or maybe? *Frontiers in Psychology, 6*(1055). Jung, R. E. (2015). Evolution, creativity, intelligence, and madness: "Here be dragons." *Frontiers in Psychology, 5*(784). Kaufman, S. B., & Paul, E. S. (2014). Creativity and schizophrenia spectrum disorders across the arts and sciences. *Frontiers in Psychology, 5*(1145).

20. De Manzano, Ö., Cervenka, S., Karabanov, A., Farde, L., & Ullén, F. (2010). Thinking outside a less intact box: Thalamic dopamine D_2 receptor densities are negatively related to psychometric creativity in healthy individuals. *PLoS ONE, 5*(5), e10670. Kuszewski, A. M. (2009). The genetics of creativity: A serendipitous assemblage of madness. *METODO Working Papers, 58.*

21. Karolinska Institutet. (2010, May 19). Dopamine system in highly creative people similar to that seen in schizophrenics, study finds. *ScienceDaily.* sciencedaily.com/releases/2010/05/100518064610.htm.

22. Fink, A., Weber, B., Koschutnig, K., Benedek, M., Reishofer, G. et al. (2014). Creativity and schizotypy from the neuroscience perspective. *Cognitive, Affective and Behavioral Neuroscience, 14,* 378–387. Cavanna, A. E. (2006). The precuneus: A review of its functional anatomy and behavioural correlates. *Brain, 129*(3), 564–583.

23. Karlsson, J. L. (1970). Genetic association of giftedness and creativity with schizophrenia. *Hereditas, 66,* 177–182. Kinney, D. K., Richards, R., Lowing, P. A., LeBlanc, D., Zimbalist, M. E., and Harlan, P. (2001). Creativity in offspring of schizophrenic and control parents: An adoption study. *Creativity Research Journal, 13,* 17–25.

24. Kyaga, S., Landén, M., Boman, M., Hultman, C. M., Långström, N., and Lichtenstein, P. L. (2013). Mental illness, suicide and creativity: 40-year prospective total population study. *Journal of Psychiatric Research, 47,* 83–90.

25. Batey, M., & Furnham, A. (2008). The relationship between measures of creativity and schizotypy. *Personality and Individual Differences, 45*(8), 816–821. Beaussart, M. L., Kaufman, S. B., & Kaufman, J. C. (2012). Creative activity, personality, mental illness, and short-term mating success. *Journal of Creative Behavior, 46,* 151–167.

26. DeYoung et al., From madness to genius. Nelson, B., & Rawlings, D. (2010). Relating schizotypy and personality to the phenomenology of creativity. *Schizophrenia Bulletin, 36*(2), 388–399.

27. Nelson & Rawlings, Relating schizotypy and personality to the phenomenology of creativity.

28. Carson, S. (2011). Creativity and psychopathology: A shared-vulnerability model. *Canadian Journal of Psychiatry, 56*(3), 144–153.

29. Takeuchi, H., Taki, Y., Hashizume, H., Sassa, Y., Nagase, T., Nouchi, R., & Kawashima, R. (2011). Failing to deactivate: The association between brain activity during a working memory task and creativity. *NeuroImage, 55*(2), 681–687.

30. Ritter, S. M., Damian, R. I., Simonton, D. K., van Baaren, R. B., Strick, M. et al. (2012). Diversifying experiences enhance cognitive flexibility. *Journal of Experimental Social Psychology, 48*(4), 961–964. Damian, R. I., & Simonton, D. K. (2014). Diversifying experiences in the development of genius and their impact on creative cognition. In D. K. Simonton (Ed.), *The Wiley Handbook of Genius* (pp. 375–393). Oxford, UK: Wiley. Damian, R. I., & Simonton, D. K. (2015). Psychopathology, adversity, and creativity: Diversifying experiences in the development of eminent African Americans. *Journal of Personality and Social Psychology, 108,* 623–636.

31. Simonton, D. K. (1997). Foreign influence and national achievement: The impact of open milieus on Japanese civilization. *Journal of Personality and Social Psychology, 72*(1), 86–94.

32. Sternberg, R. J., & Lubart, T. I. (1995). *Defying the Crowd: Cultivating Creativity in a Culture of Conformity.* New York: Free Press.

33. Tadmor, C. T., Galinsky, A. D., & Maddux, W. W. (2012). Getting the most out of living abroad: Biculturalism and integrative complexity as key drivers of creative and professional success. *Journal of Personality and Social Psychology, 103*(3), 520–542.

34. Colvin, G. (2010). *Talent Is Overrated: What Really Separates World-Class Performers from Everybody Else.* New York: Portfolio Trade.

35. Simonton, D. (2000). Creative development as acquired expertise: Theoretical issues and an empirical test. *Developmental Review, 20*(2), 283–318.

36. Simonton, D. K. (2014). Creative performance, expertise acquisition, individual differences, and developmental antecedents: An integrative research agenda. *Intelligence, 45,* 66–73.

37. Gruber, H. E. (1989). Networks of enterprise in creative scientific work. In B. Gholson, W. R. Shadish Jr., R. A. Neimeyer, & A. C. Houts (Eds.), *The Psychology of Science: Contributions to Metascience* (pp. 246–265). Cambridge, UK: Cambridge University Press. Simonton, D. K. (2004). *Creativity in Science: Chance, Logic, Genius, and Zeitgeist.* Cambridge, UK: Cambridge University Press. Simonton, Creative performance, expertise acquisition, individual differences, and developmental antecedents.

38. Root-Bernstein, R. S., Bernstein, M., & Garnier, H. (1995). Correlation between avocations, scientific style, work habits, and professional impact of scientists. *Creativity Research Journal, 8,* 115–137; Root-Bernstein, R., Allen, L., Beach, L., Bhadula, R., Fast, J., Hosey, C. et al. (2008). Arts foster scientific success: Avocations of Nobel, National Academy, Royal Society, and Sigma Xi members. *Journal of the Psychology of Science and Technology, 1,* 51–63.

39. Simonton, D. K. (2012). Foresight, insight, oversight, and hindsight in scientific discovery: How sighted were Galileo's telescopic sightings? *Psychology of Aesthetics, Creativity, and the Arts, 6,* 243–254.

40. Carr, E. (2009). The last days of the polymath. *Intelligent Life.* more intelligentlife.com/content/edward-carr/last-days-polymath.

41. Broad, W. J. (2014, July 7). Seeker, doer, giver, ponderer. *New York Times,* p. D1.

42. Broad, Seeker, doer, giver, ponderer.

43. Teitelbaum, R. (2007, November 27). Simons at Renaissance cracks code, doubling assets. Bloomberg. bloomberg.com/apps/news?pid=newsarchive&sid=aq33M3X795vQ.

7. MINDFULNESS

1. Keegan, M. (2014). *The Opposite of Loneliness: Essays and Stories*. New York: Scribner.

2. James, H. (1884, September). The art of fiction. *Longman's Magazine, 4*.

3. Didion, J. (2008). On keeping a notebook. In *Slouching Towards Bethlehem* (pp. 131–141). New York: Farrar, Straus, & Giroux.

4. O'Keeffe, G. (1976). *Some Memories of Drawings*. New York: Viking Press.

5. Weingarten, Gene. (2007, April 8). Pearls before breakfast: Can one of the nation's greatest musicians cut through the fog of a D.C. rush hour? Let's find out. *Washington Post*. washingtonpost.com/lifestyle/magazine/pearls-before-breakfast-can-one-of-the-nations-great-musicians-cut-through-the-fog-of-a-dc-rush-hour-lets-find-out/2014/09/23/8a6d46da-4331-11e4-b47c-f5889e061e5f_story.html.

6. Langer, E. Personal communication, November 7, 2014.

7. Langer, E., personal communication.

8. Langer, E. J. (1989). *Mindfulness*. Reading, MA: Addison-Wesley.

9. Sheldon, K. M., Prentice, M., & Halusic, M. (2015). The experiential incompatibility of mindfulness and flow absorption. *Social Psychological and Personality Science, 6*, 276–283.

10. Kashdan, T., & Biswas-Diener, R. (2014). *The Upside of Your Dark Side: Why Being Your Whole Self—Not Just Your "Good" Self—Drives Success and Fulfillment*. New York: Hudson Street Press.

11. Konnikova, M. (2013). *Mastermind: How to Think like Sherlock Holmes*. New York: Penguin Books.

12. Konnikova, M. (2012, December 16). The power of concentration. *New York Times*, p. SR8.

13. Kabat-Zinn, J. (2006). Mindfulness-based interventions in context: Past, present, and future. *Clinical Psychology: Science and Practice, 10*(2), 144–156.

14. Mindfulness. (n.d.). Greater Good Science Center. greatergood. berkeley.edu/topic/mindfulness/definition.

15. Goldberg, P. (2013). *American Veda*. New York: Three Rivers Press.

16. Rosenthal, N. E. (2012). T*ranscendence: Healing and Transformation Through Transcendental Meditation*. New York: Tarcher.

17. Rosenthal, *Transcendence*.

18. Lynch, D. (2007). *Catching the Big Fish: Meditation, Consciousness, and Creativity*. New York: Tarcher.

19. Gregoire, C. (2014, October 3). Our digital device addiction is causing a "national attention deficit." *Huffington Post*. huffingtonpost. com/2014/10/03/neuroscientist-richard-da_n_5923648.html.

20. Stone, L. (n.d.). Continuous partial attention: What is continuous partial attention? [Blog post.] Linda Stone. lindastone.net/qa/continuous-partial-attention.

21. Nielsen. (2014). An era of growth: The cross-platform report Q4 2013. nielsen.com/us/en/insights/reports/2014/an-era-of-growth-the-cross-platform-report.html.

22. Meeker, M., & Wu, L. (2013). Internet trends. KCPB. kpcb.com/blog/2013-internet-trends.

23. Hough, A. (2011, April 8). Student "addiction" similar to "drug cravings", study finds. *Telegraph*. telegraph.co.uk/technology/news/8436831/Student-addiction-to-technology-similar-to-drug-cravings-study-finds.html.

24. Tamir, D. I., & Mitchell, J. P. (2012). Disclosing information about the self is intrinsically rewarding. *Proceedings of the National Academy of Sciences USA, 109*(21), 8038–8043.

25. Stothart, C., Mitchum, A., & Yehnert, C. (2015). The attentional cost of receiving a cell phone notification. *Journal of Experimental Psychology: Human Perception and Performance*. doi: http://dx.doi.org/10.1037/xhp0000100.

26. Levitin, D. J. (2014). *The Organized Mind: Thinking Straight in the Age of Information Overload*. New York: Dutton.

27. Heeren, A., Van Broeck, N., & Philippot, P. (2009). The effects of mindfulness on executive processes and autobiographical memory specificity. *Behaviour Research and Therapy, 47,* 403–409.

28. Schoenberg, P. L. A., Hepark, S., Kan, C. C., Barendregt, H. P., Buitelaar, J. K., & Speckens, A. E. M. (2014). Effects of mindfulness-based cognitive therapy on neurophysiological correlates of performance monitoring in adult attention-deficit/hyperactivity disorder. *Clinical Neurophysiology, 125*(7), 1407–1416.

29. Fassbender, C., Zhang, H., Buzy, W. M., Cortes, C. R., Mizuiri, D., Beckett, L., & Schweitzer, J. B. (2009). A lack of default network suppression is linked to increased distractibility in ADHD. *Brain Research, 1273,* 114–128.

30. Kaufman, S. B. (2014, October 21). The creative gifts of ADHD. [Blog post.] *Scientific American.* blogs.scientificamerican.com/beautiful-minds/2014/10/21/the-creative-gifts-of-adhd. Kaufman, S. B. (2014, November 11). Resources to help your child with ADHD flourish. [Blog post.] *Scientific American.* blogs.scientificamerican.com/beautiful-minds/2014/11/11/resources-to-help-your-child-with-adhd-flourish.

31. Brief mindfulness training may boost test scores, working memory. (2013, March 26). Association for Psychological Science. psychologicalscience.org/index.php/news/releases/brief-mindfulness-training-may-boost-test-scores-working-memory.html.

32. Jha, A. P., Krompinger, J., & Baime, M. J. (2007). Mindfulness training modifies subsystems of attrition. *Cognitive, Affective, & Behavioral Neuroscience, 7*(2), 109–119.

33. Loh, K. K., & Kanai, R. (2014). Higher media multi-tasking activity is associated with smaller gray-matter density in the anterior cingulate cortex. *PLoS ONE, 9*(9).

34. Zeidan, F., Martucci, K. T., Kraft, R. A., McHaffie, J. G., & Coghill, R. C. (2014). Neural correlates of mindfulness meditation-related anxiety relief. *Social Cognitive and Affective Neuroscience, 9*(6), 751–759.

35. Fox, K. C. R., Nijeboer, S., Dixon, M. L., Floman, J. L., Ellamil, M., Rumak, S. P. et al. (2014). Is meditation associated with altered brain structure? A systematic review and meta-analysis of morphometric neuroimaging in meditation practitioners. *Neuroscience & Biobehavioral Reviews, 43,* 48–73. doi:10.1016/j.neubiorev.2014.03.016

36. DeYoung, C. Personal communication, January 29, 2015.

37. Brewer, J. A., Worhunsky, P. D., Gray, J. R., Tang, Y.-Y., Weber, J., & Kober, H. (2011). Meditation experience is associated with differences in default mode network activity and connectivity. In *Proceedings of the National Academy of Sciences of the United States of America, 108*(50), 20254–20259.

38. Schooler, J. W., Mrazek, M. D., Franklin, M. S., Baird, B., Mooneyham, B. W. et al. (2014). The middle way: Finding the balance between mindfulness and mind-wandering. In B. H. Ross (Ed.), *The Psychology of Learning and Motivation* (Vol. 60, pp. 1–33). Burlington, MA: Academic Press.

39. Josipovic, Z. (2013). Freedom of the mind. *Frontiers in Psychology, 4*(538).

40. Davidson, R. J., & Lutz, A. (2008). Buddha's brain: Neuroplasticity and meditation. *IEEE Signal Process Mag, 25*(1), 174–176.

41. Colzato, L. S., Ozturk, A., & Hommel, B. (2012). Meditate to create: The impact of focused-attention and open-monitoring training on convergent and divergent thinking. *Frontiers in Psychology, 3*(116).

42. Xu, J., Vik, A., Groote, I. R., Lagopoulos, J., Holen, A. et al. (2014). Nondirective meditation activates default mode network and areas associated with memory retrieval and emotional processing. *Frontiers in Human Neuroscience, 8*(86).

43. Baas, M., Nevicka, B., & Ten Velden, F. S. (2014). Specific mindfulness skills differentially predict creative performance. *Personality and Social Psychology Bulletin, 40*(9), 1092–1106.

8. SENSITIVITY

1. Kaufman, S. B. (2011, March 6). After the show: The many faces of the performer. *Huffington Post.* huffingtonpost.com/scott-barry-kaufman/creative-people_b_829563.html.

2. Jackson, M. (1992). *Dancing the Dream.* London: Doubleday.

3. Taraborrelli, J. R. (2010). *Michael Jackson: The Magic, the Madness, the Whole Story, 1958–2009.* New York: Grand Central Publishing.

4. Csikszentmihalyi, M. (1996, July 1). The creative personality. *Psychology Today.* psychologytoday.com/articles/199607/the-creative-personality.

5. Grimes, J. O. Personal communication, January 2, 2015.

6. Grimes, J. O., & Cheek, J. M. (2011). Welcome to the personality construct jungle: Dispelling the myth of the extraverted rock star. [Unpublished manuscript.] Wellseley, MA: Wellesley College, Department of Psychology.

7. Aron, E. (1997). *The Highly Sensitive Person: How to Thrive When the World Overwhelms You.* New York: Broadway Books.

8. Aron, E. N., Aron, A., & Jagiellowicz, J. (2012). Sensory processing sensitivity: A review in the light of the evolution of biological responsivity. *Personality and Social Psychology Review, 16*(3), 262–282.

9. Aron, *The Highly Sensitive Person.* Kagan, J. (2013). *The Human Spark: The Science of Human Development.* New York: Basic Books. Kagan, J. (2010). *The Temperamental Thread: How Genes, Culture, Time and Luck make Us Who We Are.* New York: Dana Press.

10. Kristal, J. (2005). *The Temperament Perspective: Working with Children's Behavioral Styles.* New York: Brookes Publishing Company.

11. Aron, et al., Sensory processing sensitivity.

12. Flora, C. (2005, May 1). The X-factors of success. *Psychology Today.* psychologytoday.com/articles/200505/the-x-factors-success.

13. Bartz, A. (2011, July 5). Sense and sensitivity. *Psychology Today.* psychologytoday.com/articles/201107/sense-and-sensitivity.

14. Ward, D. (2011, October 30). The sensitive mind is a creative mind: Why sensitivity is not a curse, but a blessing. *Psychology Today.* psychologytoday.com/blog/sense-and-sensitivity/201110/the-sensitive-mind-is-creative-mind.

15. Smolewska, K. A., McCabe, S. B., & Woody, E. Z. (2006). A psychometric evaluation of the Highly Sensitive Person Scale: The components of sensory-processing sensitivity and their relation to the BIS/BAS and "Big Five." *Personality and Individual Differences, 40*(6), 1269–1279.

16. Sobocko, K., & Zelenski, J. M. (2015). Trait sensory-processing sensitivity and subjective well-being: Distinctive associations for different aspects of sensitivity. *Personality and Individual Differences, 83*, 44–49.

17. Cheek, J. M., Bourgeois, M. L., Theran, S. A., Grimes, J. O., & Norem, J. K. (2009, February). Interpreting the factors of the highly sensitive person scale. Presented at the annual meeting of the Society for Personality and Social Psychology, Tampa, Florida.

18. Jagiellowicz, J., Xu, X., Aron, A., Aron, E., Cao, G. et al. (2011). The trait of sensory processing sensitivity and neural responses to changes in visual scenes. *Social Cognitive and Affective Neuroscience*, *6*(1), 38–47.

19. Acevedo, B., Aron, A., & Aron, E. (2010, August). Association of sensory processing sensitivity when perceiving positive and negative emotional states. Paper presented at American Psychological Association, San Diego, CA. Aron et al., Sensory processing sensitivity.

20. Craig, A. D. (2009). How do you feel—now? The anterior insula and human awareness. *Nature Reviews Neuroscience*, *10*(1), 59–70.

21. Lewis, G. J., Kanai, R., Rees, G., & Bates, T. C. (2014). Neural correlates of the "good life": Eudaimonic well-being is associated with insular cortex volume. *Social Cognitive and Affective Neuroscience*, *9*(5), 615–618. For more on Carol Ryff's model of eudaimonia, see: Ryff, C. D. (2014). Psychological well-being revisited: Advances in the science and practice of eudaimonia. *Psychotherapy and Psychosomatics*, *83*, 10–28.

22. Aron et al., Sensory processing sensitivity.

23. Ellis, B. J., & Boyce, W. T. (2008). Biological sensitivity to context. *Current Directions in Psychological Science, 13*(3), 183–187.

24. Belsky, J., & Beaver, K. M. (2011). Cumulative-genetic plasticity, parenting and adolescent self-regulation. *Journal of Child Psychology and Psychiatry, 52,* 619–626. Grazioplene, R. G., DeYoung, C. G., Rogosch, F. A., & Cicchetti, D. (2013). A novel differential susceptibility gene: CHRNA4 and moderation of the effect of maltreatment on child personality. *Journal of Child Psychology and Psychiatry, 54*(8), 872–880. Ellis, B. J. & Boyce, W. T. (2005). Biological sensitivity to context: I. An evolutionary-developmental theory of the origins and functions of stress reactivity. *Development and Psychopathology, 17,* 271–301. Ellis, B. J., Essex, M. J., & Boyce, W. T. (2005). Biological sensitivity to context: II. Empirical explorations of an evolutionary-developmental theory. *Development and Psychopathology, 17,* 303–328. Dobbs, D. (2009, December). The science of success.

The Atlantic. theatlantic.com/magazine/archive/2009/12/the-science-of-success/307761/. Belsky, J., & Pluess, M. (2009). The nature (and nurture?) of plasticity in early human development. *Perspectives on Psychological Science, 4,* 345–351. Cain, S. (2012). *Quiet: The Power of Introverts in a World That Can't Stop Talking.* New York: Broadway. Belsky, J., Bakermans-Kranenburg, M. J., & van IJzendoorn, M. H. (2005). For better and for worse: Differential susceptibility to environmental influences. *Current Directions in Psychological Science, 6,* 300–304. Aron et al., Sensory processing sensitivity.

25. Blair, C., & Diamond, A. (2008). Biological processes in prevention and intervention: The promotion of self-regulation as a means of preventing school failure. *Development and Psychopathology, 20*(3), 899–911.

26. Csikszentmihalyi, M. (1994). *The Evolving Self: A Psychology for the Third Millennium.* New York: Harper Perennial.

27. Piechowski, M. M. (1993). Is inner transformation a creative process? *Creativity Research Journal, 6*(1–2), 89–98.

28. Chávez-Eakle, R. A., Eakle, A. J., & Cruz-Fuentes, C. (2012). The multiple relations between creativity and personality. *Creativity Research Journal, 24*(1), 76–82.

29. Nietzsche, F. W. (2008). *The Birth of Tragedy.* New York: Oxford University Press. (Original work published in 1872.)

30. Piechowski, M. M., & Cunningham, K. (1985). Patterns of overexcitability in a group of artists. *Journal of Creative Behavior, 19*(3), 153–174.

31. There is evidence that highly creative individuals have a tendency to be physiologically overreactive to stimulation. Martindale, C., Anderson, K., Moore, K., & West, A. N. (1996). Creativity, oversensitivity, and rate of habituation. *Personality and Individual Differences, 20*(4), 423–427.

32. Piechowski, M. M. (1997). Emotional giftedness: The measure of intrapersonal intelligence. In Colangelo, N., & Davis, G. A. (Eds.), *Handbook of Gifted Education* (2nd ed., pp. 366–381), p. 367.

33. Ackerman, C. M. (2009). The essential elements of Dabrowski's theory of positive disintegration and how they are connected. *Roeper Review, 31*(2), 81–95.

34. Ackerman, The essential elements of Dabrowski's theory of positive integration.

35. Poe, E. A. (1910). Imp of the perverse. In *The Works of Edgar Allan Poe*. New York: Harper and Bros. http://etc.usf.edu/lit2go/147/the-works-of-edgar-allan-poe/5233/the-imp-of-the-perverse/.

36. Harrison, G. E., & Van Haneghan, J. P. (2011). The gifted and the shadow of the night: Dabrowski's overexcitabilities and their correlation to insomnia, death anxiety, and fear of the unknown. *Journal for the Education of the Gifted, 34,* 669–697. Lamont, R. T. (2012). The fears and anxieties of gifted learners: Tips for parents and educators. *Gifted Child Today, 35*(4), 271–276.

37. Ackerman, The essential elements of Dabrowski's theory of positive disintegration and how they are connected.

38. Piechowski, Emotional giftedness.

39. Mendaglio, S., & Tillier, W. (2006). Dabrowski's theory of positive disintegration and giftedness: Overexcitability research findings. *Journal for the Education of the Gifted, 30*(1), 68–87. Wirthwein, L., & Rost, D. H. (2011). Focusing on overexcitabilities: Studies with intellectually gifted and academically talented adults. *Personality and Individual Differences, 51*(3), 337–342. Piechowski, M. M., Silverman, L. K., & Falk, R. F. (1985). Comparison of intellectual and artistically gifted on five dimensions of mental functioning. *Perceptual and Motor Skills, 60,* 539–549.

40. Piechowski, M. M. (2008). Discovering Dabrowski's theory. In S. Mendaglio (Ed.), *Dabrowski's Theory of Positive Disintegration* (pp. 41–78). Scottsdale, AZ: Great Potential Press.

41. Greene, R. (2013). *Mastery.* New York: Penguin Books.

42. Brennan, T. P., & Piechowski, M. M. (1991). A developmental framework for self-actualization: Evidence from case studies. *Journal of Humanistic Psychology, 31*(3), 43–64.

43. Ackerman, The essential elements of Dabrowski's theory of positive disintegration and how they are connected.

44. Piechowski, Is inner transformation a creative process?

45. Piechowski, M. M., & Tyska, C. (1982). Self-actualization profile of Eleanor Roosevelt, a presumed nontranscender. *Genetic Psychology Monographs, 105,* 95–153.

46. Roosevelt, E. (1940). *The Moral Basis of Democracy.* New York: Howell, Soskin.

47. Gilbert, E. (2007). *Eat, Pray, Love: One Woman's Search for Everything Across Italy, India, and Indonesia.* New York: Penguin Books.

48. Kübler-Ross, E. (1969). *On Death and Dying.* New York: Routledge.

49. Lind, S. (2001). Overexcitability and the gifted. *SENG Newsletter, 1*(1), 3–6.

9. TURNING ADVERSITY INTO ADVANTAGE

1. Kahlo, F. (2005). *The Diary of Frida Kahlo: An Intimate Self-Portrait.* New York: Abrams.

2. Marcus Aurelius. *The Meditations of Marcus Aurelius* (Vol. II, Part 3). Trans. George Long. The Harvard Classics. New York: Collier, 1909–1914. Bartleby.com. For additional reading, see Holiday, R. (2014). *The Obstacle Is the Way: The Timeless Art of Turning Trials into Triumph.* New York: Portfolio.

3. Frankl, V. (1959). *Man's Search for Meaning.* Boston: Beacon Press.

4. Nhất Hạnh, T. (2014). *No Mud, No Lotus: The Art of Transforming Suffering.* Berkeley, CA: Parallax Press.

5. Roberts, G. D. (2005). *Shantaram.* New York: St. Martin's Griffin.

6. Interview with Bill Zehme. (1988). In J. S. Wenner & J. Levy (Eds.), *The Rolling Stone Interviews* (p. 265). New York: Back Bay Books, 2007.

7. Tedeschi, R. G., & Calhoun, L. G. (2004). Posttraumatic growth: Conceptual foundations and empirical evidence. *Psychological Inquiry, 15*(1), 1–18.

8. Linley, P. A., & Joseph, S. (2004). Positive change following trauma and adversity: A review. *Journal of Traumatic Stress, 17*(1), 11–21.

9. Interview with Ben Fong-Torres. (1973). J. S. Wenner & J. Levy (Eds.), *The Rolling Stone Interviews* (p. 66). New York: Back Bay Books, 2007.

10. Simonton, D. K. (1994). *Greatness: Who Makes History and Why.* New York: Guilford.

11. Frankl, *Man's Search for Meaning.*

12. Tedeschi & Calhoun. Posttraumatic growth.

13. Staub, E., & Volhardt, J. (2008). Altruism born of suffering: The roots of caring and helping after victimization and other trauma. *American Journal of Orthopsychiatry, 78*(3), 267–280.

14. Tedeschi & Calhoun, Posttraumatic growth.

15. Tedeschi & Calhoun. Posttraumatic growth.

16. Simonton, *Greatness.* Ludwig, A. M. (1995). *The Price of Greatness: Resolving the Creativity and Madness Controversy.* New York: Guilford Press.

17. Forgeard, M. J. C. (2013). Perceiving benefits after adversity: The relationship between self-reported posttraumatic growth and creativity. *Psychology of Aesthetics, Creativity, and the Arts, 7*(3), 245–264.

18. Forgeard, M. Personal communication, July 27, 2014.

19. Forgeard, Perceiving benefits after adversity.

20. Forgeard, M. J. C., Mecklenburg, A. C., Lacasse, J. J., & Jayawickreme, E. (2014). Bringing the whole universe to order: Creativity, healing, and post-traumatic growth. In J. C. Kaufman (Ed.), *Creativity and Mental Illness* (pp. 321–342). Cambridge, UK: Cambridge University Press.

21. Forgeard et al., Bringing the whole universe to order.

22. Kaufman, S. B., & Kaufman, J. C. (2009). Putting the parts together: An integrative look at the psychology of creative writing. In S. B. Kaufman & J. C. Kaufman (Eds.), *The Psychology of Creative Writing* (pp. 351–370). Cambridge, UK: Cambridge University Press. Forgeard, M. J. C., Kaufman, S. B., & Kaufman, J. C. (2013). The psychology of creative writing. In G. Harper (Ed.), *Blackwell Companion to Creative Writing* (pp. 320–333). Oxford, UK: Wiley-Blackwell.

23. Pennebaker, J. W., & Chung, C. K. (2011). Expressive writing: Connections to physical and mental health. In H. S. Friedman (Ed.), *Oxford Handbook of Health Psychology* (pp. 417–437). New York: Oxford University Press.

24. Burton, C. M., & King, L. A. (2004). The health benefits of writing about intensely positive experiences. *Journal of Research in Personality, 38,* 150–163. Burton, C. M., & King, L. A. (2008). Effects of (very) brief writing on health: The two-minute miracle. *British Journal of Health Psychology, 13,* 9–14. Kaufman, S. B., & Kaufman, J. C. (Eds.). (2009). *The Psychology of Creative Writing.* New York: Cambridge University Press. King, L. A. (2001). The health benefits of writing about life goals. *Personality and Social Psychology Bulletin, 27,* 798–807. Greenberg, M. A., Wortman, C. B., & Stone, A. A. (1996). Emotional expression and physical health: Revising traumatic memories or fostering self-regulation? *Journal of Personality and Social Psychology, 71,* 588–602.

25. Pennebaker, J. W., & Seagal, J. D. (1999). Forming a story: The health benefits of narrative. *Journal of Clinical Psychology, 55,* 1243–1254. Sexton, J. D., & Pennebaker, J. W. (2009). The healing powers of expressive writing. In S. B. Kaufman & J. C. Kaufman (Eds.), *The Psychology of Creative Writing* (pp. 264–276). Cambridge, UK: Cambridge University Press.

26. Forgeard, M. (2008). Linguistic styles of eminent writers suffering from unipolar and bipolar mood disorder. *Creativity Research Journal, 20*(1), 81–92.

27. Forgeard, Perceiving benefits after adversity.

28. Verhaeghen, P., Joorman, J., & Khan, R. (2005). Why we sing the blues: The relation between self-reflective rumination, mood, and creativity. *Emotion, 5*(2), 226–232.

29. Zausner, T. (1998). When walls become doorways: Creativity, chaos theory, and physical illness. *Creativity Research Journal, 11*(1), 21–28.

30. Sandblom, P. (2000). *Creativity and Disease: How Illness Affects Literature, Art and Music.* London: Marion Boyars.

31. Betlejewski, S., & Ossowski, R. (2009). Głuchota a psychika w malarstwie Franciszka Goi [Deafness and mentality in Francisco Goya's paintings]. *Otolaryngologia Polska, 63*(2), 186–190.

32. Monet, Claude Oscar (1840–1926). (n.d.). University of Calgary. psych.ucalgary.ca/PACE/VA-Lab/AVDE-Website/Monet.html.

33. Stone, I. & Stone, J. (Eds.). (1995). *Dear Theo: The Autobiography of Vincent van Gogh.* Quoted in Popova, M. (2014, June 5). Van

Gogh and mental illness. Brain Pickings. brainpickings.org/2014/06/05/van-gogh-and-mental-illness.

34. Roepke, A. M. (2013). Gains without pains? Growth after positive events. *Journal of Positive Psychology*, *8*(4), 280–291.

10. THINKING DIFFERENTLY

1. MacBoock. (2013, November 5). *Apple Confidential—Steve Jobs on "Think Different"—Internal Meeting Sept. 23, 1997.* [Video.] youtube.com/watch?v=9GMQhOm-Dqo.

2. Turnbull, C. (1913). *Life and Teachings of Giordano Bruno: Philosopher, Martyr, Mystic.* San Diego, CA: Gnostic Press.

3. Gamarekian, B. (1989, June 14). Corcoran, to foil dispute, drops Mapplethorpe show. *New York Times.* http://www.nytimes.com/1989/06/14/arts/corcoran-to-foil-dispute-drops-mapplethorpe-show.html.

4. A retrospective—Robert Mapplethorpe. (2012, August 3). Daily Photo News. actuphoto.com/13863-a-retrospective-robert-mapplethorpe.html.

5. Sternberg, R. J., & Lubart, T. I. (1995). *Defying the Crowd: Cultivating Creativity in a Culture of Conformity.* New York: Free Press.

6. Sternberg, *Defying the Crowd.*

7. Asimov, I. (2014, October 20). Isaac Asimov asks, "How do people get new ideas?" *MIT Technology Review.* technologyreview.com/view/531911/isaac-asimov-asks-how-do-people-get-new-ideas.

8. Galileo. (1596). Letter to Johannes Kepler. Columbia University. columbia.edu/cu/tat/core/galileo.htm.

9. Dr. Semmelweis' biography. (n.d.). Semmelweis Society International. semmelweis.org/about/dr-semmelweis-biography.

10. Campanario, J. M. (2009). Rejecting and resisting Nobel class discoveries: Accounts by Nobel laureates. *Scientometrics, 81*(2), 549–565.

11. Information for patients. (n.d.). International Society for Magnetic Resonance in Medicine. ismrm.org/resources/information-for-patients.

12. Quoted in Berns, G. (2010). *Iconoclast: A Neuroscientist Reveals How to Think Differently.* Boston: Harvard Business Press.

13. Mueller, J. S., Melwani, S., & Goncalo, J. A. (2012). The bias against creativity: Why people desire but reject creative ideas. *Psychological Science, 23*(1), 13–17.

14. Mueller et al., The bias against creativity.

15. Staw, B. M. (1995). Why no one really wants creativity. In C. M. Ford & D. A. Gioia (Eds.), *Creative Action in Organizations: Ivory Tower Visions & Real World Voices* (pp. 476–479). Thousand Oaks, CA: Sage Publications.

16. Staw, Why no one really wants creativity.

17. Griskevicius, V., Goldstein, N. J., Moretensen, C. R., Cialdini, R. B., & Kenrick, D. T. (2006). Going along versus going alone: When fundamental motives facilitate strategic (non)conformity. *Journal of Personality and Social Psychology, 91*, 281–294.

18. Griskevicius et al., Going along versus going alone.

19. Asch, S. E. (1951). Effects of group pressure on the modification and distortion of judgments. In H. Guetzkow (Ed.), *Groups, Leadership and Men* (pp. 177–190). Pittsburgh: Carnegie Press.

20. Berns, G. S., Chappelow, J., Zink, C. F., Pagnoni, G., Martin-Skurski, M. E., & Richards, J. (2005). Neurobiological correlates of social conformity and independence during mental rotation. *Biological Psychiatry, 58*(3), 245–253.

21. Buchsbaum, D., Gopnik, A., Griffiths, T. L., & Shafto, P. (2011). Children's imitation of causal action sequences is influenced by statistical and pedagogical evidence. *Cognition, 120*(3), 331–340.

22. Gopnik, A. (2011, March 16). Why preschool shouldn't be like school. *Slate.* slate.com/articles/double_x/doublex/2011/03/why_pre-school_shouldnt_be_like_school.html.

23. Westby E. L., & Dawson, V. (1995). Creativity: Asset or burden in the classroom? *Creativity Research Journal, 8*, 1–10.

24. Sternberg, R. J., & Grigorenko, E. L. (2007). *Teaching for Successful Intelligence: To Increase Student Learning and Achievement* (2nd ed.). New York: Corwin.

25. Robinson, K. (2006, February). *Do Schools Kill Creativity?* [Video.] TED. ted.com/talks/ken_robinson_says_schools_kill_creativity.

26. Wilson, C. (1956). *The Outsider.* Boston: Houghton Mifflin.

27. Kaufman, S. B. (2012, August 24). Social rejection can fuel creativity. *Psychology Today.* psychologytoday.com/blog/beautiful-minds/201208/social-rejection-can-fuel-creativity.

28. Kim, S. H., Vincent, L. C., & Goncalo, J. A. (2013). Outside advantage: Can social rejection fuel creative thought? *Journal of Experimental Psychology: General, 142*(3), 605–611.

29. Kim et al., Outside advantage.

30. Kaufman, S. B., Christopher, E. M., & Kaufman, J. C. (2008). The genius portfolio: How do poets earn their creative reputations from multiple products? *Empirical Studies of the Arts, 26,* 181–196. Simonton, D. K. (1997). Creative productivity: A predictive and explanatory model of career trajectories and landmarks. *Psychological Review, 104,* 66–89.

31. Simonton, D. K. (2003). Expertise, competence, and creative ability: The perplexing complexities. In R. J. Sternberg & E. L. Grigorenko (Eds.), *The Psychology of Abilities, Competencies, and Expertise* (pp. 213–239). New York: Cambridge University Press.

32. Simonton, D. K. (2010). Creative thought as blind-variation and selective-retention: Combinatorial models of exceptional creativity. *Physics of Life Reviews, 7,* 156–179.

33. Simonton, Creative thought as blind-variation and selective-retention. Simonton, D. K. (2011). Creativity and discovery as blind variation: Campbell's (1960) BVSR model after the half-century mark. *Review of General Psychology, 15,* 158–174. Simonton, D. K. (2015). "So we meet again!"—Replies to Gabora and Weisberg. *Psychology of Aesthetics, Creativity, and the Arts, 9,* 25–34.

34. Edison's patents. (2012, February 20). The Thomas Edison Papers. edison.rutgers.edu/patents.htm.

35. Simonton, D. K. (2014). Thomas Edison's creative career: The multilayered trajectory of trials, errors, failures, and triumphs. *Psychology of Aesthetics, Creativity, and the Arts, 9,* 2–14.

36. Fuel cell technology. (2012, February 20). The Thomas Edison Papers. edison.rutgers.edu/fuelcell.htm.

37. Simonton, Thomas Edison's creative career.

38. Simonton, Thomas Edison's creative career.

39. Simonton, D. K. (2009). The literary genius of William Shakespeare: Empirical studies of his dramatic and poetic creativity. In S. B. Kaufman & J. C. Kaufman (Eds.), *The Psychology of Creative Writing.* (pp. 131–148). Cambridge, UK: Cambridge University Press.

40. Simonton, D. K. (2015). Numerical odds and evens in Beethoven's nine symphonies: Can a computer really tell the difference? *Empirical Studies of the Arts, 33*, 18–35.

41. Simonton, Numerical odds and evens in Beethoven's nine symphonies.

42. Martindale, C. (1990). *The Clockwork Muse: The Predictability of Artistic Styles.* New York: Basic Books.

43. Lee, C. S., Therriault, D. J., & Linderholm, T. (2012). On the cognitive benefits of cultural experience: Exploring the relationship between studying abroad and creative thinking. *Applied Cognitive Psychology, 26*(5), 768–778.

44. Zynga, A. (2013, June 13). The cognitive bias keeping us from innovating. *Harvard Business Review.* hbr.org/2013/06/the-cognitive-bias-keeping-us-from.

45. Berns, G. (2010). *Iconoclast.*

46. Dyer, J., & Gregerson, H. (2011, September 27). Learn how to think different(ly). *Harvard Business Review.* hbr.org/2011/09/begin-to-think-differently.

47. Dyer & Gregerson, Learn how to think different(ly).

48. Jaussi, K. S., & Dionne, S. D. (2003). Leading for creativity: The role of unconventional leader behavior. *Leadership Quarterly, 14*(4–5), 475–498.

49. Ludwig, A. M. (1995). *The Price of Greatness: Resolving the Creativity and Madness Controversy.* New York: Guilford Press.

50. Whitman, Walt. "The Song of Myself," 1892. Poetry Foundation. poetryfoundation.org/poem/174745.

Index

About the Authors

Scott Barry Kaufman, PhD, is scientific director of the Imagination Institute in the Positive Psychology Center at the University of Pennsylvania, where he investigates the measurement and development of intelligence, imagination, and creativity. He has written or edited six previous books, including *Ungifted: Intelligence Redefined*. He is also cofounder of *The Creativity Post*, host of *The Psychology Podcast*, and he writes the blog Beautiful *Minds* for *Scientific American*. Kaufman lives in Philadelphia.

Carolyn Gregoire is a senior writer at the *Huffington Post*, where she reports on psychology, mental health, and neuroscience. She has spoken at TEDx and the Harvard Public Health Forum and has appeared on MSNBC, the *Today* show, the History Channel, and HuffPost Live. Gregoire lives in New York City.